Leadership in Context

NEW HORIZONS IN LEADERSHIP STUDIES

Series Editor: Joanne B. Ciulla
Professor and Coston Family Chair in Leadership and Ethics,
Jepson School of Leadership Studies, University of Richmond, USA

This important series is designed to make a significant contribution to the
development of leadership studies. This field has expanded dramatically in recent
years and the series provides an invaluable forum for the publication of high quality
works of scholarship and shows the diversity of leadership issues and practices around
the world.

The main emphasis of the series is on the development and application of new and
original ideas in leadership studies. It pays particular attention to leadership in
business, economics and public policy and incorporates the wide range of disciplines
which are now part of the field. Global in its approach, it includes some of the best
theoretical and empirical work with contributions to fundamental principles, rigorous
evaluations of existing concepts and competing theories, historical surveys and future
visions.

Titles in the series include:

Moral Leadership in Action
Building and Sustaining Moral Competence in European Organizations
Edited by Heidi von Weltzien Hoivik

Beyond Rules in Society and Business
Verner C. Petersen

The Moral Capital of Leaders
Why Virtue Matters
Alejo José G. Sison

The Leadership Dilemma in Modern Democracy
Kenneth P. Ruscio

The New Russian Business Leaders
*Manfred F.R. Kets de Vries, Stanislav Shekshnia, Konstantin Korotov
and Elizabeth Florent-Treacy*

Lessons on Leadership by Terror
Finding Shaka Zulu in the Attic
Manfred F.R. Kets de Vries

Leadership in Context
The Four Faces of Capitalism
Mark N. Wexler

Leadership in Context

The Four Faces of Capitalism

Mark N. Wexler

Simon Fraser University, Canada

NEW HORIZONS IN LEADERSHIP STUDIES

Edward Elgar
Cheltenham, UK • Northampton, MA, USA

Published by
Edward Elgar Publishing Limited
Glensanda House
Montpellier Parade
Cheltenham
Glos GL50 1UA
UK

Edward Elgar Publishing, Inc.
136 West Street
Suite 202
Northampton
Massachusetts 01060
USA

A catalogue record for this book
is available from the British Library

ISBN 1 84376 580 2 (cased)

Printed and bound in Great Britain by MPG Books Ltd, Bodmin, Cornwall

Contents

Figures

Preface

I have been motivated to write this book as a means of introducing those working in the field of leadership to a comprehensive model of cognitive contextualism. It has been my view as a teacher in the field that leadership books are generally of two sorts. The first, and the one I was weaned on as a student, focuses upon tightly examined empirical investigations of behaving leaders. The literature borrowing from the social sciences attempts to describe and determine the behavioural correlations among and between variables involved in a literature which depicts the leader as a problem solver dealing with collective concerns. Then there is a prescriptive literature. It is either case-based or organization-based. This work focuses on highly successful individuals or individuals who are perceived to have piloted organizations to their success. This literature either asks those involved or, like anthropologists, doggedly follows them and seeks to discern what in fact they do that if repeated by others, would in short order convert aspiring leaders into the authentic article.

This book deliberately falls between these two sorts of leadership books. It is academic. It develops a cognitive-based contextual model of leadership grounded in the social sciences. It is prescriptive. It explores the way practising leaders view their world and make sense of their leadership roles. To this end, the manuscript was read and discussed by 24 practising leaders, six from each of the four ideal types outlined in the book. They had ample opportunity for input. In early drafts of the book the skill profiles of leaders, which is the situated learning component of the book built into Chapters 6 and 7, passed muster with only 15 of my leaders. By the end of our work together, when their ideas were inserted and balanced with an anchor, all the leaders joined in. This marriage between an academic treatment and the prescriptive approach is intended to provide academics with an opportunity to test anchor cross-story transitions (ACTs) in developing questionnaires and/or pencil and paper tests using their undergraduate or MBA students. It provides practising leaders with a means of systematically identifying their worldview and determining with their own contextual reading whether their present skill portfolio is sufficient/adequate to deal with their perception of future events. Interestingly, the contextual approach to leadership is a means of bringing academics interested in the first sort of leadership treatment in touch with those who have, I believe, relied all too heavily upon the second sort of leadership literature to develop their skill portfolio.

I encourage you, once you have finished the book, to put it to use. I am very interested in academics developing studies which will assist leaders and want-to-be leaders in placing their leadership footprint within the four faces of capitalism. Those who find that they lack anchor skills in their preferred stories can, with the help of leadership coaches, learn to remedy this deficiency. Those who seek to reinvent themselves as cosmopolitan leaders are urged to go slowly and realize that success here takes time, dedication and a willingness to surround oneself with others who at one point in your life you considered irksome.

I would like to thank my extraordinary wife Judy A.E. Oberlander for providing me with a sense that when a middle-aged man holes himself in a small room for several years he is doing far more than merely escaping from the trials and tribulations of the world. To my assistants, Ms Jean Donald, Ms Betty Chung, and Ms Shirley Marcus, I offer my unreserved admiration. To the 24 leaders from Canada, Australia, the United States, Italy, Japan and Argentina, all of whom I promised anonymity, my sincere and most heartfelt recognition. Taking time from your busy day to attend to my queries and set me in new directions, was far above and beyond the leader's duty ... you are now friends. To my academic colleagues, both at Simon Fraser University and elsewhere, you are too numerous to list, my sincere gratitude. The Social Sciences and Humanities Council of Canada has been very supportive of my research on leadership and corporate governance. Lastly, but certainly not least, I would like to heap praise on Mr Alan Sturmer, the Acquisitions Editor for Edward Elgar Publishing. This is not my first book, but it is the one that taught me most about how civilized a process publishing might be. Thank you, Alan.

Despite the praise I have distributed, all the errors, omissions and points that in your mind may still need clarification are all my own doing. I urge readers interested in following up on either the errors or clarifications, or those desiring to pursue a line of reasoning stimulated by the book, to contact me at wexler@sfu.ca.

This book is dedicated to:

Pearl and Zalmon Wexler
Cornelia and Peter Oberlander
Leaders in the generation who nurtured my wife Judy and me.
Thank you.

1. Context as worldview: making sense of leadership

"To an extent, leadership is like beauty, it's hard to define, but you know it when you see it."

Warren Bennis[1]

We know leadership when we see and admire it. We are confused when we either confront another who we respect but who thinks little of our chosen leader, or when we reluctantly stumble upon information that indicts our leader as self-serving, treacherous and, worse, someone who is unable to amend his or her ways. Warren Bennis' view sums up much of our contemporary thinking on leadership. We are attracted to the concept in general, yet remain agnostic with regard to the potential of any specific leader; seeing, after all, is believing. Just as one person's beauty is another's garbage, so too, one's leader may be another's rogue or even fool. This is troubling to me. Yet it fascinates. It serves as my motive for exploring a contextualist's language to make sense of leadership and provide insight for those who aspire to the role and those who, as a consequence of their obligations in organizational life, must select effective leaders.

Why is it that leader-like behaviour in one context is seen by rational men and women as the very stuff or essence of leadership while the same behaviour in other contexts is seen as problematic, even at times the behaviour of the fool? The cunning military leader whose battlefield prowess entails strong-arm tactics, a wily deployment of selective information, and a laser-like determination to obliterate an aggressive enemy, will find these very skills underappreciated in the context of a meeting of peers seeking to outline new directions for a community-based not-for-profit organization. The military leader in the brainstorming session among stakeholders will, like a bull in a china shop, be less than prized. Similarly, a visionary high-tech leader helping participants in a network to push the envelope will, like the military leader, find his or her skills undervalued in the context of a heavily bureaucratized, "by the book" public utility. As with beauty or art, context is necessary to our comprehension of leadership.

Change the context and one person's leader is another person's irksome other. The warrior leader, replete with battlefield acumen and the loyalty of troops, shines in a context of winner-takes-all contests.[2] Here rivalry and competitiveness are unbridled. Leaders are decisive, quick and learn by immediately correcting missteps. The stakeholder meeting will call for a leader who is flexible, cooperative and learns through thoughtful ongoing dialogue with others. This is not the context where winners take all. It is, rather, a context of evolving a culture of shared values rooted in emerging trust. The "exploit your enemy's weakness" logic, so central to battlefield leadership, is not in keeping with the information sharing, collaboration and compromise needed in the emergence of leadership in the not-for-profit stakeholders' meeting.[3] In the instance of the high-tech leader transferring his or her skills to a public utility, one is likely to discover that the applause which accompanied the high-tech leader's ability to stimulate knowledge workers to take risks and try out new ideas will be met with scepticism. The risk-averse, play-by-the-rules context of a highly regulated public utility self-selects for prudent leaders. Leaders in the high-tech context seek to mobilize creative uncertainty to enhance organizational growth and stimulate the development of intellectual capital; leaders in the context of the typical public utility concertedly seek to reduce uncertainty in the pursuit of a system which is stable and dependable over time.[4]

My aim in this chapter is to introduce a contextualist's approach to leadership and the basic vocabulary necessary to begin to think of leadership within the four faces or worldviews prevalent in capitalism. When I refer to the four faces of capitalism, I am speaking less to the political economy of capitalism in its various guises in Japan, Italy, Australia and Estonia for example, but rather to the manner within modernity in which we invest our time, energy, passion and/or capital in the deliberate pursuit of desired outcomes or goals. Capitalism, in this book, is treated as the ongoing evolving realm of calculated instrumental action.[5] Leaders within the four faces or worldviews of capitalism emerge to provide followers with an acceptable return on their investment of time, energy, passion or capital. It is in this sense that followers credibly seek out military leaders in contexts in which winner-takes-all contests prevail and turn to participative leaders when compromises between different stakeholders in joint destiny contexts present themselves. In other words, as we turn to our second example, we see the beauty in the visionary high-tech leader when we look through an optimistic lens with regards to our desire to live in a future which is very different from our present experience. However, this beauty pales and that of the leader in the public utility comes to the fore when we seek to hold fast to the tried, tested and true. We move cautiously seeking assurance when we imagine the perilous nature of a terrorist-strewn future.

CONTEXTUALISM: BASIC PREMISES

In *World Hypothesis*, author Stephen Pepper looks at contextualism as one of four worldviews employed to reduce ambiguity and lend a sense of order and evidence to problems perceived as complex and unruly.[6] Worldviews are sense-making devices. Each of the worldviews discussed by Pepper – formism, mechanism, organicism and contextualism – draws its power to attract problem solvers due to its underlying "root metaphor". Formism, in Pepper's lexicon, treats logic or realism as its root metaphor and relies upon the presumed existence of an authoritative or clear map with the notion of fitting in or of corresponding a known solution to an experience of uncertainty. In formism, problems are solved by adequate rules. Mechanism, and those who see and solve the world's problems mechanistically, are empiricists. Solutions require evidence rooted in data or in an empirical account. Within the purview of the mechanistic root metaphor, to understand is to measure. Organicism, and those who adhere to this worldview (organicists), explain ambiguity as a result of the fact that people, systems, events and things develop. They do not remain static. To distil the ambiguity and wrestle the problem to the ground, organicists seek to delineate predictable stages of development, trends or trajectories. Organicists' root metaphor depicts the answers to problems in the understanding of sequences in which change is explained in terms of growth or regression. Life and events within it evolve. Some aspects regress; others evolve. Organicists seek to diminish regressions tendencies and bolster growth and development. These changes are ubiquitous. They follow us from the cradle to the grave and from one generation to the next.

In this book I am interested in expanding, developing and applying the Pepperian worldview of the contextualist to the contemporary study and practice of leadership. The contextualist makes sense, and thereby lessens ambiguity, by placing that which requires explanation in a context. The root metaphor is pragmatic – context is instrumental. From a pragmatic perspective rooted in functional accounts, how we use things, people, systems and events depends not only upon the identity of the entity, but upon our use of it as well. In the sentence "the pen is in the box", we who understand the language of the sentence understand that the pen refers to a writing utensil; however, in the sentence "the pig is in the pen" we recontextualize and understand the term pen as a home or constraining device used in the domestication of swine. A contextualist's view becomes essential when a single concept (in our case leadership) is used to make sense of a person, system, thing or idea whose identity or use alters depending upon the context.

This book in your hand or on the desk at which you are reading can, in different contexts, serve as a doorstop, a source of heat and light when burned, or as a heavy object to hurl at a cat to get it to cease clawing the couch. The saliva in your mouth is a body fluid which aids in the breakdown and digestion of food; outside your mouth it is called spit and is viewed as a defilement should it inadvertently or even more problematically intentionally land on another person. The contextualist does much more than argue that one person's terrorist is another's freedom fighter. The contextualist seeks an account in which the varied versions of terrorism, to use this as an example, albeit redolent with tension, make sense. Contextualism is a form of sense-making which assumes that, like beauty, "we know it when we see it", because not only is beauty in the eye of the beholder, it is the beholder's understanding of the aesthetic "fit" between the beautiful object or idea and its context.

Pepper anticipated that the contextualist worldview would rankle those who prized a single authoritative response. Contextualism embodies, and to some degree anticipates, the turn to postmodernism.[7] In contextualism, reality is not given, it is socially constructed. In postmodernism, identity is contingent. The contextualist world is experienced as imagistic, alterable and, when more than one context exists in a frame, fragmented. Worldviews mix and clash in an extraordinarily intense manner in our global market. Watch the television news this evening. Note that a panel of "so-called" experts (the phrase so-called frequently accompanies contextualists' analyses) will address an event or problem and the channel or network presenting the talking heads will identify each according to their point of view. The so-called aspect of contextualism emerges because most viewers identify with one or perhaps two of the experts but see the others as representing an interest group and therefore not truly representative of their preferred version of reality. In Pepper we are blind to our worldview. However, we see others as merely vested interests. The preferred version of reality, one's own anchor, confers stability, but in the midst of contextualist analysis one is asked to see the rational assumptions embedded in others' worldviews. When one cannot see this, others are viewed as so-called.

Contextualism is rooted in the cognitive views of active, involved participants in instrumental action. Identity is not fixed; it alters, dependent upon context. Contextualists see a world of multiple possibilities rooted in different cognitive lenses or worldviews and attempt to avoid viewing one of these as superior. It is in the context of ongoing change, interpretation, possible inconsistencies and multiple meanings that contextualists conclude that leaders help embody and make sense of different worldviews.[8] Leadership is a nuanced language in which different views of leadership, rooted in varying contexts, compete and cooperate for attention. Contextualization stimulates an awareness of the very polyglotism that genuine speakers use when they make sense of concepts like leadership.[9] Contextualism helps us to understand and live in complexity without simplifying the problem of rationality. Contextualism, however, is not the answer to our desire to master or control complexity. Complexity, context-ualists insist, is not mastered; rather, one becomes resilient in the face of the ambiguity borne of persistent complexity. To be a contextualist is to strive toward cosmopolitanism.

Contextualism speaks a polyglot tongue. It is not a pure language; it is not, moreover, the language of anarchy and nihilism.[10] When one becomes conscious of contextualism, the pen as a writing utensil permits one to not only work through the minor communication problem posed by homonyms, but helps us to understand why and when smart people whom one respects, using the same or similar information, come to positions that are at odds with what one believes to be perfectly apparent. The recognition of the "irksome other" as the "other" working with different basic premises is anarchistic if one assumes that this is the cause of the disorder. It is believed to be nihilistic when one assumes that nothing of any significance can be accomplished in a polyglot world where rational people speak from different basic assumptions. Let us look into the orderliness of polyglot worlds, then the basic vocabulary of worldviews which serves as our template for the four faces of capitalism.

POLYGLOT WORLDS

The root metaphor beneath contextualism conveys both the increased complexity and the uncertainty that emerges when citizens, within the relative safety of a worldview, discover that not only do other worldviews exist, but that they also have relevance. These other worldviews are getting harder and harder to dismiss as mere gibberish. An isolationist or seclusionist strategy in the face of growing uncertainty will cut one off from creative possibilities emerging elsewhere. It is not as easy as it once was to hunker down and colonize other worldviews beneath the obvious sense-making powers of one's preferred worldview. Two assumptions prevail as context-ualism meets later stages of modernity. First, while there may be a single world or reality, it is both experienced and made sense of quite differently by those within a particular worldview and, as a corollary, within a worldview participants perceive themselves and others who share their convictions as rational. Second, as a result of the increasing awareness of the simultaneous existence of diverse and even conflicting worldviews, if one seeks to become a leader, it is vital that one speak and navigate in the language and conven-tions of more than one worldview. These two assumptions are nested in an irony. While the very nature of globalization facilitates the experience of a smaller, more accessible world, intimacy among and between strangers requires the capacity to make sense of and thrive in the midst of differences.[11]

When applied to instrumental leaders, we can first understand context-ualism in an intuitive and non-threatening manner by looking at these trends in the literature. A raft of books, many very good, have emerged in the field of international business which point out that in the midst of trade liberaliza-tion, the proliferation of the transnational corporation and the Internet revolution, leaders in the business world must lose their parochial adherence to their local culture. In the jet stream of emergent cosmopolitan leaders in organizations that seek work in a world that is wider than the worldview of their birth, the leaders must not only recognize the existence of other cultures but be able to successfully navigate between and among them. Inter-cultural leadership makes it clear that this entails not merely translating other cultures into one's own, but gaining sufficient fluency in the conventions and beliefs of those cultures to make sense of the rational patterns embedded therein by their adherents.[12] Polyglot worlds require leaders who can thrive in more than one worldview.

A second, somewhat more specialized, portal through which one can grasp the significance of contextualism to the study of leadership is the rather clear divide between transactionally based managers and the call for visionary or transformationally inspiring leaders.[13] This literature marks a large divide between managers and leaders. The manager, using our view of polyglotism, is the master of a particular worldview. Managers speak with more than apparent competency to those who share their conventions. Managers enact plans. Their language is shared by those they manage. It is assumed, within the shared worldview assumption, that managers and those they manage adhere to the same rational pattern and, despite minor difficulties arising due to functional specialization or power gradients within a hierarchical system, that there is general agreement on both the organization's goals and the process required to achieve these. Within managerialism, leaders are sought when managers seriously challenge other managers and do so outside the rules and conventions of what is, within that worldview, a legitimate challenge. Leaders arise to look for alternatives rather than engage in preset transactions. To many, the comparison between managers and leaders is made most simply by referring to open and closed systems. Managers flourish in closed systems; leaders come alive in open systems. Closed systems are locked into a preferred worldview. Leading in an open system necessitates a recognition that problems and issues draw from simultaneously occurring worldviews colliding in space and time.

The call in the literature for more leaders and fewer managers (or in a less revolutionary trumpeting of this, for more managers with leadership capabilities) is, I believe, a function of the emergence of polyglotism or the recognition of the simultaneous co-existence and relevance of more than one rational worldview. To be a manager means not only that one adheres to the conventions of one worldview but, as well, that one either ignores or colonizes the positions taken by those from other worldviews. To be a leader is to work in a relatively open system, a polyglot worldview in which uncertainty increases in the face of the simultaneous co-existence of multiple and at times conflicting rationalities. Complexity breeds interdependence. As interdependence in the face of complexity escalates, leaders rely on others whose worldviews may differ from their preferred way of making sense. Leaders possess a higher tolerance for ambiguity than managers. In the midst of rising uncertainty they attempt to remain open to a search behaviour which accepts the possibility of increasing rather than decreasing options. With the emergence of complexity – whether it be dealt with using the tropes of globalization, the Internet revolution, post-industrialization or new organizational forms – leadership increasingly must embrace more than the routine of the status quo. In this interdependency and heightened complexity, leaders are reinforced for adhering to views that they may previously have thought irrelevant, irrational, or, in more vernacular terms, "loopy".

Leaders' willingness to embrace the once "loopy" is not a sign of sloppy leadership but of the increased search for alternatives in the midst of escalating uncertainty. The third and last illustrative portal we can enter to depict how polyglotism is grounded in contextualism is foreshadowed in the literature heralding the leading contemporary organization as a learning organization and the leaders of these intelligent enterprises as enabling a high involvement or learning culture.[14] Within the lens of polyglotism, the learning organization is, by definition, fighting the impulse to become a manager or expert, blind to the views of those from other worldviews. Remaining high up on the learning curve makes good sense when what one knows produces acceptable or desired results. In the environment of learning organizations, knowledge becomes rapidly obsolete. Adept experts or agile managers (leaders) learn how to move down their learning curves by taking in views and positions from other worldviews. Developing a culture of dialogue and trust, as we shall see in our exploration of the communitarian worldview, is seen as a prerequisite to publicly admitting that one's previously prized routines, those on which one is high up on the learning curve, are now in the present context not the most likely to bring desired results. Why else listen to and test the views of those who, to some degree, see the world differently?

Leaders who create adaptive learning cultures empower members within a culture to interpret rather than slavishly adhere to the rules or routines. Learning, much prized in the contemporary literature on instrumental leaders, entails hedging one's bets by increasing the capacity of the organization to hear the voices of those whose views do not confirm one's own. Escalating cognitive, structured and informational uncertainty necessitates an awareness

of the fact that old, once reliable maps have an expiration date. Contextualism addresses the manner in which leaders read contexts to learn how and
when old maps expire and new sense-making patterns must be licensed.
While this literature sensitizes us to the implicit use of contextualism, it
departs from a self-consciously contextualist method in the Pepperian sense
by championing or privileging one worldview over another. This, as I shall
argue throughout the book, draws readers and audiences to confirm their
point of view. It fails to help them recognize that what is useful now may,
like the expiring map metaphor in our discussion of the learning organization,
soon be less useful. Contextualism is rooted in the belief that users (in our
work, leaders) must be able to derive the limitations of each worldview and
the options presented by others. To state this in a contrarian fashion: when is
organizational learning contra-indicated? recruiting managers, not leaders,
prescribed? or insensitivity to others' cultures rewarded? The tendency at the
present time is to respond, "not often". But this may be problematic, not
solely because the future is unknown but more interestingly because the problem set of leaders is not determined by reading the *zeitgeist* or benchmarking
the skills at any one point in time used by excellent, sustainable, innovative
or winning organizations. In contextualism, it is not trend reading that is
rewarded, but the ability of leaders to define their situation in a vocabulary
that is rooted in the worldviews which surround them.

WHAT IS A WORLDVIEW?

Worldviews are shared sense-making paradigms.[15] Within the assumptions
and conventions of a viable worldview we feel comforted. Our actions and
thoughts, it is evident, are rational. They are rooted in the self-evident axioms
and corollaries of our worldview. Worldviews orient us towards actions and
rituals in the midst of uncertainty. They help us cope with incomplete or
changing information and reassure us that our present investment of time,
energy, capital and passion supports some good or even worthwhile causes. A
worldview helps us navigate in precarious times. Like a well-worn identity or
trusted script, we settle down within a worldview. The worldview privileges a
particular understanding of instrumental action and the role of leaders. A
viable worldview reassures us that there are those among us who, with direct
action, planning, faith and technology, can lead us into a less problematic
future. Leaders carry our aspirations within a worldview. They embody and
exemplify our desire for the good or better world. We celebrate leaders when
they deliver. We excoriate them in the midst of their own and therefore our
own failures.

It is my contention that there is a basic vocabulary from which to begin mapping our understanding of the varying worldviews of instrumental leaders. I call this, in the spirit of post-cold war geopolitics, the four faces or worldviews of capitalism. In this designation, capitalism is not privileged as a macroeconomic embodiment of free markets tied to a democratic ethos. It is not poised against communism, socialism, theocracy or despotism. Rather, capitalism, whether engaged in by the Japanese, the Italians, the Algerians or the Americans, is the process engaged in by instrumental actors investing their time, energy, passion and/or capital in the pursuit of their goals. Capitalist worldviews instrumentally envelop the notion that the future is designed, often consciously, by men and women striving to fulfil their individual and collective desires.

In Figure 1.1, I outline the four directions – the North, South, East and West – of the instrumental worldviews upon which I build this book.[16] Within an evolutionary perspective, instrumental worldviews are made coherent and credible for would-be adherents by being pulled externally or outward towards competitive exchanges with the other, inward towards systems maintenance, upward towards control by the few and downwards in recognition of the greater flexibility arising from input from the many. In Figure 1.1, each direction establishes a functional requisite or collective concern which, as we shall make clear later in this chapter, must be met or seen to have been met by those who are recognized as successful leaders within a worldview.[17] Leaders, within a contextualized reading of leadership, act as exemplars or embodiments of the values of a particular worldview. As a corollary of this, successful leaders in one worldview may not be seen as such by others in another worldview.

Worldviews are sense-making devices which assist its adherents in reducing anxiety or solving problems of being in a world of scarcities and existing in an ephemeral, often frightened, state. Worldviews and their exemplars – leaders – embody the working out of the practices, assumptions and tacit conventions required to get things done. Interestingly, each worldview has difficulty in dealing with those from different worldviews. In fact, parochial or local leaders see those from other worldviews as problematic. Theirs is a vocabulary heavily anchored in the basic premises of a worldview. Local leaders succeed by staying very close to the anchor skills required in their worldview. They have leadership, but not great reach.

Cosmopolitan leaders, on the other hand, can transition from one worldview to another. They are, however, always strongest in one instrumental worldview but they can hear the story at play in other worldviews and with work they can make themselves heard outside their worldview. At first, cosmopolitan leaders, like people learning a new language, translate the language of the new worldview they are exploring into the clear terminology of their native worldview. With work and a willingness to move down on the

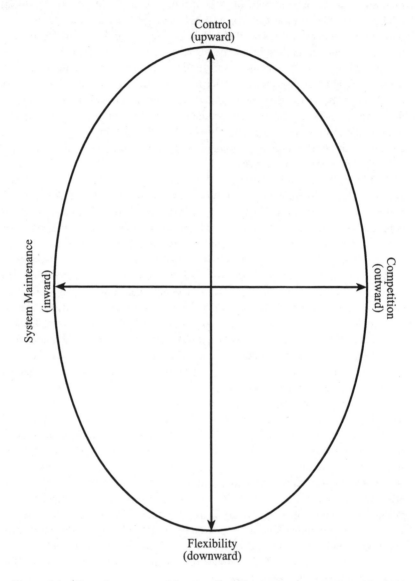

Figure 1.1   Four directions and functional requisites of instrumental worldviews

learning curve for a duration, cosmopolitan leaders can become proficient at instrumental actions in more than one worldview. Cosmopolitan leaders, as we shall learn, forge the links which hybridize worldviews. They have reach. Cosmopolitan leaders can reinvent themselves.

In the next subsections, I will focus on the four instrumental worldviews of local leaders. Two distinct qualifications should be kept in mind. First, local leaders, unlike the cosmopolitan ones I shall explore towards the end of the book, are true believers in a worldview. Local leaders limit their reach. They stay within the basic premises and assumptions that lend initial consistency to the leadership story within that worldview. The second qualification is that I steer clear of situationalist or contingency approaches to leadership.[18] These approaches argue that if one changes the situation or the external environment in which leaders and their organization operate, the effective leader must adapt. The contextualist approach to leadership, as will become more evident, is rooted in the assumption that leaders must change their cognitive lens or worldview before they attempt to realign their skill portfolios. Local leaders learn to accommodate other worldviews by translating them into the vocabulary of their worldview. Cosmopolitan leaders engage in anchor cross-story skill transitions or ACTs. They are capable of reinventing themselves as leaders. They, in time, take on others' worldviews. The third and last qualification I will bring to your attention before pushing on to examine the four faces of capitalism is that I am self-consciously limiting my discussion to "instrumental" worldviews. An instrumental worldview does not focus upon spiritual aspects or the human pursuit of the sacred. This emphasis is possible. I foresee future research in the contextualization of leadership probing non-instrumental worldviews – aesthetics, spirituality and the expressive or emotional context of relations. My focus is simply upon leaders who get things done in the material world. Leaders are people who make things happen in such a way that others seek to emulate them.

FOUR INSTRUMENTAL WORLDVIEWS

In this section I introduce four instrumental worldviews as sense-making devices used worldwide to accomplish goals. Each worldview prescribes and describes how adherents to it can live in the world and satisfy their desires. Interestingly, each worldview privileges certain desires and highlights specific anxieties as worthy of banishment. I urge the reader to resist the temptation – one that grows with one's curiosity – to start hybridizing worldviews. Let us first get into the minds and stories of local leaders, followed by cosmopolitan leaders. At this point I am interested in making you, the reader, conscious of the basic ways in which our species makes sense of what goals are worth pursuing and how. Leaders make things happen. They are those of us who crystallize goals. They call our attention to what can be done. In the act of doing, the very essence of practice, we turn to the leader for guidance, structure, support and explanatory options.

The four instrumental worldviews are: (1) the entrepreneurial worldview; (2) the regulatory worldview; (3) the communitarian worldview; and (4) the network worldview. Each worldview is made up of a series of assumptions. Each provides those within it with a sense of purpose and a belief that their goal-oriented actions are embedded in an ordered cosmos. This sense of knowing how and what one does, why and for what intrinsic and extrinsic reward, provides those within a worldview with a comforting sense of their relationship to a bigger story. As we shall see in the next section these stories tell us what it takes to become a leader or a person of influence within a particular worldview. Instrumental worldviews are templates for action and reflection. They are the archetypical stories depicting how we, relying upon leaders as winners, decision-makers, shamans and explorers, get things done. What is interesting is that what we ought to accomplish, how we do it and how we justify our expenditure of time, capital and energy are told in very different stories within each worldview.

In Figure 1.2, I outline the four instrumental worldviews as grounded in the primary goals which both bind adherents and help them make sense of their actions. Note that this Figure locates the worldviews as combinations of the directions and functional requisites made explicit in Figure 1.1. Thus the entrepreneurial worldview designated by the sign for money combines the upward pull towards control with the outward emphasis upon competition. This is the worldview of winners and losers avidly pursuing their goals in contests in which control over time goes to the winners. The entrepreneurial worldview is pragmatic. Outcomes are determined by markets. The freer or less rule-ridden the market, the more the contestants, rather than the umpires or referees, determine the outcomes. Control goes to individuals as winners. Firms or collectivities stay within the power of the invisible hand that guides the market. The $ sign (euro, pound sterling, dollar, etc.) is the symbol for this worldview because those who succeed in getting results accumulate wealth and power. Read *Fortune* or *Forbes* for depictions of this worldview and its leaders. The leader is located in the winner's circle. We seek to emulate or displace them in our quest for entry into the winner's circle. All winners must compete again another day. Losers believe that with this worldview, in time, they can become winners.

The regulatory worldview, designated by the symbol of a tiered or stratified triangle (Figure 1.2), turns our attention from the market, in which winners emerge triumphant, to a hierarchical rule-based system. The pull is inward towards system maintenance. The system is designed or engineered to

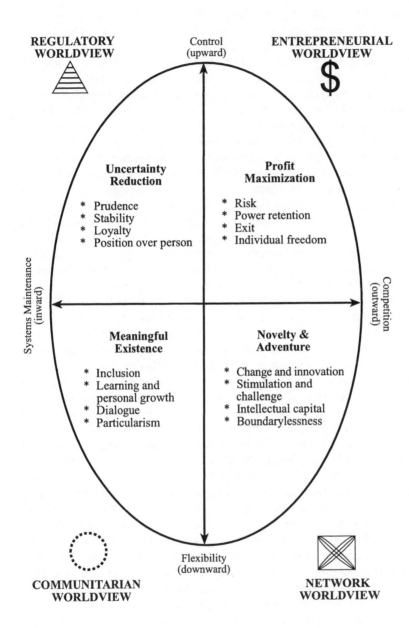

Figure 1.2   Four instrumental worldviews

continue in a stable fashion. The pull in the system, as manifested in the shape of the stratified triangle, is upward. Control via policy is rule-based and set by the few at the top or pinnacle of the hierarchy. The goal of instrumental actors in the regulatory worldview is not profit maximization but uncertainty reduction. Leaders are not self-made individualists who have, through dint of effort and decisive action, bootstrapped themselves into the winner's circle, but rather credentialed analysts who in a prudent adherence to the rules within the system have moved upward towards positions of authority over time. This is not the realm of "just do it", but the cautious effort to maintain a reliable system over time. Leaders here lead from the top; they possess position power over subordinates. It is important to recognize that competition is not absent in the regulatory worldview. It is inward driven. Rather than firms competing with others as in the entrepreneurial worldview, parts of the system, including individuals, compete for scarce resources in the system. Individuals struggle and attempt to move up within the hierarchy. Varying departments or subsystems within the hierarchical system compete for secure budgetary allocations. This competition is played out within the rules of the hierarchical or regulated system.

The communitarian worldview, depicted by the circle bound by a broken circumference (see Figure 1.2), pulls downward toward the inclusion of many within the decision-making nexus in the community and inward towards system, or in this case cultural, maintenance. While we speak of the firm and prize individualism in the entrepreneurial worldview, and speak of the hierarchical system and privilege rule-based conventions in the regulatory worldview, we talk of the collective as a community and cherish the experience of a meaningful existence in the communitarian worldview. The communitarian worldview empowers members. These are called lower participants or subordinates in the regulatory worldview and followers in the entrepreneurial worldview. Rather than adhering closely to the explicit rules prevalent in the regulatory worldview, members rely upon their use of discretion rooted in the norms used within the organization's culture. Members in a communitarian worldview interpret, using the meaning system imbedded in the community, what is to be valued and when. They downplay the meaning and impact of the bottom line – an image which rules the roost in the entrepreneurial worldview. The leader in the communitarian worldview leads from the centre. The leader is inclusive of others and is an exemplar of the values aspired to by members of the community. This is a community which values trust and dialogue-based learning.

The network worldview marries the pull outward towards competition with the desire for flexibility, a downward pull towards the use of collaboration and projects employing temporary team members. Those imbued with the network worldview, self-consciously pursue innovation and the quest for originality (see Figure 1.2). The network worldview prizes competition but, unlike that present in the entrepreneurial worldview, rewards accrue to those who do research and development that results in a new marketable output. This is not a worldview that celebrates mimicry or pirating. This is a quest for originality. Creating breakthroughs requires creativity. Flexibility in the network worldview celebrates leaders who lead from the edge. Unlike the communitarian worldview, network communities are not permanent. They are hot groups or communities of practice riveted to explore the next new thing.[19] Network leaders lead from the edge of a shifting and dynamic body of applied knowledge. Reputation is vital to network participants.[20] Networks are temporary. Each time a project comes to a conclusion the leaders from defunct or completed projects utilize information within the now-disbanded network as the basis to reinvest in the personnel and technology for new projects. This start up, stop and begin anew worldview is prone to cataclysmic bouts of creativity, often revolutionary in their implications, but equally as frequently followed by a fallow period or a meltdown.

In introducing the four worldviews – entrepreneurial, regulatory, communitarian and network – it is important to recognize that the first impulse when building a contextual vocabulary is to avoid the simultaneous occurrence of all four and to align each as a historical epoch. Thus many histories of organizations or instrumental activity tell a tale in which, out of the ashes of a land-based feudalism, there emerges an urban-based industrial society whose first footsteps are found in the owner-operated, self-made social Darwinism of the successful entrepreneur. The neo-classical economist's notion of the firm, as first espoused by Adam Smith and later tied to the logic of "creative destruction", emphasizes an era rife with those imbued with the entrepreneurial worldview. In this story the market generates a level playing field of competitors all vying to compete and become victorious. Victory is not merely staying alive, but, in winning, contributing to the wealth of the nation. Those who contribute the most to the wealth of nations are, and ought to be, our leaders.

The historicizing of worldviews creates a contingent view of contextualization rooted in temporal periods. Thus in the beginning of the industrial revolution was the entrepreneurial worldview, most frequently followed by a recognition that, as firms become large and/or as entrepreneurs began to rely upon price-fixing, free-riding and chicanery, in order to win, third-party rule makers and legislators in the guise of elected officials, managers of large firms, boards of directors and professional bodies evolved both to deal with market failures and to rein in the externalities generated by unchecked powerful entrepreneurs. The regulatory worldview comes into historical prominence as bureaucratic organizations rooted in the rules of the government or the rules imposed by cadres of professional bodies are licensed and supported. In the regulatory worldview, the winners are systems stabilizers, uncertainty reducers and bringers of law, order and systematization. In the imaging of leaders, the historical shift is from the self-made individualist to the educated, numerate official or expert spokesperson. Those in this historical telling of worldviews that are nostalgic for the old days lament the absence of freedom and the imposition of a lattice of forms and credentials that must be filled in and sat through before a man or woman can become a leader.

Within this simplified and stylized historical reading of worldviews, the communitarian worldview rises due to the inability of the entrepreneurial and regulatory worldviews which precede it to build a community in which members derive a sense that theirs is a meaningful existence. This "membership has its privileges" worldview derogates the entrepreneurial worldview as stressful, too focused upon winning and upon failing to recognize the benefits of communality, cooperation and dialogue. It similarly expresses discomfort with the cold impersonal idealization of the mechanical system attributed by communitarians to regulatory capitalists and, in lieu, lauds the organic adaptive community. The call so prevalent when conscription is being resisted that "I am a person, not a number" resonates with the tone and temper of the communitarian quest for a local and particular identity, not a systems-based label. Flexibility wins over control since problems, when they get more complex, require diverse input.

The network world, if I read business books on leadership correctly, predominates in our present historical period of white-water change, globalization, contract workers and emphasis upon innovation and knowledge creation, acquisition and transfer.[21] The network worldview borrows from its predecessors and seeks to cope with the weakness each manifests in the face of escalating uncertainty. The network worldview shares the entrepreneurial focus upon competition, but turns to problems which are complex, quickly altering, knowledge based and global. As a consequence, leadership turns from control by the few in the entrepreneurial worldview to the flexibility of knowledge inputs from the many. The network worldview looks to the regulatory worldview for capital and as a potential buyer for its new ideas and innovations, but disdains the hierarchy itself as a tradition-based model of governance incapable of modifying the rules quickly enough to engage in genuine innovation. Lastly, the network worldview shares the communitarian focus upon flexibility and collaboration, but not its interest in systems maintenance. Networks are exploratory. They neither idealize the centre, nor seek to protect it; their attention is riveted towards the edge. Here boundaries disappear and the clear, albeit evolving, language of a given community with a resilient culture gives way to an experimental culture.[22] The experimental culture is temporary. It self-consciously folds when it either fails to achieve its ends or is beaten to these by other competing networks.

This historical reading in which worldviews are temporarily aligned is, I believe, the dominant albeit tacit use of contextualization in studying instrumental action in contemporary books on leadership. Thus, when various authors speak about "revolution" in business or instrumental activities, they are addressing their reading of the various shifts from the predominance of one worldview or set of worldviews to others. Those, for example, who heralded the "managerial revolution" were calling attention to the shift from the owner-operated, non-publicly held firm run by the entrepreneur to the worldview of the trained manager or public administrator whose actions are accountable to stockholders and/or constituents. Those who trumpeted the revolutionary potential of the post-industrial or information economy were drawing attention to the shift from a goods-producing economy tied to tangible goods and measurable deliverables (entrepreneurial and regulatory) to a service-based or abstract knowledge-based economy (communitarian and network worldview) in which the exchanges required trust between buyer and seller and in which an increasingly educated population is willing to explore new options. As a final example, those speaking to the even more contemporary globalization revolution are tacitly calling attention to the shift from a worldview privileging one community, state, culture or market rooted in a common history or currency (communitarian and regulatory worldview) to a deregulated, free trade or boundaryless market in which varying cultures, currencies and languages mingle (entrepreneurial and network).

In this volume, contingent contextualism tied to a historical reading of the rise, fall and needed return of worldviews is purposefully avoided. Worldviews, I argue, exist simultaneously. They compete for the hearts and minds of individuals. This is not to say that global readings emphasizing that ours is an age in need of more leaders from the network worldview or trumpeting a return to execution oriented, end-results leaders in the entrepreneurial worldview are not credible. Who, after all, can visit a book-store without reading about the lamentable absence of compassion and ethics for leaders with skills in the communitarian worldview or the death of accountability occasioned by a serious failure to reward and promote capable leaders from the regulatory worldview into positions of genuine authority. All these positions, for varying motives borne by their authors, advocate a particular worldview to solve more problems than it causes. This is true within a world-view but, alas, is far from self-evident when viewed by others. A contextual approach to leadership systematically outlines and explains how masterful leaders develop an awareness of simultaneously occurring worldviews. Those who stay within their preferred story in a worldview develop skills which translate these stories through their preferred worldview or dominant paradigm. These are local leaders. Those who reinvent themselves by moving out of their preferred stories into others are cosmopolitan leaders. Each shares a form of masking what is recognizable to those who seek leaders.

Each worldview is cradled in a delicately coherent story which lionizes and romanticizes a distinct version of the competent or masterful leader. Let us turn to an introduction to each story and catch a glimpse of the leader within the story. In subsequent chapters, using a story template we shall explore: (a) the buccaneer leader in the "money talks" story; (b) the bureaucratic leader in the "built to last" story; (c) the participative leader in the "cooperation pays" story, and (d) the knowledge leader in the "portal to a new world" story.

STORIES AND WORLDVIEWS

Robert Coles notes that "the beauty of a good story is its openness – the way you or I or anyone reading it can take it and use it for ourselves".[23] Stories are encapsulations of worldviews. This position is an explicit recognition that we live in a world already loaded with meaning and convention, much of it we did not construct ourselves. We, as active sense-makers, must both learn these meanings or conventions and, when so driven, suggest alternatives. We recognize a worldview, or in this book "a face of capitalism", when we can hear the stories that emanate from it. In his path breaking work entitled *Ways of Worldmaking*, Nelson Goodman depicts worldviews as versions of reality that are comprehensible to a particular audience.[24] Worldviews compete for audiences. Storytellers learn to suture worldviews to audiences and, when presented with a mixed audience, to skilfully hybridize worldviews.

Worldviews are coherent stories which provide us with a means of making sense of our world. When shared with others, stories provide us with a sense of security and aid us either in trying to become a leader or in locating one. Leaders provide proof of the existence of the efficacy of the power of a particular worldview. Leaders embody, exemplify and concretize a particular story. Leaders, often called heroes in the stories we read as children, are now labelled leaders in our adult life and come in many different versions just like the heroes in our childhood. We select or are drawn to worldviews in which the leader resonates with virtue and accomplishments which, once realized, reinforce our interest in the story. As children we read or had our parents read stories to us again and again. As adults we seek to become or locate those whom we believe can help make these stories real – leaders.

Leaders put worldviews into flesh (see Figure 1.3). They concretize them and lend a sense of "real world" pragmatism to a complicated story. In our contextualization of leadership we will, using the worldviews discussed in

Chapter 1, turn to four types of leaders, each configured into a specific story. In Figure 1.3 we see where the entrepreneurial worldview – rife with the money talks story and where markets prevail – gives rise to the confident, action-oriented, self-made buccaneer leader. The regulatory view which marries control by a few people high up within a hierarchy with the pull towards tradition and rule-based systems maintenance is grounded in the built to last story. The built to last story and, within it, the bureaucratic leader, are the focus of Chapter 3. In this story emphasizing the longevity and stability of well-designed and managed systems, the authoritative figure is the prudent, loyal, analytically minded leader.

Note that the stories that emphasize control each treat it differently. In the money talks story, control rests with the ability of the buccaneer to execute and obtain bottom line results. The buccaneer leader is in control of his or her followers. They do not control the market. Control is the "just dessert" of winners – those proven to be successful in explicit high stakes contests. In the built to last story, control accrues over time to both the policy makers who succeed in stabilizing, enduring and reliable systems and to the systems themselves. The bureaucratic leader in the regulatory worldview sits at the top of a complex set of rules, structures and routines. Due to their position in the hierarchy, they see further than others within the system. Control goes to those who anticipate problems, reduce uncertainty and, working within the rules, routines and structures, build an enduring, reliable system.

In the regulatory worldview, rules take priority over markets and systems take priority over persons. The built to last story handles the succession from leader to leader well; the money talks story is rife with tragic transitions among and between buccaneers. This is, as we shall see, because in the built to last story, persons are selected for positions in accordance with the rules. They possess the credentials, certificates and past experiences required to fill the job description. In the money talks story, individuals and individualism prevail over the design and structure of rule-based hierarchical systems. In the entrepreneurial worldview, there is no job description other than "win baby, win".

The communitarian and network worldviews (see Figure 1.3) evolve, albeit with different strategies, to cope with greater uncertainty than either the entrepreneurial or the regulatory worldviews. They pull downward towards inclusion, empowerment and the decentralization of decision-making. The cooperation pays story which bolsters the communitarian worldview handles change by creating an open, organic and adaptive community which interprets the rules of the bureaucratic leader rather than obeys them. The participative leader in the cooperation pays story challenges members of the community to cope with ambiguity by developing a culture of dialogue rooted in shared information and trust. The participative leader succeeds, not

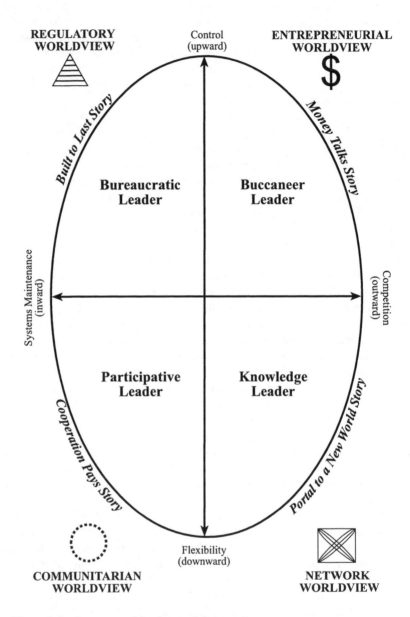

Figure 1.3   Instrumental leaders and their stories

when members increase their profit or reduce their experience of uncertainty, but rather when they feel that their involvement in the collectivity furnishes them with a meaningful identity and a sense of purpose. Those who claim that "work is my life" and then put this into practice by refusing to relocate to a higher paying job elsewhere are showing their commitment to a culture which provides them with intrinsic benefits.

The network worldview understands the "good", not in membership in a consensually based community, but in pushing the envelope. This is the portal to a new world story. It is told through the eyes of a knowledge leader who attracts creative and knowledgeable workers to the edge of a pool of knowledge in search of a breakthrough. The denizens of the network worldview live in a swiftly changing world in which knowledge becomes obsolete as new discoveries are brought on line. Just as Heraclitus, the ancient Greek philosopher said, "one cannot put one's foot in the same river twice", so too those drawn to the knowledge leader see change as inevitable, pervasive and desirable. The knowledge leader emerges as a guide in the midst of the ongoing, often frantic inquiry engaged in by participants in the loosely structured network. One may find wealth, a meaningful existence, and even a sense of security as in the built to last story, however, the primary goal in the portal to a new world story is to explore – to design and create a less burdensome human condition. The desire or call to creative invention entails radical innovation, or claims thereof, and a critical disposition towards the status quo.

Each story has a coherent thematic structure (see Figure 1.4). The money talks story idealizes the liberty of a self-made individualist and extols the virtue of freedom. Freedom holds for both winners and losers. All are permitted to exit and re-enter contests. The enemy or shadow in this story is rules. They entrench authority and prohibit the player in the actual contest from determining the outcome. Rules typically are the manifestation of a false authority. The umpires or referees, those not in the purifying flame of competition, should not determine outcomes. They are too far from the action. As authority figures they must be kept in the background in the money talks story. Neither greater clarity nor better judgement, buccaneers argue, arises from either dispassionate involvement or imposed authority. Authority and power must be won. The call to freedom in the money talks story is hot. It admits, even idealizes, the logic of active, passionate involvement as long as all succumb to the real authority – the authority of the market. Those who win should be and are rewarded; they have proven their contribution to society. We are free – winners and losers – only when we can enter and exit markets with liberty. In this story, progress is possible when free markets determine, and justly so, who gets what, when, where and why.

The built to last story privileges objectivity, prizes data, celebrates

Leadership in context

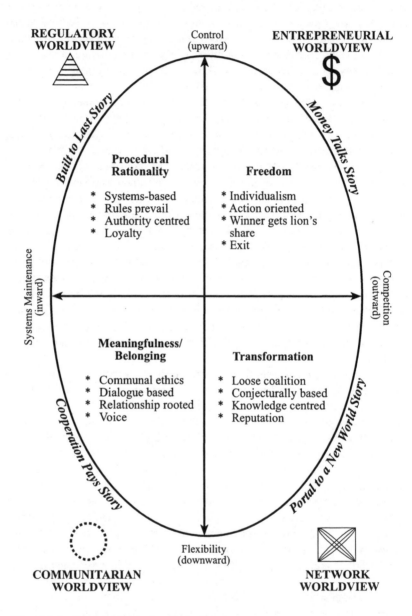

Figure 1.4   Leadership stories: basic themes

procedural rationality in the guise of and loyalty to formal rules, codes and structures. In the domain of the bureaucratic leader, position denotes authority and, the higher one's position within the hierarchy, the greater one's authority or control. Freedom, metaphorically speaking, is "cool". It is the freedom of the expert or specialist who shows their intelligence by mobilizing data and evidence to justify action. In the money talks story, experts are doers. Freedom is contested. It must be won often through hard-fought struggle. In the built to last story, experts render credible, dispassionate accounts employing evidence to support their views. Planning precedes action. Leaders are loyal agents to the system. They are subservient to the rules of the system and must follow the rules to change rules. The system takes priority over the individual. One does one's duty for the system and, in time, one will be amply rewarded by the very security and stability that is the goal of the bureaucratic leader within the built to last story. At times one may feel lonely and out of touch with others in this rule-bound system, but the stability, argued by those who buy in, is well worth the depersonalization.

The coherent theme in the cooperation pays story stewarded by the participative leader is an antidote to the feeling of loneliness, depersonalization and meaninglessness. In the communitarian value system, life is experienced as meaningful (see Figure 1.4) when one feels that one is being heard and seen by relevant others – one's input counts. This motivates. Members become committed and strive for excellence when they are empowered by a trusting community in which they feel that their views are taken seriously. What makes us lonely and compliant rather than involved and committed is the misplaced values of the other worldviews. In the money talks story, there is no community. Each of us attempts to use the other to get more of what we want. In the built to last story, blind obedience to a mechanical system and a formalized top-down communication system stifles dialogue and constrains learning. In the portal to a new world story the knowledge leader utilizes collaborative terms in a mercenary fashion by attempting to employ the appearance of a genuine community in order to extract tacit knowledge from employees. When their knowledge is obsolete, they are left to fend for themselves.

Those drawn to the portal to a new world story piloted by the visionary knowledge leader see themselves as pioneers engaged in a much needed transformation of the way we do things (see Figure 1.4). This story marries flexibility with competition. It is a story of the exciting prospect of change that, when implemented, will make a difference. The network worldview draws the best minds to large pools of money during periods in which the public is eager to push the envelope. The public seeks breakthroughs in these areas and accordingly is willing to license experimentation. Flexibility is needed to create a collaborative context for creatives who enjoy living on the edge with few rules. Varying networks aggressively compete with one another for the priority of discovery and the intellectual capital to be accrued by legitimately claiming the radical innovations as intellectual property.[25] A conjecturally based "what if" logic thrives in this story. Networks adapt to this pursuit of change under the beacon of a "what if" logic by developing an amoebic-like or *ad hoc* structure which remains unstable, yet generative. It is a story in which knowledge and its pursuit provides competitive advantage. Change is believed to be unprecedented and old maps do not cover the important territory that is emerging. While there is a tendency to associate the portal to a new world story with activities that we envision today as setting the stage for the future, the same can be said about those who adhered to this worldview in our great-great grandmother's era. New ideas have been brought, albeit not at equal rates, into our lives in each generation. It is part of our human condition that has us convinced that our generation is really on the leading edge.

A STORY TEMPLATE

In Chapters 2 through 5, I outline the money talks story as embodied in the buccaneer leader; the built to last story exemplified by the bureaucratic leader; the cooperation pays story modelled after the participative leader and then in Chapter 5, the portal to a new world story with the knowledge leader. Each of these leaders is uniquely adapted to the axioms and assumptions built into their worldviews. They are not, I argue, simply interchangeable. Moreover, and much to the point of this book, discussions of leadership frequently proceeds as if it were apparent that one of these leaders is clearly the best. In contextualism this is not so. Leaders thrive in their worldview.

In Chapter 6 following the four archetype depictions of the leaders within their leadership stories, I turn to how, in practice, leaders within a leadership story employ the anchor skill in their worldview to accommodate the pulls of the other worldviews. The local leader has the virtue of strongly signalling an archetypal message to would-be followers, subordinates, members and/or participants. The local leader's story addresses, using the four faces of capitalism model, how and why leaders within a worldview develop particular skills. As shall become more apparent, they do so to deal with those with whom they must enter into exchange and who hail from and are strongly anchored in other worldviews. The role of the local leader is limited. He or she succeeds in coping with interlopers by translating their behaviour and motivations into patterns explained by the leader's worldview.

In the final chapter of the book, I address how cosmopolitan leaders within the contextualist model of leadership, through hard work, reinvent themselves by systematically developing leadership skills that extend and even leave their preferred worldview. Cosmopolitan leaders are the epitome of reflective practitioners. They systematically extend their skills, understanding the four faces of capitalism, by developing anchor cross-story transitions (ACTs). These ACTs extend their leadership competence and expand their reach as leaders. ACTs exist at three levels of gradient – ACTs "1" to "3". The higher the number associated with the ACT, the more difficult it is for the cosmopolitan leader to successfully engage in the transition from the skills associated with his or her preferred worldview to others. ACT "3" gradient transitions involve leaders reinventing themselves or, in the contextualist model of leadership, successfully transforming anchor skills from one leadership story to another. Cosmopolitan leaders succeed, not when they extend their reach at any time, but rather when the context requires them to radically alter their skill portfolio as leaders.

One of the interesting problems that I must deal with in telling the basic leadership stories is to avoid appropriating other leaders' worldviews to mine. Each of us, the four faces of capitalism model argues, is partial to one of these worldviews over others. My own predilection is towards that of the participative leader in the cooperation pays story. Each of us believes quite earnestly that we see others' positions clearly and are not caught by the cognitive lens of our preferred worldview. To help me from reading my worldview onto others, I will use a net or template. It cannot force me into objectivity. It can, however, encourage me to be fair and, in my cooperation pays fashion, give this manuscript to buccaneers, bureaucratic, participatory and knowledge leaders to make sure that I have not given a pale version of their story.

To organize the stories at the heart of the four faces of capitalism model and to begin to make sense of the differing skills in each, I will follow an outline or synopsis. Each story in the next four chapters is divided into six story components. These are: (1) *origins* of the story and of the leader within it; (2) the *plot*, attending in particular to the role of the leader in overcoming tensions, problem solving and moving on to new issues; (3) the *audience*, or to whom the story is most frequently and successfully told; (4) the *protagonist*, a discussion of how the main character or hero is seen within the story and how they are depicted by others who hear (but do not fully buy into) the story; (5) the *genre*, or what category of storytelling most suits the tale and its tellers; and lastly, (6) the *lesson*, or what is learned by attending to the particular leadership model.

Let us now turn to the buccaneer leader in the money talks story and see the footprint it leaves in our basic understanding of leadership. While buccaneer leaders thrive in the money talks story, they, as we shall see, are frequently called upon in times of crisis and breakdown within the other leadership stories.

NOTES

1. Warren Bennis depicts the difficulty in trying to capture and put the leader under the microscope. See Warren Bennis (2003), *On Becoming a Leader*, Cambridge, MA: Perseus.
2. Robert H. Frank and Philip Cook (1995), *The Winner-Take-All Society*, New York: Free Press, point towards the problematic collective outcome of zero sum games taken to the extreme. Robert M. Axelrod (1998), *The Complexity of Cooperation: Agent-Based Models of Competition and Collaboration*, Princeton, NJ: Princeton University Press, works out some of the leadership implications of working from a cooperative versus a competitive worldview. In a more hands-on approach Robert Fulmer, Philip Gibbs and Marshall Goldsmith (2000), "Developing leaders: How winning companies keep on winning", *Sloan Management Review*, **42**(11), pp. 49–59, explore how General Electric, Hewlett Packard, and Johnson and Johnson develop a sustainable competitive advantage through their selection, training and creating incentives for leaders.
3. The rhetoric of the battlefield is used extensively in both leadership and business literature. See Paul Solman and Thomas Friedman (1982), *Life and Death on the Corporate Battlefield: How Companies Win, Lose, and Survive*, New York: Simon & Schuster. Compare this to the image of the organization in works extolling the collaboration and trusting nature of leadership. See, for example, the recent compilation of readings by Bart Nooteboom and Frederique Six (2003), *The Trust Process in Organization: Empirical Studies of the Determinants and the Process of Trust Development*, Cheltenham, UK and Northampton, MA, USA: Edward Elgar; and Kurt T. Dirks and Donald L. Ferrin (2002), "Trust in leadership: Meta-analytic findings and implications for research and practice", *Journal of Applied Psychology*, **87**(4), pp. 611–26.
4. Intellectual capital refers to the patents, licences, copyrights and other means of extracting rents from creative products or ideas. See Daniel Andriessen (2004), *Making Sense of Intellectual Capital: Designing a Method for the Valuation of Intangibles*, Amsterdam: Butterworth-Heinemann, for a useful contemporary treatment of the topic. We focus upon it when we discuss the knowledge leader in Chapter 5 of this book. A sense of the uncertainty-reducing of leaders in bureaucratic contexts can be found in the classic treatment of the topic by James D. Thompson (1969), *Organization in Action*, New York: McGraw-Hill, and Peter M. Blau and Marshall W. Meyer (1991), *Bureaucracy in Modern Society*, New York: Random House. For an updating of the role of bureaucracy and the bureaucratic leader in modern society see Gyorgy Gajduschek (2002), "Bureaucracy: Is it efficient? Is it not? Is that the question?" *Administration and Society*, **34**(6), pp. 700–22.
5. Capitalism is not employed here as the antithesis to Communism or in tension with socialism, but as the human investment of time, capital, passion and energy in either getting things done by oneself or paying others to engage in instrumental actions. See James Fulcher (2004), *Capitalism: A Very Short Introduction*, Oxford: Oxford University Press, for a solid primer. See Arlie Russell Hochschild (2003), *The Commercialization of Intimate Life: Notes From Home and Work*, Berkeley, CA: University of California Press, for the shift from capitalism as a mode of production to capitalism as a cognitive lens from which to make sense of things.
6. While Stephen C. Pepper (1942), *World Hypotheses: A Study in Evidence*, Berkeley, CA: University of California Press, has been invaluable in contributing to my understanding of contextualism, more modern treatments may be found in the critical review by E.J. Capaldi and Robert W. Procter (1999), *Contextualism in Psychological Research: A Critical Review*, Thousand Oaks, CA: Sage. Diane Gillespie (1992), *The Mind's We: Contextualism in Cognitive Psychology*, Carbondale, IL: Southern Illinois University, provides insights on the treatment of "we" which I use in my concept of worldview. For a connection between

contextualism and the relativism of worldviews, see Elaine B. Johnson (2002), *Contextual Teaching and Learning: What is it and Why it is Here to Stay*, Thousand Oaks, CA: Corwin Press.

7. While William H. Berquist (1993), *The Postmodern Organization: Mastering the Art of Irreversible Change*, San Francisco, CA: Jossey-Bass, attempts to relate postmodernism to leadership, it is Jim Norwine and Jonathan M.S. Smith (eds) (2000), *Worldview Flux: Perplexed Values Among Postmodern Peoples*, Lanham, MD: Lexington Books, who push the position to its conclusion. For a useful treatment of the social construction of key concepts in organization science from a postmodern perspective see Kenneth J. Gergen and Tojo Joseph Thatchen-Key (2004), "Organization science as a social construction", *Journal of Applied Behavioural Science*, **40**(2), pp. 228–49.

8. This susceptibility to multiple meanings and interpretations puts language and its use at the centre of making sense of leadership and organizations. See for example Graham W. Astley and Raymond F. Zammuto (1992), "Organization science, managers and language games", *Organization Science*, **10**(3), pp. 503–25. Gilbert W. Fairholm captures my sense that scholars in the field of leadership, even very good ones, treat leadership as a series of theories imposed upon leaders by researchers rather than a concerted effort to capture the differing cognitive lens used as interpretive filters by active leaders. See G.W. Fairholm (1998), *Perspectives on Leadership: From the Science of Management to its Spiritual Heart*, London: Quorum. For a more orthodox treatment of this perspective, see Murray Hiebert (2001), *The Encyclopedia of Leadership: A Practical Guide to Popular Leadership Theories and Techniques*, New York: McGraw-Hill.

9. Blending contextualism and social constructionism, Kenneth J. Gegen (1994), *Realities and Relationships: Soundings in Social Construction*, Cambridge, MA: Harvard University Press, captures this idea of ongoing change, interpretation and possible inconsistencies in our daily routines. Sven-Erik Sjöstrand, Jörgen Sandberg and Mats Tyrstrup (eds) (2001), *Invisible Management: The Social Construction of Leadership*, London: Thomson Learning, attempt to apply contextualism and social constructionism to leadership in this useful but uneven compilation of readings.

10. Polyglotism here refers to more than diversity or multiculturalism but to the relativistic framework needed when social discourse steeped in different values and assumptions clash. Richard N. Osborn, James G. Hunt and Lawrence R. Jauch (2002), "Toward a contextual theory of leadership", *Leadership Quarterly*, **13**(6), pp. 797–837, like myself, attempt to build a contextual model. Rather than using worldviews, they employ the contexts of stability, crisis, dynamic equilibrium and the edge of chaos as states in which leaders must lose the assumption that the language of leadership scholarship is necessary and sufficient for the task at hand. See Jill M.S.W. Freedman (1996), *Narrative Therapy: The Social Construction of Preferred Realities*, New York: Norton, who uses social discourse theory in a discussion of stories as a form of preferred realities. Bill Doolin (2003), "Narratives of change: Discourse, technology and organization", *Organization*, **10**(4), pp. 751–70 captures this in the leadership literature.

11. James W. Cortada (2001), *21st Century Business: Managing and Working in the New Digital Economy*, Upper Saddle River, NJ: Financial Times/Prentice Hall, captures the paradox between globalization as a distancing process and, in it, the potential for digitization to create community and intimacy. For a discussion of how IKEA's CEO Anders Dahlvig recognizes this paradox in building the organizational culture in his global firm, see Katarlnia Kling and Ingela Goleman (2003), "IKEA CEO Anders Dahlvig on intentional growth and IKEA's unique culture and brand identity", *Academy of Management Executive*, **7**(1), pp. 31–8.

12. This process, frequently called sense-making, has been thoroughly and creatively explored by Karl Weick. See for example, Karl E. Weick (2001), *Making Sense of the Organization*, Oxford: Blackwell Publishing and Karl E. Weick (2002), "Leadership when events don't play by the rules", *Reflections*, **4**(1), pp. 30–3. To capture this idea in the literature on intercultural leadership, see C. Brooklyn Derr and Sylvie Roussilov (eds) (2002), *Cross-Cultural Approaches to Leadership Development*, Westport, CT: Quorum Books.

13. The literature on visionary and transformational leaders is developed, explored and applied

by M. Bass (1998), *Transformational Leadership: Industrial, Military, and Educational Impact*, Mahwah, NJ: Lawrence Erlbaum. Gary Yuk (2002), *Leadership in Organization*, 5th edn, Upper Saddle River, NJ: Prentice Hall, provides a comprehensive and well researched literature review, which spans both the manager and the leader.

14. High involvement cultures have been explored quite thoroughly by Edward E. Lawler III (1992), *The Ultimate Advantage: Creating High Involvement Organizations*, San Francisco, CA: Jossey-Bass and Fred E. Schuster (1998), *Employee Centered Management: A Strategy for High Commitment and Involvement*, Westport, CT: Quorum Books. For the classic treatment of the learning organization, see Peter Senge (1990), *The Fifth Discipline: The Art and Practice of the Learning Organization*, New York: Doubleday/ Currency.

15. With the emphasis upon learning, Yasmin Kafai and Michael Resnick (eds) (1996), *Constructionism in Practice: Designing Thinking and Learning in a Digital World*, Mahwah, NJ: Lawrence Erlbaum, in their compilation of readings explore the rudiments of sense-making paradigms in practice. Diarmuid O. Murchu (2000), *Our World in Transition: Making Sense of a Changing World*, New York: Crossroad Publishing, uses sense-making paradigms to explore worldviews. Karl E. Weick (1995), *Sense Making in Organizations*, Thousand Oaks: Sage, outlines the seven properties of sense-making and applies these in organizations.

16. In this regard I am indebted to Ronnie Lessem and Sudhanshu Palsule (1992), *Managing in Four Worlds: From Competition to Co-creation*, Cambridge, MA: Blackwell, and Ronnie Lessem (2001), "Managing in four worlds: Culture, strategy and transformation", *Long Range Planning*, **34**(7), pp. 9–32. Lessem, in this work, ties the pulls to the cognitive model I employ.

17. The model which serves as the basis for the figures in this book is culled from the work of several scientists and leadership scholars. What they have in common is their reliance upon a value-based interpretation of the works of Talcott Parson (1977), *Social Systems and the Evolution of Action Theory*, New York: Free Press, with its AGIL framework but interpreted by those interested in leaders of instrumental action. I rely upon Max Boisot (1995), *Information Space: A Framework for Learning in Organizations, Institutions and Cultures*, New York: Routledge, for his treatment of instituted governance – market, bureaucracy, clan, fiefdom; Robert E. Quinn (1998), *Beyond Rational Management: Mastering the Paradoxes of Competing Demands of High Performance*, San Francisco: Jossey-Bass, for his treatment of organizational types with the functional model, and Peter Koestenbaum (1991), *Leadership: The Inner Side of Greatness*, San Francisco: Jossey-Bass, for his leadership diamond.

18. Paul Hersey (1985), *The Situational Leader*, New York: Warner Books, provides the most popular account of the situational approach to leadership. Contingency theories of leadership are rooted in the work of Fred E. Fielder and Martin M. Chemeus (1974), *Leadership and Effective Management*, Glenview, IL: Sort, Foresman and Fred E. Fielder (1990), "The leadership situation: A missing factor in selecting and training managers", *Human Resource Management Review*, **8**(4), pp. 335–50.

19. Etienne Wenger and his colleagues have explored the informal nature of learning in communities of practice. See Etienne Wenger, Richard McDermott and William Snyder (2002), *Cultivating Community Practice: A Guide to Knowledge*, Cambridge: Harvard Business School Press, and Etienne Wenger (1998), *Communities of Practice: Learning, Meaning and Identity*, Cambridge: Cambridge University Press. Peruse Jean Lipman-Blumen and Harold J. Leavitt (1999), *Hot Groups: Seeding Them, Feeding Them and Using Them to Ignite Your Organization*, Oxford: Oxford University Press, for a discussion of the creation potential of short-lived groups.

20. For a far-reaching discussion of reputations in technology-based virtual communities, see D. Bernstein (2001), "Managing reputations in cyberspace", *Journal of Communications Management*, **5**(3) pp. 300–8; J. Dukerich and S. Carter (2000), "Distorted images and reputational repair", in M. Schultz, M.J. Hatch and M. Lorsa (eds), *The Expressive Organization: Linking Identity, Reputation and the Corporate Brand*, Oxford: Oxford University Press, pp. 97–112. For the classic in the field of corporate identity and its

vicissitudes see Charles J. Fombrun (1996), *Reputation: Realizing Value from the Corporate Image*, Cambridge: Harvard Business School Press.

21. Efforts to categorize and lend significant meaning to the factors propelling us into a knowledge-based network worldview are explored by Robert M. Grant (2000), "Shifts in the world economy: The drivers of knowledge management", in Charles Despren and Danielle Chauvel (eds) (2000), *Knowledge Horizons: The Past and the Present and the Promise of Knowledge Management*, Oxford: Butterworth-Heinemann, pp. 27–54. In a more applied sense, Richard E. Caves (2000), *Creative Industries*, Cambridge, MA: Harvard University Press, explores how these faces strengthen and alter the relations between commercial enterprises and creative endeavours.

22. Ronald N. Ashkenas and his colleagues have compiled a thoughtful set of readings on the causes, significance and prevalence of boundaryless organizations. See R.N. Ashkenas et al. (eds) (2002), *The Boundaryless Organization: Breaking the Chains of Organization Structure*, San Francisco: Jossey-Bass. To shadow this literature, an interesting series of discussions of the boundaryless career has developed. For example, see Lilian T. Eby, Marcus Butts and Angie Lockwood (2003), "Predictions of success in the era of the boundaryless career", *Journal of Organizational Behaviour*, **24**(6), pp. 689–708.

23. See Robert Coles (1989), *The Call of Stories*, Boston, MA: Houghton Mifflin, p. 1. For an understanding of the power of stories in leadership and relationship building, see Terrence L. Garguilo (2002), *Making Stories: A Practical Guide for Organizational Leaders and Human Resource Specialists*, Westport, CT: Quorum Books.

24. See Nelson Goodman (1978), *Ways of Worldmaking*, Indianapolis: Hackett Publishing. For a broad based background to the emergence of relativism as a cultural worldview, see Richard D. Lewis (2003), *The Cultural Imperative: Global Trends in the 21st Century*, Yarmouth, ME: Intercultural Press.

25. Clayton M. Christessen (1997), *Innovator's Dilemma: When Technologies Cause Great Firms to Fail*, Boston, MA: Harvard Business School Press, captures the notion of radical innovation in his discussion of discontinuous innovation and disruptive technologies. Wolfgang Grulke (2002), *Lessons in Radical Innovation*, London: Financial Times/Prentice Hall, explores the funding and leadership implications of the radical innovator. For a first-rate treatment of the importance of intellectual capital in the network worldview, see Alan Burton-Jones (1999), *Knowledge Capitalism: Business, Work and Learning in the New Economy*, Oxford: Oxford University Press. David J. Teece (2000), *Managing Intellectual Capital: Organizational Strategies and Policy Dimensions*, Oxford: Oxford University Press, looks at practical strategies in developing intellectual capital.

2. Buccaneer leaders: the money talks story

> "Money talks because money is a metaphor, a transfer and a bridge. Like words and language, money is a storehouse of communally achieved work, skill and experience."
>
> Marshall McLuhan[1]

In the money talks story the leader gets results. The bottom line is sovereign and those who contribute to it and make others aware of their contributions are leaders. This is not the quiet leader with integrity or the mentor fiercely proud of his or her contributions to the next generation, but the confident, decisive individualists who by dint of hard work and relentless intensity bootstrap themselves into a pivotal role in the story. They make a fortune. Buccaneer leaders advertise themselves as indispensable. They possess money, lots of it. As McLuhan puts it, "Money is a storehouse of communally achieved skill and experience" and by virtue of their ability to talk and walk the language of money successful buccaneers are leaders. Money confers power, the freedom to access privileged venues and the ability to extricate oneself from costly and less than desirable situations.[2] Money talks because it is the ultimate form of expression in the entrepreneurial worldview. It is concretized, embodied and legitimized in the personality of the buccaneer leader.

The money talks story locates the buccaneer leader as the alpha dog loose in a dog-eat-dog landscape. Talk in this landscape is of battles, strategic runs and raids. In this story getting results, or winning the battle, means competing with others. In its simplest version, winners get results; losers are those who do not make it into the winner's circle. Buccaneers are winners in a world which is relatively blind to also-rans. At its core, the story uncoils around the struggle for all players' desire to become winners. The symbol of winning is money – plenty of it. Over time, the persons, companies and institutions which develop a reputation for continually winning or enlarging their fortune find themselves surrounded by minions of followers seeking to ingratiate themselves with the winner.

The relationship between buccaneer leaders and their followers in the money talks story, and between buccaneer leaders and other buccaneers is a story of a dynamic struggle punctuated by possible upheavals. This is a game of snakes and ladders. Skill, chance and timing meld. If one happens upon a snake, one loses ground in the struggle to win; landing upon a ladder moves one towards one's goals. Followers compete with followers. Moving into the winner's circle is hard work.[3] Winners compete with other winners to move up in the stakes played for in the quest for success, fame and fortune.[4] Followers have an eye, also open, to displace and replace winners. Winners cannot rest on their laurels. They must put their success on the table and face all comers, again and again. This constant pressure to perform, the very public accounting of success and the loss of face that accompanies a winner's fall from grace, all make the money talks story a relentless pressure cooker.

Despite this, the story, as we shall discover in more depth, draws an audience of "wanna be" winners willing to buy into this pressure-filled story. Those disdainful of the money talks story lament the plight of the loser and portray the story as a self-serving outlet for megalomaniacs whose ambition is to take charge and operate exploitive sweatshops. Adherents to the money talks story – the largest number of which are losers – do not see it this way at all. Three interrelated explanations for this exist. First, the identity of the loser is skilfully framed. The loser is a player who has not yet won. This rags to riches melody entices.[5] The more one is in rags, the greater the enticement. Second, all players in this story – winners and losers – determine their destiny by their actions. No one is a slave. Each can exit. Freedom is a haunting theme. It attracts those who, failing to advance, can at least point to their independence as a hard fought victory. Third and last in this story, as seen by true believers in the money talks story, there are no fakes or windbags who pass as leaders. Players who win must remain active. They cannot bluster their way to success. Buccaneer leaders cannot fake it. Markets discern impostors from the genuine item swiftly and decisively. They are clear in distinguishing winners from losers. This calms losers. At least in the money talks story, their leaders are genuine. They make things happen. They act swiftly and decisively. Leaders must be able to show their superior ability. Like the prototypical boss, they take charge. They excel at taking existing ideas and/or prototypes and pushing them towards the bottom line results faster and more profitably than others.

In a paradoxical manner, what buccaneers are not is precisely the reason I employ the term buccaneer. It differentiates them from leaders in other stories. Buccaneers are neither prudent nor careful. Bureaucratic leaders are. Buccaneers do not facilitate trust. Participative leaders facilitate a culture in which dialogue rooted in shared values enhances members' involvement. Last, buccaneer leaders neither originate new ideas nor self-consciously seek to innovate. Theirs is a story which marries success and profits. Leaders in the entrepreneurial worldview are swashbucklers. They lead raids. They create packs of fellow travellers interested in maximizing the spoils of their adventure. They leave for other packs when rewards are better elsewhere. They are forced out when their contribution to the pack and their ability to protect themselves are low. Lastly, it is clear that since buccaneers are so end-results oriented, while certainly not compelled to bend the rules or laws, they do both unabashedly. They reward those who win and ask very few questions regarding how.[6]

The buccaneer leader, as a bold action-oriented figure, possesses strong vested interests in protecting the money talks story. As contextualists, let us first hear each leader's story from their own point of view. The buccaneer leader's money talks story is one of the voices interwoven into the tapestry of the four faces of capitalism. It speaks of a need to reward proven winners, keep rules at a minimum, trust others but only when they can aid you in getting a leg up. Ideas or prototypes, once entered into the competitive market, are public and they can and must be copied, improved and disseminated to the public. Let us hear the money talks story from the buccaneer's perspective. We will systematically focus on the six-point story template – origin, plot, audience, protagonist, genre, and lesson – discussed in Chapter 1.

ORIGINS: BUCCANEER LEADER

Within a contextualist reading of instrumental worldviews, "in the beginning" there is not the word but the problem. Instrumental leaders in each of these stories concretize and embody the skills necessary to overcome or solve a problem. While all the stories we will look at owe their names to the solutions they offer, it is the problems that they do not acknowledge which tell us about their origins. Thus one of the dominant motifs in the array of stories available to tale-tellers is the quest or journey to find or, in more modern parlance, earn a fortune. The money talks story has reach. It is global. From the smallest fishing village in coastal Greenland to the crowded storefronts of Hong Kong, this story is told and retold. It is archetypal. It resonates with a strong solution – make a fortune in order to put to rest a strong and recurrent fear, a basic insecurity, the fear of losing.

The money talks story directly addresses those whose greatest fear is seeing themselves and/or being seen by others, as a loser. Losers, the story would have us believe, lead lives of quiet desperation. These lives pass beneath the radar registering those among us who lead lives worth tracking. Those who are marginalized – the homeless, the insane and those who have, as the money talks phrase goes, "hit bottom", are losers. Still further, and somewhat above the bottom rung of losers are those who, in doing the bidding of others, are given little, not even recognition, in return. To lose is to go unnoticed when you would like to be seen and heard. It is to fail so frequently and publicly that others, eventually even your loved ones and you yourself, begin to discount your views and, even in time your presence. In the money talks story, to be a loser is to flirt with a hellish existence on earth, to be bypassed, neglected and collectively reviled.[7]

The critics seek to rein in the buccaneer and modify the money talks depiction and treatment of the loser. The bureaucratic leader calls for rules and a system in order to regulate the free-wheeling fortune hunter and, in so doing, protect the loser from undue exploitation and abuse. The call to justice, understood in formal legal terms, is rooted in the belief that all – not merely winners – are protected by the law. The participative leader in the communitarian worldview envisions an all-inclusive, trust-based community in which all, regardless of rank, wealth or family background, are heard and seen. Members have rights. This is not a community of rabid egalitarians as portrayed by buccaneers, but one in the midst of diversity which respects all. Last, the knowledge leader in the network worldview reframes the buccaneer's conception of the loser. The losers in the knowledge leader's story are those unable or unwilling to keep up in the midst of the information and technological revolutions. Rich or poor, first world or third, these are Luddites. They turn away from globalization, cower at the prospect of genetically modified foods and resist the key experiments that are creating a portal to a new world. In the eyes of network leaders, buccaneers, even winners are often the wrong stuff.

While the origin of the money talks story glosses and remains optimistic that some losers will make it into the winners circle in the story, it is unabashedly vocal and strident regarding the role of the buccaneer leader as the winner. Winners are the glue that hold together the tales of struggle, freedom and just desserts. In the money talks story, the unit of analysis is the contest.[8] The world is awash with rivals. In this environment, winners not only establish themselves in the hand-to-hand combat that marks the struggle of each for their fortune, but motivates others to raise their efforts. Buccaneer leaders goad followers into higher levels of productivity. Winners stimulate other winners to raise their game. Winners are the Joneses. Others must keep up with them. They push. They set a demanding pace. This is what has euphemistically been called the "rat race". Moreover, in all this they are emulated by those who seek to displace them and claim their rewards within the winner's circle. The "good" in the money talks story is the material abundance that results from wealth generation. Buccaneer leaders are depicted as the prime force responsible for wealth generation in the entrepreneurial worldview (see Figure 2.1).

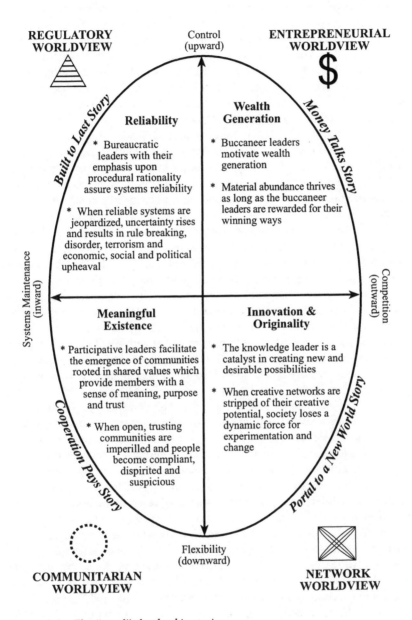

Figure 2.1 The "good": leadership stories

Interestingly, in all leadership stories, the leader within that story is depicted as the primary force for the triumph of the "good". What is equally worthy of note is how the "good" within each story is seriously questioned by those from other worldviews. Thus material abundance – the result of wealth generation piloted by the buccaneer leader – is called into question by, for instance, the bureaucratic leader's insistence that increased numbers of rules and regulations will rein in free-wheeling buccaneers and render them accountable. Reliability is the "good" in the regulatory worldview and it is embodied in the story of the virtuous bureaucratic leader. A system is reliable when it reduces uncertainty. Reliable systems are orderly. Those in charge of them plan carefully. They follow rules rooted in precedent. They attend to the costs and benefits of the system as a whole. Reliability reduces breakdowns, eliminates bottlenecks, trounces errors and lowers the rate at which laws are violated. In the regulatory worldview, we are all richer when good order prevails. When prudent men and women, those with a distaste for gambling and playing hunches and who are loyal to the system, get their just desserts. Just desserts in this story are not a mercurial rise in wealth, but a slow rise towards a good living and adequate security for one's twilight years.

The participative leader in the communitarian cooperation pays story thwarts the lionization of the buccaneer leader by degrading the dog-eat-dog nature of a world nested in and glorifying winners in zero sum games. To be rich in the cooperation stories is to be surrounded with significant others who, in a trust-filled context, help one through one's perilous journey. The cooperation pays story speaks to the "good" of a meaningful existence made possible when leaders manifest the values of openness, sincerity and a willingness to enter into genuine dialogue.[9] Adherents to the communitarian worldview worry about the plight of those who must pay others to hear their personal problems or provide them with a sense of self-worth. Communitarians depict the buccaneers as crass materialists, untrustworthy and disingenuous. They critique the buccaneers for their wavering principles or propensity towards self-serving behaviour and a desire to increase rather than reduce status differences. These critiques are given credence in earnest efforts to penalize those who are seen as having violated community norms. For example, those who push themselves forward with little regard for others ought to be scolded rather than rewarded. In the cooperation pays story, participative leaders are called to the centre of the community by members. The celebration of the individual ego, so apparent in the money talks story, is decried in the communitarian call to compromise, civility and fair play.

Lastly, the unbridled fascination with wealth generators as leaders in the entrepreneurial worldview (depicted in Figure 2.1) is strongly modified and selectively heard by knowledge leaders in the network worldview. In the portal to a new world story, the knowledge leader modifies the winner as a wealth generator. The winner in the knowledge leader's story is seen as a catalyst or stimulator of new and original ideas or innovations.[10] The wealth strategies of buccaneers steer wide of investing time, energy and capital in attaining original results. If the results are economically valuable, they will, in the blink of an eye, be imitated by others. Buccaneers see nothing wrong with this. They wait for others to make costly investments in innovation, then copy with impunity. While some may argue that imitation is the highest form of flattery, this position pales, network advocates insist, when the imitator deprives the originator of benefits. In the buccaneer's story there are benefits to be distributed to society as a whole. These, however, come with the invisible hand in the struggle for wealth itself. Good ideas, buccaneers insist, are just that – ideas. Winners must make money On the other hand, network advocates treat good new ideas as the basic DNA of a new world order in which, even in years gone by, new breakthrough ideas with great potential must be nurtured. In the portal to a new world story, genuine leaders think outside the box. They may not realize a profit or even accumulate wealth, but knowledge leaders agree we must find a means of motivating the creatives to step forward even if their rewards are offered posthumously to their survivors.

The buccaneer story celebrates the get-rich-quick leader as the epitome of the story. In the dog-eat-dog jungle, the get-rich-quick leader moves with confidence, lightning speed and a retinue of followers. When and if a buccaneer succeeds in locating the coveted pot of gold at the end of the rainbow, the number of followers or even sycophants willing and eager to do the bidding of the buccaneer leader grows. While the money talks story originates in an understated moment of insecurity – the fear of being and/or being seen as a loser – it moves loudly and publicly to the celebration of the buccaneer leader enjoying the pot of gold at the end of the rainbow.

The plot line from insecure origins to the liberating pot of gold is marked with and by an ongoing and continuous struggle. The struggle is not a free-for-all. It is contained within a loose governance notion called the market. In the market, the story is clear. While few can own the pot of gold, the colourful hues of the rainbow light up the sky for all to see and nurture the joint desires of both getting close to winners or more ambitiously taking one on. Pots of gold can be wrestled from others' hands within the market. The struggle is pervasive. Even winners have but momentary respite. As the rainbow lights up the sky, the buccaneer must prepare to stave off aggressive efforts by those who seek both to be and to be seen as winners.

PLOT: BUCCANEER LEADER

Struggle is cathartic. Adherents to the entrepreneurial worldview firmly believe that if a thing or idea is worth having, others will want it. Moreover, "to have" in this story is to own and thereby control. It is important to note that while control is high over that which is mine, the buccaneer has little or no control over the market. As in property rights, control entails the right to exclude others or at least those of your choosing, from access to that which you control. The words "my" or "mine" understood in their various guises are the territory upon which the struggle motif runs its course. Losers have little option to use and have others accept their "my or mine" claim; winners, on the other hand, lay claim and have others accept theirs. In the plot line of the money talks story, it is the struggle itself, not the motive of the contestants, that generates the catharsis. Those who see markets as the basis for justifying who gets what, when, where and why, embrace the notion of struggle and the value of contests, and celebrate the tactical intelligence and daringness of the buccaneer leader.

Each of the plot lines we shall discuss is bolstered by a rational form of discourse; in other words, a preferred vehicle to move the plot and perception of the leader as an intelligent participant. Thus, as outlined in Figure 2.2, in the money talks story the tale itself focuses upon the ubiquity and purifying aspects of struggle. Struggle flourishes when contests are licensed and openly acknowledged as the primary means of solving problems and determining outcomes. Those who win at contests, and thus are justly rewarded in markets, are players who possess a highly focused end-results intelligence and are willing to act and take risks in situations in which information is imperfect. The tactically intelligent are affirmed in their intelligence when they not only fulfil their desires, but do so by beating others to the punch. The spoils go to the swift. Tactical intelligence involves getting to where there is value first and winning the contest. The plot line is rendered meaningful under the overarching protective layering of market rationality.

The point here as outlined in Figure 2.2 is that while the idealization of struggle in open contests is prized by those who privilege market rationality, it is heard but viewed as problematic by adherents to other stories. Thus those who champion the bureaucratic leader and see the "good" in the reliability of uncertainty reduction, view market rationality as entirely suitable when selling shoes or soft drinks, but far less so in setting accounting standards, reducing mortality in the population as a result of obesity, or creating a system to deal thoroughly with airport security. Struggle is replaced by coordination via planning and prudent design in the built to last story. Experts relying upon careful data gathering, forecasting and state-of-the-art

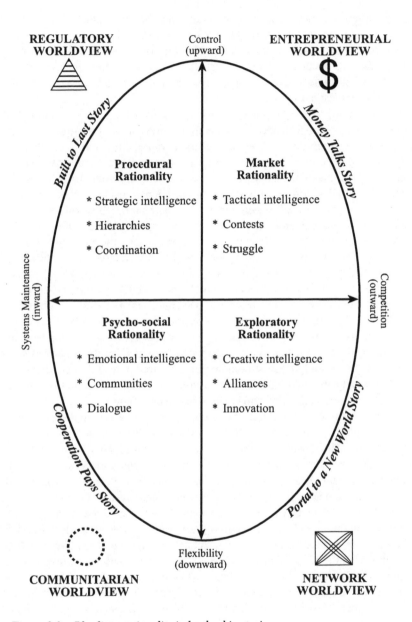

Figure 2.2   Plot line: rationality in leadership stories

information generate strategic options or plans before action.[11] The built to last story is not anchored on the "puts", "calls" and options of tactically minded contestants, but upon the stable platform of structural hierarchies. Procedural rationality replaces or curtails market rationality when the plot is rooted not in the cathartic notion of struggle, but in the tale of a deliberately coordinated design or plan.

Communities pursuing the quest for a meaningful existence as embodied in the participative leader's cooperation pays story join those in the regulatory worldview in hearing market rationality, but feel that its application to selling shoes or soft drinks is less than adequate. Advocates of the cooperation pays story insist that the dog-eat-dog struggle of the entrepreneurial worldview does nothing but alienate people from their work and turn neighbour against neighbour. The communitarian worldview, as we shall see in much greater depth in Chapter 4, emphasizes the quality of one's life over the quantity of material possession in it as the measure of one's success. The plot is all about building bridges of understanding within the self and between the self and others. Dialogue replaces struggle.[12] Emotional intelligence – the quest for balance – replaces the quick hit, take-no-prisoners tactical intelligence of the buccaneer. Psycho-social rationality protects the notion of dialogue in the plot of the cooperation pays story. Advocates of the emotionally intelligent leader argue that trust, sharing and dialogue – the building blocks of cooperation – ought to prevail over the idealization of struggle. In the end, insist communitarians, we are all dead. Let us, therefore, invest wisely in building our future through creating the conditions which nurture the next generation and create a sustainable future.

Finally, those imbued with the network worldview are comfortable with struggle, but uncomfortable with how buccaneers tie struggle into the quest for control. Those who hear the portal to a new world story seek to take the participative leader's fascination with cooperation and collaboration, tie it to the bureaucratic leader's quest for design, and marry both of these with creative intelligence. Exploratory rationality brings together the best minds in a problem area in order to create alliances with the potential to generate breakthroughs or radical innovations. Advocates of the network worldview worry about the tendency within the tactical intelligence of the buccaneers to think within the box, simplify problems, go for quick returns on investments, and generally ignore the costly outlay required to engage in experimentation. They see the knowledge leader as an explorer willing to engage in the arduous task of dealing with complex problems requiring the input of many bright minds, originality, imagination and business acumen. These genuine leaders are knowledge leaders. They push into the unknown. They explore in a rational manner. In the midst of a loose network of shifting alliances and a competitive call to claim priority of discovery, knowledge leaders open new vistas.

The general struggle motif and the celebration of market rationality in the buccaneer leader's story results in three persistent subplots each at a different level of struggle. At the individual level of the entrepreneur, struggle is demanding. Burnout issues, mental health and the inability to balance work and home life remain dogged issues. I shall discuss this in greater depth in Chapter 3 (see Figure 3.2). At the level of the organization, the buccaneer must not only get results but avoid scandal and law violations, and walk the hard line of integrity in a story where the ends often justify the means. At a systems level, the buccaneer's struggle means living with the possibility of having to make a new start. There is no tenure, no respite from struggle. Each challenge requires one to seriously entertain the possibility of needing to start anew. You cannot play this game at its pitched frenzy with the fear of losing.

The plot of the money talks story, rooted in the idealization of the effects of market rationality, the prevalence of open contests as well as the purifying aspects of struggle, needs little assistance in protecting itself from the hoots and catcalls of those intrigued by the plots of other stories. Market rationality appeals to a vast audience. A story derives its power from its ability to draw and retain listeners. From this vantage point, the story of the buccaneer leader is, I believe, the most popular story on the planet at this time. Popularity in this statement is not measured by the aggregate capital accumulated by adherents to the entrepreneurial worldview, but by the number of people worldwide attracted to the clear simple lines of this end-results story.

AUDIENCE: BUCCANEER LEADER

A diverse audience – originating from very different economic, political and social views – is drawn to the buccaneer leader's story. It is precisely because of its reach that it is one of the four master stories in a contextualist treatment of leadership. It appeals to a wide audience of winners, "wanna be" winners, end-results champions and no nonsense types who seek leaders that take charge when the going gets tough. In economic terms, winners hear the story, but so too do those who, with little cash in hand, aspire to the winner's circle. In political terms, those on the political right resonate with the story. They hear the clarion call to efficiency as a good reason to cut government, privatize, downsize and, in general, put power in the hands of those who have proven that they can get results. Interestingly, those on the political left, especially activists or radicals, admire the story for its unabashed call to action and dedication to overcoming the banal rules of ineffective and even at times corrupt but well-ensconced authority figures. Finally, in social terms, those who seek out strong boss-like or directive leaders to help curb their worries regarding imminent crises are drawn to the story, but so too are those who want to blame the very visible buccaneer and hold him or her accountable for all that has gone wrong.[13]

These diverse audiences are drawn to the buccaneer leader's story because they see them as a credible sense-making device which explains their actions. Thus in this story, not only do winners receive the rewards that are justly theirs, but, in this version of just desserts, society is made all that much better. The theory of progress in this story is propelled by markets, but given flesh in the actions of the buccaneer. The buccaneer leader reduces inefficiency. The buccaneer motivates others to raise their game. Prices are lowered. Goods and services are disseminated and in the midst of the ever present struggle – framed as a form of creative destruction – the inefficient sink while the cream rises to very visible leadership roles.[14] Progress is imperilled when buccaneer leaders are denigrated, curbed by regulation or forced to hide their light under a bushel. In the money talks story, the freedom of action required to keep contests open and markets free is everyone's business.

This duty to protect the struggle, insist true believers in the entrepreneurial worldview, benefits all – not merely winners. Three interrelated components in the buccaneer leader's story make this viable. The first we can call the rags to riches theme; the second, the riches to rag motif; and the last, the multiple league proposition. This first theme focuses upon a small number of school drop outs, the physically or mentally handicapped or those born again after imprisonment who have accumulated a fortune. Despite the small number of these cases, they prove to be beacons. Those who struggle and lose are reminded of those who exploded forward by bootstrapping themselves out of obscurity into positions of prominence. These instances not only enhance the credibility of the story, but add to it a realism that travels easily and well as the buccaneer leader's story becomes a global story. The self-made leader emerges in a new buccaneer image of China. Tales of buccaneers emerging in the previously over-regulated regions of Eastern Europe and in the midst of strife-ridden Africa all speak both to the dogged determination of winners and to the ubiquity of the story.

The rags to riches theme is intensified in its call to audiences who have not yet been in the winner's circle when one adds to it the riches-to-rags motif. In these few instances, tellers tell of the rich and powerful who have been forced out of control due to their inability to remain competitive. The image of the humbling of the wealthy buoys the spirits of the humble most when the once-mighty are replaced by the once-humble. The combination of the rags-to-riches and the riches-to-rags creates a cycle within the money talks story. This cycle suggests that, while barriers between winners and losers in the entrepreneurial worldview exist, they are neither fixed in stone nor without exception. Elites circulate. Old money gives way to new. Recently arrived immigrants can, within a generation, play at casino tables undreamed of by their ancestors. The heady tone here is not one intimating that equality is near at hand but rather the assurance that all are better off with an unequal distribution of harms and benefits providing that the struggle is open. The money talks story is rooted in an optimistic eschatology. It is not the meek who shall inherit the earth, but the competent and ambitious who must get their fair share. It they do not, the story abandons its optimism.

The reassuring optimism that attracts diverse audiences to the buccaneer story rests in a third assumption within the money talks story. This is the multiple league proposition. In it there is not one vast struggle to win, but a series of graduated markets, each set at different levels of intensity and with varying rewards accruing to those who take on risk at a particular level and succeed. Metaphorically speaking, the individual who plays at the poker table with minor stakes can, with consistent winning, choose to compete at tables with more money riding on the outcome. Winning in this context both signals one's skills and provides the medium (money) which enhances choice or freedom. Success at one level or league provides one with the option of moving up or into new and different leagues. Even in a scrabble poor neighbourhood, becoming wealthy within the money talks story – like being poor – is relative to one's reference group. At the top of the hill in deluxe neighbourhoods, feeling poor may entail nothing more than the absence of a swimming pool.

What is reassuring in the multiple league proposition within the money talks story is that it is the individuals themselves who determine if they choose to move up into a higher league or into a different one. One can elect to be a big fish in a small pond, or one can strive to become a big fish in a bigger pond with more "wanna be" big fish. This freedom to frame one's ambitions by active personal choice goes a long way in explaining the immense appeal of the money talks story. The tale of individual freedom attracts. Individuals are free to exit as long as they are willing to pay the consequences of leaving once-binding relations and entering into new leagues. Buccaneer leaders are those in the story who relentlessly seek to push towards larger ponds and poker tables which they believe are both worthy of their skills and will reward these amply. The fact that not all buccaneer leaders end up in the big leagues is less important than the fact that the story permits them not only to have this dream but to retain it as well.

This freedom to frame one's ambitions, struggle to find the league with the best payout and dream the big dream of success for oneself or one's children is not found in other stories as advocates of the money talks story maintain. They have, I believe, a good point. Loyalty and patience, not freedom and exuberance, are rewarded in the built to last story.[15] In hierarchical systems seeking to reduce uncertainty, one must wait for the voice of authority to recognize one's skills or talents and call one upward or into new leagues. In the cooperation pays story, one is selected by the community or team inward towards the centre and towards more significant and meaningful relationships. Pushing oneself outwards toward the exit violates group norms. In the communitarian worldview, freedom involves membership in one happy family; exit is framed as a cowardly, self-serving form of desertion. As well, in the network worldview one can push oneself forward and exit a particular project, but it is the network that selects and pushes one in new directions. Project-based networks are temporary. Those who move from project to project are those who have built excellent reputations. In the portal to the new world story, the leader develops a reputation of being on the edge of knowledge. There is no exit, only innovation. To innovate and reap the reward of one's talent, one must have a claim to priority and intellectual capital, and earn the respect of participants in the network.

Those who hear and feel comfortable with the call to individual freedom are drawn to the money talks story. They want to be the boss, the person in charge or the hero who lives well precisely because he or she delivers results and gets the job done. The buccaneer leaders are framed, and frame themselves, as the chief characters or protagonists in the story, and not only as a force with which one must reckon, but one which must be taken seriously. Money talks precisely because the buccaneer gives it voice. The golden rule in this story is not the search for moderation or a call to treat others as one would treat oneself, but a simple and powerful recognition that whoever has the gold determines the rule. Let us turn to the character of the buccaneers and take their measure – a measure weighed first by true believers in the money talks story, then by advocates of the other three faces of capitalism.

PROTAGONIST: BUCCANEER LEADER

It is difficult not to identify with the hero in a story we hear and believe to be important. Those enamoured with the money talks story lionize the buccaneer leader. Those who find fault and remain uncomfortable with the money talks story evaluate the buccaneer leader much more critically. In these stories, the buccaneer leader is disruptive and can only be tolerated in very narrow instances. The distance between the buccaneer leader's self-portrait and depictions in other stories becomes our focus more fully when we look at the practical implication of those who possess leadership skills and seek to have these recognized outside their story. This real world problem is, I argue in Chapters 6 and 7, best handled within a contextualist treatment of leadership. At this point, my portrayal of the buccaneer leader focuses less on specific skills than on character. As well, it is less focused on the evaluation within the four faces of capitalism of each leader by others from different worldviews.

The buccaneer leader is a fulfilment of the wishes of those drawn to the money talks story. The buccaneer leader, as shown in Figure 2.3, is a confident, decisive realist who, by taking charge and keeping things under control, gets significant results. The claim to be a realist is grounded in the assumption that buccaneers live in the present. They rely not upon models or projections of future trends, but upon things as they see them. They do not blindly follow community pressures. They get results. Buccaneer leaders are tough skinned. They can take the heat. As the bumper sticker prized by buccaneers states, they "show no fear". They are revered as bold risk takers, genuine bosses whose favourite song is always some variant of "I Did it My Way". They are rewarded by our awe and envy and our desire to ingratiate ourselves to them, and thereby partake of the bounty that accrues to those who have allied themselves with a genuine buccaneer. Within the money talks story the buccaneer leader is the catalyst. No action worthy of emulation occurs without the buccaneer leader. No sharp, clear, bottom-line directions are drilled into the minions of attentive aspiring winners. The buccaneer leader is the motor which makes the story move. He or she is indispensable.

Within a contextualist reading of leadership, the hero in one story is not equally esteemed in others. With all the self-importance of those who unabashedly push to the front of the line, the buccaneer leader reads badly as a hero in other stories. In the regulatory worldview buccaneers are seen as devious, pushy and overly conspicuous characters always calling attention to themselves. The buccaneer is not prized in prudent systems dedicated to reducing error and achieving high degrees of stability. The buccaneer leader does not show deference to authority. Buccaneer leaders are viewed as impulsive, rash, short-term, self-serving decision makers who are likely to bend the rules in pursuit of a win. In a system seeking to reduce uncertainty, the risk-taking propensities of the buccaneer leader are understood as satisfying personal career ambitions at the expense of the system's needs. The buccaneer leader can direct but not delegate. Buccaneer leaders lead from the front; they have difficulty collecting data. They are in the action. They lack the objectivity required to be an effective bureaucratic leader. The only context in which adherents to the built to last story embrace the buccaneer leader is in crisis situations where the system is in immediate peril unless it can act decisively and even uncharacteristically violate precedent in the struggle to survive. The role of the buccaneer leader as the crisis leader in the regulatory worldview is understood as a short-lived flirtation.[16] As soon as the system returns to equilibrium, the system returns to its strong preference for bureaucratic leaders.

The buccaneer leader in the communitarian worldview is like a bull in a china shop. The evolution of characteristics suited to win in the struggle at the core of the money talks story fares poorly in a story centred around character traits which enhance trust, facilitate cooperation and create a culture of shared values. As noted in Figure 2.3 the buccaneer is seen as an untrustworthy, ruthless egoist who is unable and unwilling to become a team player. The buccaneer barks out orders. They do not listen.[17] Dialogue is not sought, it is far too time consuming. Talk, in the lexicon of the buccaneer, is cheap; action is precious. In the communitarian worldview, talk is a prerequisite to consensus building and the primary tool in building significant relationships between and among members in a community. The buccaneer leader is seen as too political, keeping people at a distance with power tactics, too secretive and far too tactical. The leader in the money talks story is not open, inclusive and empowering. The participative leader, the protagonist in the cooperation pays story, attempts to develop others' potential so that, within the community, learning and adaptation to change become possible. The participative leader engages in appreciative inquiry.[18] The buccaneer leader is embraced in the communitarian worldview when he or she is willing to serve as a public advocate of the values espoused by the community or to provide an infusion of funds (philanthropy) with a minimum of demands to assist the community in its mission. Interestingly, buccaneer leaders eager to repair their reputations, particularly as seen by those outside the money talks story, often turn to philanthropy at some stage in their lives.

Lastly, the buccaneer leader as noted in Figure 2.3 comes across as an unimaginative, control-driven simpleton in the network worldview. The knowledge leader as the hero in the network worldview is fascinated with making the world a better place through applied creativity, radical innovation and the deliberate invention of new ideas, technologies and processes. This is a problem set which is difficult to filter through the mind of one, even an incredibly gifted, buccaneer leader. It needs a network of agile minds working in concert with leaders who are at the outer edges or the frontier in their knowledge domains. The buccaneer is seen as a mimic, at best, and a plagiarist in a less flattering portrayal by those drawn to the network worldview. The buccaneer, in their view, is unable or unwilling to share ideas lest these be appropriated by others or used, in time, to undermine the buccaneer's control. The buccaneer is viewed as too controlling. He or she directs others rather than stimulating in them a quest for new options or possibilities. The "just do it" mantra of the time-pressed, shoot-from-the-hip buccaneer bypasses careful research, costly experimentation and consultation

Bureaucratic Leader's View of Buccaneer	Buccaneer Leader's Self-Portrait
Character * unprincipled * pushy * conspicuous *Evaluation* * rash, short-term decision makers * no respect for the rules * unable to delegate * useful only in extreme crises	*Character* * decisive * realistic * in control *Evaluation* * get results * risk takers * the boss * indispensable in all circumstances
Participative Leader's View of Buccaneer	**Knowledge Leader's View of Buccaneer**
Character * egotistical * untrustworthy * ruthless *Evaluation* * no team player * too political * unable to listen * useful only as an advocate or philanthropist when demands can be kept low	*Character* * controlling * unimaginative * simplistic *Evaluation* * unable or unwilling to share ideas * pushes rather than leads * bypasses research * useful only to disseminate innovation but must not be allowed to control or pirate

Figure 2.3   Buccaneer leader: portraits

with others. Moreover, the knowledge leader is often enraged by the "chutzpah" of buccaneers who, despite their disdain for research and experimentation, claim to be the genuine motor of innovation. The advocates of the portal to a new world story do embrace the buccaneer leader as a potential disseminator of innovation. They, however, have grave reservations regarding tenets of intellectual property in their rush to claim a possible fortune.[19]

One of the reasons that the hero in one context is a flawed character in others is because each story is imbedded in a genre. Each genre focuses upon the hero for attenuating the positive dynamics of the story and curtailing the negative. In the money talks story, the genre is that of an ongoing, action-packed drama. The drama is open ended. The forces of good battle evil. The forces of good do not pertain to who wins in the competitive struggle itself, but rather to those who believe in the struggle to create the conditions in which individuals are free to compete. Enemies of the story, those who oppose the buccaneer, oppose freedom. The fate of an open society driven by the freedom of individuals to compete is in peril in the continuing drama of the buccaneer leader's story.

GENRE: BUCCANEER LEADER

Not all leaders' stories are within the same genre. The buccaneer leader's story is an ongoing action-packed drama – some even insist, melodrama – in which the open society hangs precariously in the balance. The genre in which the bureaucratic leader's story is best understood is the tightly scripted stage play. In Figure 3.3 in Chapter 3, the buccaneer leader's story genre is compared to that of the bureaucratic leader's. In this genre, adherence to precedent-based clear routines and the elimination of error over time enhances the actors' view that they are making progress. The participative leader's story is an open-line talk show in which diverse voices are drawn to shared values in the search for a meaningful community. Finally, the knowledge leader's tale is a futuristic genre – one part cybertale, one part imaginative creation and one part science. The genre applauds exploratory intelligence and intimates the unsatisfactory nature of the status quo. It tantalizingly promises a future rife with new possibilities. Each genre creates certain conventions which frame the leader as a particular embodiment of virtue.

In the money talks story the buccaneer leader is a freedom fighter. This is not to be confused, especially in contemporary geo-political events, with the terrorist. Indeed, it will become clear that the terrorist within the buccaneer leader's story is framed as a threat to freedom. In the lexicon of the buccaneer, there is no more righteous struggle for freedom than the struggle to keep the markets for goods, services and ideas free of interference. This is the basis of our collective wealth. All other freedoms, insist buccaneers, flow from this. It is the procrustean bed of individual liberty. The hero in the story is the genuine buccaneer leader who is entrusted with protecting this core value. The buccaneer leader protects this value through deeds and actions. He or she protects our right to struggle. The genuine buccaneer is the champion of the open society; enemies are all those who oppose the buccaneer's version of this open society.

The story rivets. For those drawn to this story, freedom is not assured. There are those among us who can for various reasons rip our fragile freedom apart. From within the money talks story, I will address two versions of the enemy. Then we will turn to how and when buccaneers see each story outside its genre as rising to the status of the enemy. In the struggle imbedded in the money talks story, the enemy is recurrent and ongoing. He or she is both inside and outside the story. The fragility of freedom is an existential condition. It is built into the fabric of the narrative. One does not, for once and for all, vanquish the enemy and then assume that freedom is safe. The hero in the buccaneer's story must remain vigilant. The battle with the enemy is not scheduled; it is ever present. It requires those who are willing to protect the struggle itself from being manipulated or planned. Kowtowing to authority is to be resisted. Authority must prove itself a winner.

The first illustrative notion of the enemy within the story is the lapsed buccaneer. The lapsed buccaneer is a winner who seeks to collude with others to fix prices and assure that they need not take on greater risk once they have established a winning hand. Collusion erodes freedom because winners begin to conspire to protect themselves at the expense of "wanna be" winners. This tactic is not only not in the spirit of the game, it prevents the game. It attracts and legitimizes the call to third parties, like regulators, to intervene in the free markets. It unfairly raises the gradient for individuals with new, better or less-pricey products, ideas or services. It drives highly motivated players who seek to break into the winner's circle to either reduce their effort or go elsewhere in search of a game which is not fixed. The lapsed buccaneer is an anti-hero. In colluding, the anti-hero joins others of the same ilk in turning their backs on the openness of the game precisely when the game, in extending control to them, assumes that they have become imbued with the spirit of the game. The spirit of the game is simply that, in the game being open, winners must fairly take on all challengers. Winners are not acting fairly when, for example, they fix prices or collude with others to close the game or refuse to take on challenges.

Buccaneers, I argue, feel uncomfortable with the lapsed buccaneer. They are publicly outlawed, but privately there is ambivalence. After all, what is the "win, baby, win" mantra except a call to use one's winnings to continue winning. There is, however, far less ambivalence with the second inside enemy. This is the collectivist option. In this, rather than winners colluding, losers or "wanna be" winners collectivize. Just as we can speak of those who collude as lapsed leaders within the story, those who collectivize are lapsed losers. Genuine losers persist in the struggle. Lapsed losers seek an edge. They are willing to trade in their individual freedom for the benefits of group membership. They form unions, guilds, trade associations, social movements and, to the most dedicated believers in the buccaneer's story, even professional associations. Collectivizing is acceptable as a tactic, but not when it forms an impediment to freedom and efficiency. Efforts as in the communitarian worldview to privilege certain groups are acceptable, but only when these groups freely compete with others and get results. The telltale story of unions versus management is heard quite differently, as we shall see, in the buccaneer leader's story than in the bureaucratic or participative leaders' stories.

The enemy within our illustration – lapsed winners who destroy freedom (for example, by fixing prices) and lapsed losers who collectivize – can be tolerated as long as they are isolated. When they are joined by those outside the story, individual freedom is truly imperiled. Within the genre of the continuing drama the buccaneer leader rides the range in this version of cowboy capitalism and makes certain that the enemies of freedom do not form alliances. This emphasis upon neutralizing and isolating both lapsed buccaneers and outsiders makes the genre one whose outcome is always in question. Virtuous are those who struggle to keep the flame of freedom burning. Those who are perceived by the true believer as endangering this flame are seen as problematic. As the numbers of those viewed as problematic rise and calls for putting these people in their places rise in intensity and frequency, those outside the money talks story see the buccaneer leader as histrionic or even paranoid. Within the drama, the buccaneer is celebrated as an icon of freedom and a pillar of strength

Bureaucratic leaders in the built to last story are likely to support unions, guilds and professional associations.[20] Moreover, those who seek to plan, reduce uncertainty and create stable systems are not so disturbed by the collusive tendency of price fixers and cartel makers as are the buccaneers. This is paradoxical since they are typically entrusted with regulating them. The regulatory worldview supports those who believe that systems – when and wherever possible – take priority over individuals. This is a red flag to buccaneers who champion individual freedom over the duties and constraints required to subordinate oneself before the rules of the system. Thus, in the typical entrepreneurial firm in the money talks story, individuals suture the job to fit their skill set; in the hierarchical system of the built to last story, the individual must satisfy the pre-specified demands of a job description. When one hears the call, often fierce and strident, to reduce the power of big business, government and labour, one is more often than not eavesdropping on the voice of the defender of freedom in the buccaneer story. Those threatening freedom are typically bureaucrats who seek to bring order and stability to the land.

What aspect of freedom, as understood by the buccaneer, is imperilled by the story told by outsiders from the communitarian worldview? The drama here develops as a consequence of the participative leader's reframing of the buccaneer's notion of freedom. The participative leader reframes the ideals of freedom through struggle to freedom via cooperation. One is free in the cooperation pays story when one can give voice to one's concerns without struggle and have this heard, assessed and, as appropriate, championed by the community. The open society, insists communitarians, is the compassionate society. The hero as a leader is one who feels deeply the problems and pains of others. This reframing both imperils the buccaneer's conception of freedom and, worse, seems to make of it an enemy of compassion. It substitutes a community ethos for the views of individual actors, talk for action and, most egregiously, rewards those who are deemed appropriate by the community rather than those who, through continuing struggle, challenge it. When one hears the call, often a bellicose one, to reduce the influence of bleeding-heart liberals, fuzzy-headed leftists, leaders of social movements, mindless cults and grass-roots organizations, one is eavesdropping on the voice of the defender of freedom in the buccaneer's story.

Finally, the game of the knowledge leader's cybertale rife with the licence to collaborate (albeit in temporary networks) and to reward explorers, innovators and creatives, threatens the buccaneer leader's version of freedom in two interrelated manners. First, the buccaneer's notion of freedom is not threatened by driving competition away, but by tying it to flexibility. Rather than winners producing concrete results which, like a pair of shoes, can be tried and tested in the marketplace, knowledge leaders stress innovation, originality and creativity. The portal to a new world story presents an array of promises of a better future with no clear direction. Exploratory logic after all is conjectural. In the buccaneer leader's story, the provision of an array of options with no directions stupefies and induces a narcotic-like effect rather than liberates. The cornucopia of dreamy possibilities paralyses action. Second, buccaneers see freedom as imperilled in the knowledge leader's strategic aim of expanding the territory covered by intellectual property law.[21] Freedom, insist buccaneers, entails the ability to take what is and should be available in the public domain. The buccaneers lament the knowledge leader's snuffing out of freedom in claiming more and more territory for thinkers and dreamers rather than doers. In essence, the buccaneer rails against those who provide leadership without direction and who, while failing to provide direction, insist that larger and larger parts of the public domain rightfully belong to them.

The buccaneer leader is a restless figure fighting the battle for individual freedom on many fronts simultaneously. In this ongoing and compelling drama, it is clear to all who resonate with this drama that, without the vigilance of the buccaneer we would forfeit our individual freedoms. In this drama we learn by entering into the fray, in other words, taking action. The lesson in the story – that which is conveyed from generation to generation of storytellers – is to remain as independent as one can, to be prepared for the unexpected and to know your desires. The lessons in each of the four leadership stories we look at are bold, simple and clear (see Figure 2.4). This, in part, is why these stories endure.

LESSON: BUCCANEER LEADER

All stories reveal both a mode of learning and lessons to be learned. While it is the allure of the plot line (struggle and you will be rewarded) and the genre (the buccaneer as a freedom fighter) that draws in the audience, it is the mode of learning and the lesson that they are left with that keep the audience there. The mode of learning in the story is buried in the way in which the leader deals with problematic events, people and ideas. In the buccaneer leader's story, the mode is action oriented. The "just do it" mantra of those hawking running shoes speaks to this form of direct, non-hesitant, quick-to-commit line of action. There is no pretence that one can get it perfect with enough data gathering, discussion, or experimentation. This is time consuming. The buccaneer's worldview requires lightning speed. One must, in an instant, avoid threats, capitalize on opportunities and always know the bottom line. Markets change. Information is either unavailable or distorted. Experimentation is best done, not in theory, but in practice. Buccaneer leaders learn by doing.

The preference for practice is tailor-made to suit the buccaneer leader dynamics in the entrepreneurial plotline. Action learning is a form of learning by immersion.[22] Those "wanna be" winners learn from proven winners. The learning occurs, not in the classroom, but in the red hot action on the shop floor. To use the parlance of those who coach athletes and other competitors, action learning involves getting in the zone. This is the psycho-physiological marriage that occurs when competitors are so visibly at the top of their game. They execute faultlessly. They see the whole playing field. In action learning, those in the zone experience time as a smooth flow. There is a sense of being in the game. Worries drop off. Anxieties drift away. This is the catharsis that

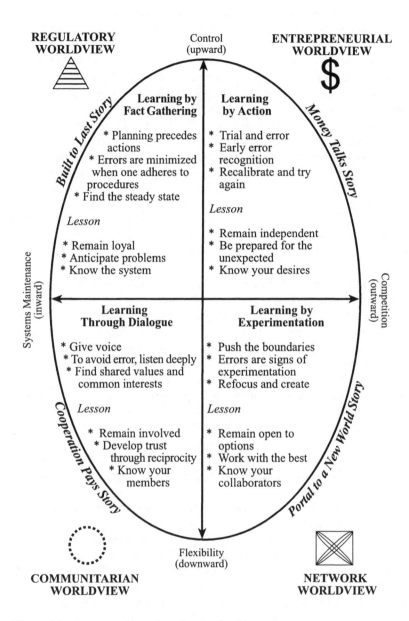

REGULATORY
WORLDVIEW

Control
(upward)

ENTREPRENEURIAL
WORLDVIEW

$

Built to Last Story

**Learning by
Fact Gathering**

* Planning precedes
  actions
* Errors are minimized
  when one adheres to
  procedures
* Find the steady state

Lesson

* Remain loyal
* Anticipate problems
* Know the system

**Learning
by Action**

* Trial and error
* Early error
  recognition
* Recalibrate and try
  again

Lesson

* Remain independent
* Be prepared for the
  unexpected
* Know your desires

Money Talks Story

Systems Maintenance
(inward)

Competition
(outward)

**Learning
Through Dialogue**

* Give voice
* To avoid error, listen deeply
* Find shared values and
  common interests

Lesson

* Remain involved
* Develop trust
  through reciprocity
* Know your
  members

**Learning by
Experimentation**

* Push the boundaries
* Errors are signs of
  experimentation
* Refocus and create

Lesson

* Remain open to
  options
* Work with the best
* Know your
  collaborators

Cooperation Pays Story

Portal to a New World Story

Flexibility
(downward)

COMMUNITARIAN
WORLDVIEW

NETWORK
WORLDVIEW

Figure 2.4   Lesson and learning: four leadership stories

accompanies the winner in the struggle. It is, of course, the passion of those who consciously and relentlessly pursue excellence and recognize it when they win.

Immersion in the zone within action learning is a state of knowledge not easily transferred by buccaneer leaders to others. The problem may be equivalent to that experienced by the polished actor who tries, in a classroom context, to get others to act with equal skill. The buccaneer does not, or cannot, share ideas easily with others. On the one hand, being in the zone may entail tacit or difficult knowledge to communicate, or it may be in the interest of successful buccaneers to hoard their knowledge, thus maintaining its scarcity and assuring that the ample rewards that accrue to those in control of scarce resources go to the buccaneer leader. Staying in control entails an ongoing ability by leaders in the money talks story to close the distance between themselves and followers when they need the latter's assistance and increasing the distance when they do not. The aspiring buccaneer, however, usually has a method in his or her desire to emulate or displace those in the zone.

The method is rooted in the age-old apprenticeship system.[23] This is the glue that binds leaders and followers within the struggle in the plot line of the buccaneer leader's story. Action learning in the apprenticeship mode begins with observation and mimicry. The apprentice shadows the master – sometimes overly, at other times less so. The apprentice attempts to emulate first the style and then the specific actions of the master. The apprentice begins to try out actions and learns to use trial and error to guide him or her through variations and repetitions. It is important to recognize that trial and error is neither theoretical or self-evaluative in the buccaneer leader's game. There is a bottom line. Score is kept. The feedback is clear, immediate and trustworthy. The key to action learning by trial and error is to be able to recognize one's errors early, recalibrate and then act again. This is an iterative process. Mastery requires repetition, focus and, as veterans call it, the "touch" (see Figure 2.4).

Interestingly, the lesson in the buccaneer's story is a learning method very much at odds with that in the other leaders' stories. The lesson in the entrepreneurial worldview, given its focus upon struggle and individual freedom, is a call – clear and palpable – for buccaneer leaders to remain independent. The leader, so to speak, must keep aloof from his or her followers. To succeed, the buccaneer leader must be prepared for the unexpected. The emphasis is not upon improvisation, but agile reaction and swift commitment to a line of action. However, as noted in action learning, all lines of action are tentative. As soon as better options emerge or others threaten one's trajectory, recalibration is essential. The lesson is clear – to be a leader in this story one must be able to live with surprises and turn these into bottom-line results. Perhaps the most important lesson in the buccaneer leader's story is that the buccaneers must know their desire. Getting money, for the master player, is the means to an end. Those who obtain a fortune but do not know their desire, win the battle but stumble in the war. They are recognized as players but not as masters. They lack the grace and fluidity of action that accompanies one who is fulfilling his or her desire or, as Joseph Campbell, the master analyst of stories puts it, following their bliss.[24]

One leader's bliss through the mastery of action learning is, in a contextualist reading of leadership, not necessarily that of leaders in the other stories. The bureaucratic, participative and knowledge leaders, each within their own tale, hold neither the action mode of learning nor the lessons tacitly conveyed in the buccaneer story in high esteem. The bureaucratic leader insists that prudent fact gathering and careful adherence to the rules and rational planning trump action learning. One must, bureaucrats insist, not merely react to, but anticipate, problems. One must not lead with one's gut feeling but with one's head. The participative leader views both action learning and the buccaneer's lessons as failures. They fail to enhance learning through dialogue. The "win, baby, win" attitude central to the buccaneer leader's story vaporizes trust. Rather than learning which involves the genuine manifestation of one's views, communitarians insist that it degenerates into an impression management contest. The knowledge leader views action learning and the buccaneer's lessons as celebrations of skill development in the individual rather than as a concerted effort to build intelligent collaborative teams. The skilled leader as solo boss or director, while not derogated in the knowledge leader's story, is not prized. He or she cannot carry the burden of complexity required to deal with interdependent issues and global problems. Complexity, insists the experimentally minded knowledge leader, requires networks that marry the best minds with state-of-the-art technology and adequate funding to leaders who stimulate others to think "outside the box".

Let us now turn to the built to last story. It originates in a quest for security, safety and predictability. The genre here is of a tightly scripted, carefully planned stage play. The fear at the root of the regulatory worldview is the likelihood of crises, disorder and chaos. Imagine, if you will, being lost, out of control and not aware of what is next. In the bureaucrat's reading of the buccaneer's story, the struggle, if left untended, cannot be contained. It will result in a deadly and devastating war of each against the other. To eliminate this nightmare, those who are rational will enter into a contract. We will compromise our individual freedoms. We will become specialists and work within the rules of a system. The plot is simple. It is powerful. We must devise a means of thwarting disorder and reducing uncertainty. The hero in this story is the well-trained, objective, big picture analyst or system administrator. The lesson in the story is a continuing mantra which insists that by carefully gathering facts, creating stable routines and relying upon the talents of well-trained specialists, it is possible to create and operate a system which provides the greatest good for the largest number of people.

NOTES

1. Marshall McLuhan (1964), *Understanding Media: The Extensions of Man*, New York: McGraw-Hill, p. 189.
2. Geoffrey Ingham (2004), *The Nature of Money*, Cambridge: Polity Press, explores the language, cultural and socio-emotional aspects of money in a very useful manner. Benjamin J. Cohen (2004), *The Future of Money*, Princeton, NJ: Princeton University Press, takes a less culturally oriented trajectory through contemporary issues in international finances to show how money in the entrepreneurial worldview impacts those who follow the leader.
3. Attempting to capture the scope, depth and intensity of the idea of competition in the money talks story is difficult. See Ulrich van Suntum (2004), *The Invisible Hand: Economic Thought Yesterday and Today*, translated by Caroline Hemingway, Berlin: Springer, for a solid discussion of the neo-classical economic position and efforts to update it. For how the literature on instrumental leadership is taking early conceptions and orthodox economic versions of competition in new directions, see C.K. Prahalad and Venkat Ramaswahy (2004), *The Future of Competition: Co-creating Unique Value with Customers*, Cambridge, MA: Harvard Business School Press.
4. Leo Braudy (1986), *The Frenzy of Renown: Fame and Its History*, Oxford: Oxford University Press, captures the quest for fame in the buccaneer leader's story. With a biographical approach, Paul G. Schervish, Platon E. Coutsoukis and Ethan Lewis (1994), *Gospels of Wealth: How the Rich Portray Their Lives*, Westport, CT: Praeger, explore how the wealthy tell their stories. Michael Silverstein and Neil Fiske (2003), *Trading Up: The New American Luxury*, New York: Portfolio Press, discuss the sociology, economics and psychology of leaders who relentlessly trade up.
5. Variations on this rags-to-riches melody are discussed by James Champy and Nitin Nohria (2000), *The Arc of Ambition: Defining the Leadership Journey*, Cambridge, MA: Perseus Books. For a more controversial position which aims to make sense of the male rhetoric underlying this relentless ambition, see James V. Cantano (2001), *Ragged Dicks: Masculine, Steel and the Rhetoric of the Self-made Man*, Carbondale, IL: Southern Illinois University Press.
6. Philip Deane (2002), *Power and Greed: A Short History of the World*, London: Constable, gives a big picture account of the clash between buccaneers in their quest for power and utilitarian ethics. Stephen Young (2002), *Moral Capitalism: Reconciling Private Interest with the Public Good*, San Francisco: Berrett-Koehler, juxtaposes the money talks story with calls for moral capitalism.
7. The roots of the neglect of the loser are discussed in Roger A. Salerno (2003), *Landscapes of Abandonment: Capitalism, Modernity and Estrangement*, Albany, NY: State University of New York Press. At the micro-analytic level of international competition, Pascal G. Zachary (2000), *The Global Me: New Cosmopolitan and the Competitive Edge: Picking Globalism's Winners and Losers*, London: Nicholas Brealey, presents a stimulating view of the new cosmopolitan winners.
8. Liam Fahey (1999), *Competitors: Outwitting, Outmanoeuvring and Outperforming*, Chichester: Wiley, captures the mindset of individuals in the grip of an all-consuming context. Linda Woodhead explores the nature of rivalry by focusing upon two ardent competitors in the winner-take-all world of cosmetics. See Linda Woodhead (2004), *War Paint: Madame Helena Rubinstein and Elizabeth Arden: Their Lives, Times and Rivalry*,

Hoboken, NJ: John Wiley & Sons.
9. To arrive at a sense of the ideological roots and values embedded in the communitarian worldview, attend to the recent works of two classically trained, structural, functional, sociologists: Amitai Etzioni (2000), *A Third Way to a Good Society*, London: Demos; and Philip Selznick (2002), *The Communitarian Persuasion*, Washington, DC: Woodrow Wilson Center Press.
10. A.D. Amar (2001), *Managing Knowledge Workers: Unleashing Innovation and Productivity*, Westport, CT: Quorum Books, discusses the knowledge leader's focus on intellectual capital, not immediate profits. Thomas A. Stewart (1997), *Intellectual Capital: The New Wealth of Organization*, New York: Doubleday/Currency, explains how both the buccaneer and the knowledge leader use competition but towards different ends. The former emphasizes control; the latter flexibility.
11. See Harald Alard Mieg (2001), *The Social Psychology of Expertise: Case Studies in Research, Professional Domain and Expert Rules*, Mahwah, NJ: Laurence Erlbaum, and compare this with Albert John Dunlap (1996), *Mean Business: How I Save Bad Companies and Make Good Companies Great*, New York: Times Business, to arrive at a sense of how bureaucratic leaders frame the notion of struggle differently from buccaneer leaders.
12. Communitarians make dialogue a central ingredient of their worldview. This is not the trial and error learning of the action-oriented buccaneer. See Geoffrey Rockwell (2003), *Defining Dialogue: From Socrates to the Internet*, Amherst, NY: Harmony Books, for a review of the classic positions in the cooperation pays story. Daniel Yankelovich (1999), *The Magic of Dialogue: Transferring Conflict Into Cooperation*, New York: Simon & Schuster, applies dialogue to the participative leader in the communitarian worldview.
13. In the midst of crisis, all the four faces of capitalism become much more predisposed towards an action-oriented, turnaround leader. See John Laye (2002), *Avoiding Disaster: How to Keep Your Business Going When Catastrophe Strikes*, New York: Wiley, for a discussion of this turn to end-results leadership. John O. Whitney (1987), *Taking Charge: Management Guide to Troubled Companies and Turnarounds*, Homewood, IL: Dow Jones-Irwin, emphasizes the need for the take-charge leader in the midst of imminent breakdown.
14. Buccaneer leaders rhetorically emphasize the valuable items and ideas now rising from the ashes of the recently destroyed. Tyler Cowen places an entrepreneurial spin on globalization by optimistically discussing the dislocation period as a necessary phase before moving up to a more desirable one. See Tyler Cowen (2002), *Creative Destruction: How Globalization is Changing the World's Culture*, Princeton, NJ: Princeton University Press. Richard Foster and Sarah Kaplan (2001), *Creative Destruction: Why Companies That Are Built to Last Underperform the Market, and How to Successfully Transform Them*, New York: Currency/Doubleday, expand on why the built to last story is inefficient.
15. My thinking of the use of voice (communication), exit (entrepreneurial), and loyalty (regulatory) is informed by the classic treatment by Albert Hirschman (1970), *Exit, Voice and Loyalty: Response to Decline in Firms*, Organizations and States, Cambridge, MA: Harvard University Press. Philipp H. Lepenies (2004), "Exit, voice and vouchers: Using vouchers to train microentrepreneurs – observations from the Paraguayan voucher system," *World Development*, **32**(4), pp. 713–25, explores the application of Hirschman's logic to the network worldview. Donald W. Light, Ramon Castellblanch, Pablo Arredondo and Deborah Socolor (2003), "No exit and the organization of voice in Biotechnology and Pharmaceuticals," *Journal of Health Politics, Policy and Law*, **28**(2/3), pp. 473–507, turn from Lepenies's notion of external financing to new forms of voice as a means of framing how knowledge workers collectively attempt to shape their destiny in their favour.
16. The crisis leader is seen as useful only as long as the crisis in the regulatory worldview persists. Once it is under control there is a concerted preference to return to the bureaucratic leader. Business planning replaces emergency action. See, for example, Dominic Elliott, Ethné Swartz and Brahim Herbane (2002), *Business Continuity Management: A Crisis Management Approach*, London: Routledge. Carole Lalonde (2004), "In search of archetype in crisis management," *Journal of Contingencies and Crisis Management*, **12**(2), pp. 76–88, captures the need for the crisis leader to shift from adrenalin and action to a more restrained form of planning as the crisis moves from start to finish.

17. This is a continual reminder to successful leaders that, if they are to continue with their success, they must improve their capacity to listen. See, for a practical approach, Theo Theobald (2002), *Shut Up and Listen! The Truth About How to Communicate at Work*, London: Kogan Page. Kenneth J. Hatten and Stephen R. Rosenthal (2000), "Listening: The foundation for leadership," *Strategic Communication Management*, **14**(3), pp. 34–9, focus on what leaders should listen for in their acoustical environment. Ira David Welch (2003), *The Therapeutic Relationship: Listening and Responding in a Multicultural World*, Westport, CT: Praeger, captures the role of listening in counselling and mentoring done by participative leaders and psychotherapists.

18. For a communitarian approach to appreciative inquiry, see Suresh Srivastua and David L. Cooper (1990), *Appreciative Management and Leadership: The Power of Positive Thought and Action in Organizations*, San Francisco: Jossey-Bass, and for an application of these principles see Diana Whitney and Amanda Trosten-Bloom (2003), *The Power of Appreciative Inquiry: A Practical Guide to Positive Change*, San Francisco: Berrett-Koehler.

19. Kerry Seagrave (2003), *Piracy in the Motion Picture Industry*, Jefferson, NC: McFreland and Company, gives a thorough depiction of piracy in film making. Laurence Jacobs, A. Coskan Samli and Tom Jedlik (2001), "The nightmare of international product piracy," *Industrial Marketing Management*, **30**(6), pp. 499–510, explore the nature of cross-cultural piracy.

20. Paul du Gay (2000), *In Praise of Bureaucracy: Weber, Organization and Ethics*, London: Sage, has a positive view of this much-maligned organizational structure. Richard Hamilton (2001), *Mass Society, Pluralism and Bureaucracy: Explanation, Assessment and Commentary*, Westport, CT: Praeger, explains the ability of bureaucratic structures to both support and provide for many different groups seeking stability.

21. This expanded territory is reviewed with stimulating insight by Ove Grandstrand (1999), *The Economics and Management of Intellectual Property: Towards Intellectual Capitalism*, Cheltenham, UK and Northampton, MA, USA: Edward Elgar. Lawrence Lessig (2002), *The Future of Ideas: The Fate of the Common in a Connected World*, New York: Vintage Books, probes the costs and benefits of the knowledge leader's expanding domain.

22. Yury Boshyk (ed.) (2002), *Action Learning Worldwide: Experiences of Leadership and Organization Development*, Basingstoke: Palgrave Macmillan, has compiled a useful set of readings on action learning across cultures. Michael J. Marquardt (2004), *Optimizing the Power of Action Learning: Solving Problems and Building Leaders in Real Time*, Palo Alto, CA: Davies-Block, gives insight into the 12 action learning steps.

23. Wendy Smits and Thorsten Stromback (2000), *The Economics of the Apprenticeship Systems*, Cheltenham, UK and Northampton, MA, USA: Edward Elgar, lay out a solid history of the apprenticeship system. Noami Lamoreaux, Daniel Raff and Peter Temin (1999), *Learning by Doing in Markets, Firms and Countries*, Chicago, IL: University of Chicago Press, focus on the active modelling that accelerates learning from active masters.

24. For the classic treatment of the varying ways leaders embody the notion of follow your bliss, see the classic statement by Joseph Campbell (1949), *The Hero With a Thousand Faces*, New York: Pantheon Books. To capture Campbell's reflections on this theme, use the edited commentary by Phil Cousineau (1991), *The Hero's Journey: The World of Joseph Campbell*, San Francisco: Harper.

3. Bureaucratic leaders: the built to last story

"I'm not a rigid person. I have modified the organization design fairly regularly to tune it to reflect what I believe I need and how I can best design a structure that is responsive ... No design is perfect, you're always striving to adjust and modify the structure, usually to facilitate or focus accountability and responsibility."

George Warrington[1]

Running Amtrak, a large bureaucracy, as George Warrington the executive in charge of the railway company notes, requires prudence and attention to detail, not rigidity. Warrington, as a bureaucratic leader, is not alone in attempting to deflect the accusation of rigidity by pointing to what hierarchical systems do best. They are carefully planned, designed and operated. They reduce uncertainty. Competition is driven internally. Individuals following a clear set of rules tied to the system struggle to move up within the hierarchy. In lieu of markets, so prevalent in the money talks story, the built to last story focuses on the prudent presentation of the best of the past with an eye to slowly and judiciously adding to it. In lieu of the "just do it" appeal to adrenalin that in a staccato manner marks the action-oriented buccaneer's story, the bureaucrat's credo is "when in doubt, don't". The bureaucratic leader lives in his or her head. Action is preceded by fact-gathering, testing and careful screening.

The bureaucrat is a consummate big-picture decision maker.[2] Bureaucratic leaders, metaphorically speaking, do not drive the buccaneer's sleek mobile sports car which can, even in the hands of a mediocre talent, stop on a dime; they are like George Warrington running a complex railway with precise schedules, carefully designated routes and a series of cross-hatched expectations. Passengers expect to arrive at their destinations safely and on time. Communities living along the rails expect a minimum of disruption to their citizens. Stockholders in the railway expect their investment to return dividends. Employees in the railway, many of whom may be unionized, expect the railway to live up to its contractual agreements. The railway is a hierarchical system that is designed to follow clearly specified routines. In the hierarchical system, varying expectations are aligned and made orderly.

Where these cross-hatched expectations meet is in the position of the bureaucratic leader. The bureaucratic leader is an agent for those who can legally, morally and/or economically make a claim to be stakeholders in the system.[3] This agency role simplifies, and in other ways complicates, the bureaucratic leader's story when compared to the buccaneer's. In the money talks story, the leader is an agent for him or herself. To act rationally in the buccaneer leader's story is to act in one's self-interest. Thus winning in the money talks story puts rationality in the service of the self. Moreover, it insists that, by so doing, the unfettered market will, after some small perturbations, result in the best of all worlds – one in which individuals are free. Those who generate wealth are in control and "wanna be" winners are highly motivated to either challenge and displace existing winners or select those who provide high payoffs to follow in the eventual hope of learning the ropes. In this story all are free to exit.

In the bureaucrat's story, the leader is an agent of the system. In most instances the system both precedes and will outlive the bureaucratic leader. As an agent of the system, the bureaucratic leader is required or duty-bound to forgo short-term, self-interested behaviour and both think and act in accordance with the rules of the system. This loyalty, in time, will be rewarded. The leader is an agent for his or her department, organization and industry. The bureaucratic leader acts rationally when he or she makes prudent decisions, adheres to the policies of the system and acts in accordance with standard operating procedures. The loyal agent serves the system by reducing uncertainty and maintaining order and stability. The local agent can proudly announce to others that "nothing untoward occurred on my watch". Moreover it is expected that within the system bureaucratic leaders who are competent show their loyalty to the system by grooming their successors – those who take on the duty of the next watch.

A prerequisite of the loyal agent is time logged into the system. Senior agents who are seen as rational decision makers are highly rewarded. Senior agents are leaders. Rationality is procedural. Within the rules of a system, those who are rational make few mistakes. This simplifies the role of the bureaucratic leader if one believes that within a system rules are clear, shared throughout the system and require only fine-tuning; it complicates the role if one views rules as unclear, controversial and requiring constant redesign. As we shall see once we get more fully into the built to last story, those who are outside this story elect to tell the simplified version and then show how it fails.[4] Those who are true believers in the built to last story view procedural rationality as requiring a masterful leader who, as Warrington notes, recognizes that no design is perfect and strives to facilitate accountability and responsibility. To true believers in the built to last story the bureaucratic leader stands at the helm of a great ocean-going vessel and sees that it remains on course in fair and stormy seas.

Those drawn to the tale of procedural rationality, prudence and accountability resonate with the fable of the tortoise and the hare. They are not at all surprised when the tortoise crosses the finish line first. In the hierarchical systems of big government, business, labour and religion, the prize of control goes to those who provide a sense of order. These are the sure footed, the mistake free and the agenda makers. These all use logic and the rules of evidence to give a creditable account, often called a strategic plan, that promises to bring stability to new and emerging problems. To accomplish this, the task of the bureaucratic leader is to identify, elaborate and protect a series of ongoing repeatable routines that form the core technology of the system. These routines (delegated downward within the top-down communication channels of the vertically aligned hierarchy) provide the ongoing standard operating procedure that is crucial to the system.[5] Bureaucratic leaders who work with elaborate routines and protect them from uncertainty are viewed as heroes. The bureaucratic leader is an integrator, information synthesizer and systems stabilizer. He or she monitors and oversees the reliable system.

In achieving stability and order over time, the hierarchical system and those at its helm or apex strive to achieve legitimacy.[6] In the regulatory worldview, legitimacy is a double-edged sword. On the one hand, legitimacy enhances the system's opportunity for self-regulation and the creation and monitoring of codes of conduct; on the other hand, violators, especially those at the top, are held to account for systems failures. The shift from markets as the governing principle in the buccaneer's story to hierarchy in the bureaucrat's is accompanied by an increased public call for responsibility. Morality in the regulatory world is more complicated than merely following the law of the land; it requires a duty to the extra-legal codes imbedded in the procedural rationality of the system. These frequently include a call to a professional ethos and a series of standard contracts that bind the person as an occupant of a position within a hierarchy to the system itself. This bond is fortified when the person avoids conflicts of interest and other systems code violations and contributes to the orderliness, predictability and good governance of the system.

Those who aspire to good governance in the regulatory worldview walk a thin line between a reverence for traditions, as rooted in procedure, rules and previous authoritative rulings within the system, and the need to adapt to change.[7] Balance is key. Those bureaucratic leaders who act as caretakers for the past, bureaucratic fundamentalists, are accused of mounting campaigns of red tape and ritual-like procedure. Those bureaucratic leaders who play to win and revere the buccaneers are seen as Machiavellians using the rules of the system to hide an entrepreneurial pursuit of self-interested behaviour. In the mood of contemporary public opinion, it is increasingly hard in the regulatory worldview to get the balance just right. Bureaucratic systems are seen either as a shell game for thieves running a protected scam on unsuspecting shareholders and constituents[8] or as a monolithic sheltered workshop providing refuge to the mediocre, inefficient and insecure.

The story of the bureaucratic leader, while told worldwide, is suffering a troubled image. Advocates of the built to last story are having difficulty getting their version of the story accepted. Other stories' framing of it are getting the upper hand. The regulatory worldview has been portrayed as inefficient and wasteful by buccaneer leaders. They call for privatizing and/or downsizing public sector hierarchies and introducing efficiency to the story by outsourcing in the private sector.[9] Communitarians see bureaucracies as inhuman, soul-destroying and increasingly corrupt.[10] The participative leader portrays the bureaucratic leader as an agent of big business, labour or government who, in following the dictates of a top-down system, is not to be trusted. Those in the network worldview are attracted to the deep pockets of bureaucrats, but view the bureaucracy as an anathema to innovation and the passionate quest for a new and better world order.[11] The bureaucratic leader, insists the visionary leader, is less than capable under conditions of mounting uncertainty. The calls to improvise, create and pioneer are not strong suits to those who pride themselves in the systematic reduction of uncertainty.

In this chapter, using the six-part story template – origins, plot, audience, protagonist, genre and lesson – I will explore the bureaucratic leader's story as told by its champions. In a counter-intuitive manner, I shall show how the grey-flannelled bureaucrat's[12] story originates in a series of assumptions regarding faith or spirituality resting in the "call to duty". The origins of the built to last story rest in the belief that, if rational men and women put their faith in a consciously designed and carefully operated system, the greatest good will accrue to the largest number.

ORIGINS: BUREAUCRATIC LEADER

When chaos looms, all eyes turn to the stability and promise of reduced uncertainty in the regulatory worldview. The attraction of the built to last story is highest and most credible in the advent of expected chaos. Chaos is not framed, as knowledge leaders would have it, as an opportunity for creativity and exploration, but as a dreadful loss of control. Chaos breeds waste. It is a state of disorder in which innocent people, acting dutifully, are often the recipients of harm. Chaos causes collateral damage. The advocates of the regulatory worldview portray chaos as the result of failures in the other three stories. Chaos and uncertainty, if left unchecked, will prove costly. Bureaucratic leaders are lionized when they are seen as wrestling chaos to the ground.

Chaos, bureaucrats admonish, is the result of market failure in the buccaneer leader's story.[13] There is a war in which each blindly lashes out against the other in pursuit of their individual interests. This is permissible, bureaucrats sagely counsel, in running pizza parlours, manufacturing soft drinks and the like where substitutes quickly and easily spring into place soon after the failure of a player. It is less permissible when dealing with national defence, pharmaceuticals or orphans. Markets have a limited reach. They do not work well, insist advocates of the regulatory worldview, when monopolies or oligopolies are better at tackling the problem. They are deficient when in heated competition the social costs of buccaneers' activities outweigh the benefits. If permitted and encouraged to thrive without restrictions, the buccaneer leader's story produces chaos. Not only do all eventually lose, but in the midst of the battlefield strewn with the dead, wounded, psychologically debilitated and burned-out combatants, it is hardly reassuring when a few can say that once these were winners.

The bureaucrats see chaos emanating from a reliance upon the communitarian worldview quite differently from the failure of markets. While the bureaucratic leader celebrates the participative leader's ability to generate shared values and a sense of purpose within a community, these are achieved by jeopardizing order. The bureaucrat worries about the tribal basis upon which communitarian claims are developed. Tribalism is problematic. Those within a tribe, while comforted by the shared values and trust within the group, are often not as easy going when those in other tribes challenge their values. The espoused openness and ability to compromise lauded in the talk of communitarians is, insist bureaucrats, often absent in their walk. When challenged, especially by those perceived as outside their communities, communitarians rally around their core values and uncompromisingly defend what they take to be privileged principles rooted in consensus.[14] Bureaucrats see this as originating in the communitarians' lack of objectivity, detachment and the search for standardized systems. This results in chaotic tribal wars, factionalism and concerted efforts to derogate those who, over the years, are taken to be the enemy.

Bureaucratic leaders view knowledge leaders in the portal to a new world story as potentially unleashing pandemonium. This story, insist bureaucrats, must be kept as a small outlet within a predominately regulatory worldview. The knowledge leader's call to experimentation is an acceptable call if experimentation is properly and carefully regulated. Knowledge, in the bureaucratic worldview, is for good or evil. In the network worldview, knowledge is by definition good. The difference between these two worldviews rests on bureaucrats' spiritual faith in the need for and reliance upon systems as a distillation of rational authority. The knowledge leader's animated call to the future, the insistence that we are on the edge of the new, exciting and apparently better, requires sober second thought. It requires careful checks and balances lest we unleash another drug like thalidomide to be used by pregnant women or enter too recklessly, if at all, into the domain of cloning humans. Bureaucratic leaders seek to impose order upon the network worldview by reminding knowledge leaders that we must make a distinction between what it may be possible to do and what is good for the largest number of people within a system.

It is order that is the "good" in the regulatory worldview and chaos that creeps in when one relies too heavily upon other stories. Order, like justice, is a call to recognize a higher authority. The regulatory worldview, I argue, originates in the spiritual call to duty (see Figure 3.1). The loyal and dutiful agent, as we shall see in our discussion of the bureaucratic leader as protagonist, places his or her faith in the system. The system is under the control of its leaders, but the controllers are not free to do as they please. We are inheritors of a past, much of which works very well. The bureaucratic leader inherits a consciously constructed system designed to inculcate the best and most authoritative views from the past and fine-tune these to deal with new and emerging problems. The bureaucratic leader places her or his faith in the need to humble the ego, to defer gratification, and to sacrifice quick and easy victories for that which is best for the system. Piety in the built to last story is service to the system. The placing of one's portrait or photograph in the hallway with one's predecessors, with room left for one's successors, is part of the aspiration to this form of dutifulness. We are part of the great design we are slowly evolving. We are not the creator or the prime mover – we are the prudent means for making things orderly.

The spiritual origins of the bureaucratic leader as hearing "the calling" and becoming a dutiful servant of the system in pursuit of the greatest good for the largest number are treated as a joke by those in other stories. The buccaneers see bureaucratic leaders as credentialled ideologues hiding their personal ambitions behind the sanctimonious facade of a system. The assumption that authority is and should be vested in systems is problematic. In the buccaneer worldview we are all hustlers. We are deeply and irrevocably self-interested. Those who claim to have the best interests of the system in mind are cloaking their aspirations in the guise of the loyal servant. Be wary of the loyal servant insist the buccaneers. They will rob you in the name of a higher authority and insist, somewhat paternally, that in the long run this is in your best interest. Those who put their faith in experts and systems players are bound to get stale advice, become caught up in the rules and slowed down. One will either be prohibited from practising buccaneer

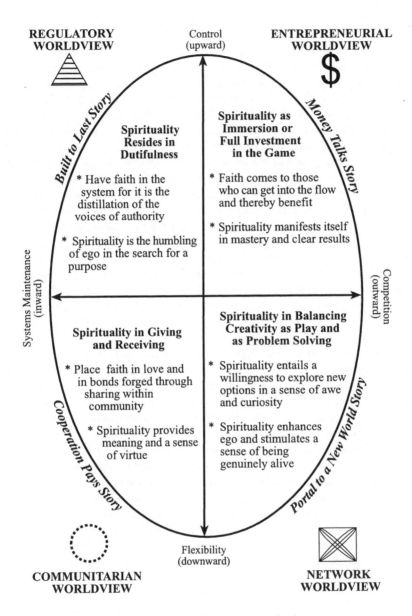

REGULATORY WORLDVIEW

Control (upward)

ENTREPRENEURIAL WORLDVIEW

Built to Last Story

Money Talks Story

Spirituality Resides in Dutifulness

* Have faith in the system for it is the distillation of the voices of authority

* Spirituality is the humbling of ego in the search for a purpose

Spirituality as Immersion or Full Investment in the Game

* Faith comes to those who can get into the flow and thereby benefit

* Spirituality manifests itself in mastery and clear results

Systems Maintenance (inward)

Competition (outward)

Spirituality in Giving and Receiving

* Place faith in love and in bonds forged through sharing within community

* Spirituality provides meaning and a sense of virtue

Spirituality in Balancing Creativity as Play and as Problem Solving

* Spirituality entails a willingness to explore new options in a sense of awe and curiosity

* Spirituality enhances ego and stimulates a sense of being genuinely alive

Cooperation Pays Story

Portal to a New World Story

Flexibility (downward)

COMMUNITARIAN WORLDVIEW

NETWORK WORLDVIEW

Figure 3.1   Spirituality (secular forms): the four leadership stories

spirituality (see Figure 3.1) in the midst of the regulatory worldview or permitted to do so only if one succumbs to periodic forms of monitoring. When in the zone, action learners and end-results achievers are viewed as rule violators, free-riders and players requiring close scrutiny.

The participative leaders view the call to duty in a top-down hierarchy as the triumph of dispirited compliance. Bureaucratic systems are death traps of the human spirit. The call to standardization, objectivity and dispassionate specialization and expertise disenchants. Rather than eliminating disorder, it generates an iron cage.[15] Within this cage people are expected to comply with its rules. The system is intrusive. It demands attention and promises security. However, upon clear inspection, it is capable of downsizing or privatizing, cancelling contracts and placing those dependent upon it in dire straits. Moreover, the system entraps, so once one has invested time in the system, it is hard to exit or to give voice. The real payoff comes later – always later. The communitarians seek to escape the iron cage by insisting that spirituality in its secular form entails modifying the iron cage-like qualities of a mechanistic system. It entails the quest for authentication (see Figure 3.1). Duty ought to be replaced by choice, objectivity and detachment along with subjective involvement and debate with dialogue. The spiritual task of the participative leader is to turn a series of subordinate–superordinate relations defined by clear rules into a community in which members use norms and are empowered to employ discretion in solving problems.

Lastly, the knowledge leader views the bureaucrat's call to duty as a form of spirituality grounded in a failure of nerve. While ostensibly celebrating the powers of the mind, the bureaucrats fail to embrace either the creative or the playful capacity to explore new options and boldly go where others have not yet been. In the network worldview, spirituality entails a delicate balancing of creativity as both play and problem solving.[16] As outlined in Figure 3.1 it entails a willingness to explore new options in a sense of awe and curiosity. Spirituality in the knowledge leader's story enhances the ego, as it does in the buccaneer's, but in the network worldview it calls for egoism in the sense of willingness to undergo a challenge in collaboration with other creative participants. Spirituality is generative. The knowledge leader recognizes that while innovation is often sought in the regulatory worldview, it is not licensed. It increases rather than reduces uncertainty. It talks the language of play in a setting that honours duty. It exalts a future which can be ours only if we are willing to experiment in the midst of a system dedicated to precedent, rule adherence and deference to authority.

In the true believers' view of the built to last story, the bureaucratic leader neither blindly nor ritualistically defers to authority. Authority is achieved by very skilled leaders who blend the skills of the monitor, fire fighter, evaluator and strategist (as we shall see in Chapter 5). The bureaucratic leader brings clarity to chaos, justice with a capital "J" to markets, civility and tolerance to xenophobic clans and due diligence and care to those fascinated with experimentation. The spirituality of the dutiful or loyal agent arises not in the pursuit of excess, newness or solidarity but in a call to balance. In the built to last story the prudent or moderate bureaucratic leader oversees a collective quest for the virtues of reliability, order and legitimacy.

PLOT: BUREAUCRATIC LEADER

At first one might suspect that a plot centring on the quest for greater degrees of certainty and reliability would be as dull as watching paint dry. It is not. It is the story of how procedural rationality is mobilized. The built to last story is the tale of how the establishment gets, and at times loses, its authority. Those who are drawn to the built to last story are interested in one of three options. One option is to seek authority to make rules and provide governance in hierarchical systems. Second, they may seek to depose those who possess authority either by using the very rules of the system or by challenging the legitimacy of those in authority. Third, very large numbers seek the security and stability promised by those at the top within a well-governed system whether this is run by either the old guard or new challengers. Bureaucratic leaders' quest for greater certainty and reliability takes place within systems that are never as stable as those who run them would have those who rely upon them believe.

To achieve order, the hierarchical system must be able to absorb, buffer and tame disorder. Moreover, in the built to last story, this taming, unlike the money talks story, must be made to look easy. The bureaucratic leader is rarely romanticized or lionized. In fact, when order is achieved within the built to last story, the success is attributed to the system; when it fails, the bureaucratic leader is held accountable. The dynamics of this attribution are revealing. In the built to last story, competition is driven inward towards systems maintenance. The power of external markets is driven inward. Individuals chase positions – higher positions with greater authority and increments of increasing salary. In general, the tests which differentiate those who rise swiftly from others who do not, are not market tests fixed to end results, but the ability to argue and show that one, if given the opportunity, can contribute to systems maintenance. Indeed, the plot line (see Figure 3.2) in the bureaucratic leader's story is that greater control goes to those who can maintain or return the system to order.

Order is generated within three subplots in the bureaucratic leader's story. Each subplot addresses a different level of analysis – the individual, the organization and the system as a whole. A subplot illustrates the tensions that

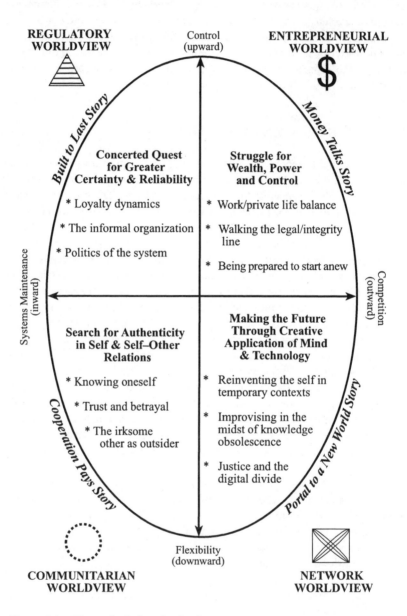

Figure 3.2   Plot and subplots: leadership stories

bind the quest for greater certainty and reliability in the built to last story. At the individual level, the tension is best understood in the loyalty dynamics required of systems' participants. One is loyal to the system or socialized when one acknowledges the rules, defers to one's superordinates and is willing to subordinate one's work to the measures and evaluative criteria established by the system. The plot thickens when loyalty dynamics imposed by the system create order, but unintendedly generate other problems. For example, the ineffective, tyrannical or even substance-abusing superordinate may be protected in a system that insists that subordinates do not bypass their superordinates when reporting problems. Whistleblowers or those who go public with tales of wrongdoing and/or corruption within the system are seen and often treated as disloyal in a bureaucratic setting.[17] Participants whose productivity soars when compared with their peers are seen as failing to understand that long-term stability takes precedent over self-promotion and other options.

At the organizational level, the bureaucratic leader's plot line, the tension between order and disorder, resonates in the ongoing relationship between the formal organization and the shadow or informal organization (see Figure 3.2). This tension is equivalent to that between rules and the rules in use. The two differ. The idealized, rule-based, prescriptive organization rooted in formal procedural logic must be enacted. The perfect plan or architectural drawing must be put into practice. The informal organization is the enactment of the idealized formal structure. Decision makers in the formal organization, for example, are idealized as cool, detached analysts with the information required to act rationally in rendering effective decision outcomes. In the informal system, decision makers are attached to certain outcomes, constrained by time and always in search of higher quality, more reliable information. As the perceived difference between the idealized or espoused organization, redolent with the potential for orderliness, and the actual informal organization grows, so too do the challenges for bureaucratic leaders.

At the systems level, the bureaucratic plot thickens when we acknowledge the prevalence of politics within the system.[18] Ideally, the subsystems or departments within a system employ the same procedural rationality to arrive at the very stability assumed to exist at the core of the system as whole. In this sense there is a belief that a standardized language, much like mathematics with rules that bind, prevails. The system as a whole is embodied in the rules. Politics emerge when subcomponents of the system not only disagree, but argue from the system's perspective for a new or idiosyncratic interpretation of the rules. In the advent of the politicization of systems, the whole may not stay together and buccaneer factions may crystallize. In this subplot, the rules fail to thwart the emergence of self-serving behaviour. These buccaneers seek to maximize short-term subsystem goals at the expense of the system's stability. In time, they place themselves and their needs above those of the system.

The bureaucratic leader in this plot line walks a narrow line between taking a caretaker role emphasizing the status quo at all costs or attending to the subplots that create tensions within the quest for systems with greater certainty and reliability. Balance between the caretaker and the adapter roles is essential. The bureaucratic leader is not the winner (entrepreneurial), the well-loved colleague (communitarian) or the visionary (knowledge). In lieu, the bureaucratic leader is the loyal agent who operates, sustains and adapts a hierarchical system over time so that, if successful, it achieves greater and greater legitimacy. Legitimacy is a measure of the respect for the authority of a system held by its stakeholders. As legitimacy rises, societal monitoring and the call to socially responsible behaviour by those in at the head of that system go down. In this idealized plot, the sequence is clear. As leaders achieve systems stability, their control over the system is enhanced and this both increases the public perception of the system's legitimacy and, over time, generates even greater stability. The circle goes on and the stable system persists. It is built to last.

The plot twist that makes the built to last story newsworthy does not occur when the bureaucratic leader successfully reduces uncertainty, but rather when, despite the best of efforts, it rises. In this brief discussion, I will focus on uncertainty arising from within the system itself. In the subsection entitled "Lessons: bureaucratic leader" near the end of this chapter, I tackle the lessons we learn in the bureaucratic story when the crisis emerges from outside the system. Uncertainty arising within the built to last story is a clear sign that the bureaucratic leader is in trouble. The regulatory worldview rewards those who maintain systems with greater control. When they do not and it is credibly believed that uncertainty is rising in the system, control is taken away from the head of the system – the bureaucratic leader.

To regain control and return the system to its core routine, the bureaucratic leader, often urged on by rising discontent from subordinates, begins to experiment – at times voluntarily and at other times under some coercive influence – with the means of reducing uncertainty used in other stories. The bureaucratic leader in the midst of fiscal pressures caused by the discrediting of the system due to its inability to reduce uncertainty may be pushed into or experiment with downsizing, privatization or outsourcing. All this pulls the regulatory worldview towards the entrepreneurial. Control is relinquished or size is diminished to cut costs and emphasize end results. What is germane from our perspective is that, as bureaucratic leaders act entrepreneurially in the face of rising uncertainty, they are seen as failing to show loyalty to the system. They are seen as playing politics, acting with vested interests and violating the rules. The shift from a systems maintenance (inward) to a competitive (outward) stance by the head of the system is seen as violating the basic premises of the regulatory worldview.

Those who are drawn to the built to last story opt for security rather than the high risk and potentially large payoffs associated with the entrepreneurial worldview. However, when the bureaucratic leader turns entrepreneurial and asks subordinates to increase their risks with little increase in their rewards, they scream foul. It is difficult to sustain the balance between the formal and informal organization when subordinates are irate. As their discontent grows they tend to comply with the rules and let the chips fall where they will. My job description, insists the disgruntled subordinate, requires me only to pick up the following chips. Interestingly and paradoxically, when systems that are designed to follow the rules do not, they become vulnerable. Participants lower down the hierarchy recognize this and employ it in various guises to capture the attention of bureaucratic leaders.

To quell the rising disquietude of subordinates in the midst of uncertainty arising from within (as in the pull to the entrepreneurial worldview), the bureaucratic leader often embraces the communitarian worldview. The cooperation pays story attracts the bureaucratic leader when the rising uncertainty in the system is seen to emerge from subordinates' dissatisfaction. This bolstering of the informal organization in order to offset the growing politics comes at a price. The participative leader achieves cooperation because he or she empowers subordinates and moves toward a flat, flexible and participative structure. The participative leader turns subordinates into members and systems into communities. The bureaucratic leader who attempts to achieve consensus and heighten subordinates' satisfaction, yet retain the formal structure of an uncertainty-reducing system, is doomed to disappointment. A vicious spiral sets in. Subordinates raise their expectations and soon demand a shift from a duty-based system to a community forum in which rights and entitlements are given priority. This, as we shall see, escalates trust and motivates personal development and learning, but does little to reduce uncertainty.

Lastly, in a moment of rising uncertainty within the system, bureaucratic leaders are often attracted to the idea of innovating or hiring someone to help them extricate themselves from the mess. This shift to a knowledge leader by a bureaucrat under duress is problematic. In the midst of rising uncertainty and confusion, the bureaucratic leader soon finds that innovation and change are far from quick fixes.[19] Those that succeed in eventually stabilizing and standardizing systems do so by first increasing the uncertainty and confusion before they diminish it. In turning to innovation in the midst of rising uncertainty in the system, the bureaucrat must show prudence. He or she must show that the option is justifiable. However, at the time of purchase, the promise of an innovator, like all promises, is difficult to measure or assess. Within bureaucratic rules, this makes justification difficult. Therefore, not surprisingly, to quell uncertainty through innovation, buccaneers rely upon the public reputation of those to whom they turn for out-of-the-box thinking. This often results in a bureaucrat doing the innovation talk and seeking a safe, tested and tried innovator like one of the top consulting firms to do the innovation walk.

Bureaucratic leaders are much more adaptable than their critics would have us believe. The audience drawn to this story, however, is captivated by their drive for security and the prevalence of stability. Over time, systems which fail to reduce uncertainty are pulled, often kicking and screaming into other stories. In Chapters 6 and 7 we will discuss the skill transitions required to either adapt one's story to the pulls of other worldviews or reinvent oneself as a leader.

AUDIENCE: BUREAUCRATIC LEADER

If life is a gamble, rampant with chance, then there must be a system – well designed, competently led and readily accessible – which would reduce uncertainty for the largest number. The bureaucratic leader draws those who defer to and believe in authority, pine for a routine and clear standards, to ground themselves and believe that in contributing to an enduring system they are part of something that will both outlive them and contribute to the planet for years to come. The regulatory worldview marries system maintenance and the pull inward with the pull upward towards control by the few. True believers in the regulatory worldview rarely worry about the autocratic or Kafkaesque potential of hierarchical systems overseen by the few. They see systems as well designed, full of checks and balances, and are reassured by the fact that everyone, even those at the top, has agreed to defer to the rules.

In the bureaucratic leader's story, the leader is an authority figure who embodies the administrative power and rational procedures of the system as a whole. The system draws together a diverse array of credentialled specialists, trained practitioners and analytic experts to work on interdependent, complex tasks which cannot be handled by individuals working alone or in small buccaneer-like raiding parties. Authority is necessary as interdependence increases. When people do different things and speak varying technical languages, there must exist a strong authority to lend structure and priority to the complexity. Authority figures are not merely those above one in a hierarchical system, they have been called upward by a legitimate system. They have the right to oversee and evaluate your input into the system. They are those who, as you rise in the hierarchy, you replace and become. Moreover, and to take the sting out of the ongoing levels of subordinate–superordinate relations within a system, there is no ultimate authority except the system itself.

The legitimate system is seen as a fair broker by those who assemble under its big tent. It is an attempt to calm the duelling buccaneers. It serves as a neutral space for communitarians whose values jar despite efforts to generate dialogue. In time it is the site where most innovations eventually find their steady and reliable customers. Yet despite this, not everyone trusts the authority of the bureaucratic leader's story. The buccaneers see bureaucratic authority as corruptible. This is self-fulfilling to a degree. Buccaneers often approach the system, money in hand, to seek favours or exceptions to costly rulings. It is difficult, on the one hand, to lobby those entrenched in the system and, at the same time, frame them as beyond influence. The communitarians view bureaucratic authority as too top-down, legalistic and universalist to deal with grassroots issues deeply embedded in the value system of specific cultures. Knowledge leaders laughingly see bureaucratic authority as the single greatest enemy of experimentation, innovation and exploration. Instead of playing an authoritative role, bureaucrats are overly bound by tradition and caught in the paralysing safety of routine.

The audience drawn to the bureaucratic story does not scoff at the standardization and routinization at the core of the system. In the midst of complexity, insist bureaucratic leaders, not everyone can innovate. Innovation is not a breaking away from routine, tradition and authority, but an integration of what is potentially promising in the new with the best of what proved to work in the past. Routine is celebrated in the built to last story. It is the building block of stability. It reassures. Like a well-known and often-repeated chant or refrain, it calms in the midst of uncertainty. Routine in the bureaucratic leader's story is understood as that which can be brought under control, repeated, perfected over time and, like facts, easily transferred to others.

Nowhere is the routine more evident in the built to last story than in the hierarchical system's rapacious appetite for explicit fact-based information. Where there are routines, there are forms. There are standardized data-gathering entry points intended to build, feed and improve routines. The hierarchical system measures and monitors. It compares these against standards created from ongoing routines. Progress in the bureaucratic system is measured against past performances on routines. As errors diminish, the system learns. It learns to slowly yet incrementally adapt new variations within the basic routines. This occurs, insist true believers in the built to last story, with little if any shock to the system as a whole. Indeed, those who are learning within hierarchical systems are rarely aware of it. They are relatively high up on the learning curve within their routine or specialty. It all appears as if this has been seen before. These routines alter ever so slightly in the system as a whole, but the minor variations taken aggregatively and over a long time frame result in very perceptible and noticeable impacts.

The very routine at the core of adaptation in the built to last story is seen as a form of mindlessness by buccaneers.[20] Buccaneers see bureaucrats as mindless specialists who are easily lulled into a narcotic-like stupor or trance. They keep repeating routines even when it is apparent to anyone who watches the bottom line that these, in buccaneer terms, are doomed to failure. The communitarian views routine in the bureaucratic leader's story as fostering robot-like and mechanistic responses clearly out of touch with the needs of the organizational culture within that system. Routines, insist communitarians, are helpful only if those so engaged understand the purpose of the ritual. In the communitarian worldview, as we shall see in Chapter 4, tacit knowledge is valued much more than the explicit knowledge embedded in bureaucratic routine. Those who are drawn to the portal to a new world story frame bureaucratic routines as at the very core of what prevents hierarchical systems from experimenting, innovating and licensing the search for originality. Those drawn to the built to last story celebrate that which endures. This is significant. They are unwilling to jettison what clearly works for what might work. Patience, the psychological engine beneath the belief in routine, is a virtue of the bureaucratic leader.

Patience becomes more virtuous as time frames lengthen. The built to last story takes the long view of time.[21] Those drawn to the built to last story are attracted to the long view. Those who contribute to systems are convinced that they are building something enduring, something important. Systems which pass the classic test of enduring over time are proof, at least to the champion of the bureaucratic leader, that something right is being done. Time is the great test. It establishes that not only does the system have great leaders but they have developed a succession plan which enables these skills embedded in ongoing routines, rules and policies to be perpetuated. Tradition is revered in this emphasis upon perpetuation. The bureaucratic leader honours the best of the past and adapts this to deal with emerging events. There is a sense of security in knowing that history, discipline and a long line of talented leaders are behind decisions that will impact a large number of us.

Those who resonate with the thought that "the future is best made by those who understand and respect the past" will be drawn to the built to last story and the tale of the dutiful bureaucrat as a loyal agent. In this story, the bureaucratic leader is disciplined, analytical and impartial. Things happen in this worldview for good reasons. Chance is reduced. Clear policies prevail. Bureaucratic leaders take the best practices of the past and slowly, with great skill and attention to detail, use these to manage new and emerging problems. When the hierarchical system is rightfully in the hands of the bureaucratic leader and not poached upon by those from other stories, it works like a charm. It is indefatigable. Day in and day out, like clockwork, it keeps ticking despite the fact that it takes an enormous beating.

PROTAGONIST: BUREAUCRATIC LEADER

Being called a bureaucrat, even in the heartland of the regulatory worldview, can hardly be construed as a compliment. In a contextualist treatment of leadership, language and its use sensitize us to threats and opportunities in that leader's world. Bureaucratic leaders prefer to be called the head of the hierarchical system. Words like "chief" often precede executive officer. President, prime minister and executive all convey the bureaucratic leader's desire to associate themselves, not with the run-of-the-mill employee within a hierarchical system, but with the small set of individuals – the elite – who oversee the system. In the regulatory worldview leaders rise to the top. They pass tests. They show that they can deliver the very stability and reliability sought by the system.

We can say that bureaucratic leaders lead from the top. Buccaneers, in their fascination with the race or struggle, lead from the front. Communitarians lead from the centre and knowledge leaders in the network worldview lead from the edge. What is important here is that the protagonist who leads from the top, speaks with and as the authority of the system. Those who arrive at the top within hierarchical systems do not arrive in the elite positions of control by chance. They can provide proof of their abilities as an elite member in the system or in systems considered to be similar to the focal hierarchy. This proof entails the ability to convincingly employ information as evidence that rational procedures are being put in place. The leader embodies the stability and reliability of the system. To be an elite is to be tried, tested and found to be true or reliable.

The tests issued by the system to verify the abilities of bureaucratic leaders – those who would be at the head of the system – all address the discipline, analytical skills and detached impartiality of the incumbent. Bureaucratic leaders are disciplined. They have specialized in developing skills in a body of knowledge and practice that is in demand by the system. They have manifested their discipline by showing to those at lower levels of the hierarchy that they know their stuff. The opportunity to be called upward is certainly aided by solid credentials and a skill in presenting information in a clear and convincing fashion. They must be able to interpret data, convert it into information and manage explicit knowledge.[22] In hierarchical systems, information is power. Those who can develop the analytical skills to harness information to stabilize the system are precisely those deemed talented by the system. The impartiality of the bureaucrat is a function of the fact that he or she cannot be seen as a partisan favouring one subsystem over others. The bureaucratic leader consciously deliberates on the evidence, weighing options and alternatives. This not done on the basis of whim, favouritism or subjective preference.

The head of a hierarchical system, as seen by true believers in the bureaucratic leader's story, is a competent decision maker. The emphasis is not upon action, but as the term "head" suggests, on the ability to think through a problem, gather facts, look at options, weigh and evaluate costs and benefits and finally plan to act in a manner that is deemed best for the long-term stability of the system. While competent decision making entails monitoring the facts, it also calls for the ability of the bureaucratic leader to evaluate data, information and documents sent upward by advisers in the system. This input is not only technical, but also requires the ability to make sense of the organizational culture within the system. The bureaucratic leader's decision skills require that they anticipate emerging issues/problems and develop a strategic ability to reposition the system long before the problems take root. However, when this fails and the hierarchical system and stakeholders of it begin to experience the dreaded "state of crisis", the bureaucratic leader must be able to mobilize fire fighters or, when the time is right and the danger clear and present, act as a fire fighter him or herself.

Within the built to last story, bureaucratic leaders are heroes. They have a robust skill set and have proven capabilities. The bureaucratic leader is far from a glory hound. As the head, they are accountable for the system in fair and foul weather. All those in the system and critics outside it know where to find the head. When stakeholders to the system are dissatisfied with the head, they do not fire them. They attempt to push them to the side. They are given a special project. At first they are offered a large payout with incentives encouraging them to leave earlier than expected. This not because hierarchical systems are tender hearted, but rather because they are stable. They solve problems with a minimum of fuss. This is the essence of reducing uncertainty. The very series of routines at the core of the system – its standard operating procedure – stabilized in policies and enshrined in rules and regulations keeps on working out is variations.[23] Leaders come and go. Stock markets rise and fall. New technologies explode on the scene. Throughout this the hierarchical system absorbs change slowly, carefully and in such a way that as few as possible get an unnecessary poke in the eye. This is the sensible story of those who toil to reduce uncertainty.

The buccaneers do not buy this story at all (see Figure 3.3). They view the head of the hierarchical system, like the system itself, as a slow, ineffective

Bureaucratic Leader's Self-Portrait	Buccaneer Leader's View of Bureaucratic Leader
Character * disciplined * analytical * impartial *Evaluation* * competent decision maker * accountable * adaptable * indispensable for handling all complex problems	*Character* * slow * demanding * biased *Evaluation* * inefficient and wasteful * possess a hidden agenda * out to get the "little guy/gal" * useful when they stay out of the way
Participative Leader's View of Bureaucratic Leader	**Knowledge Leader's View of Bureaucratic Leader**
Character * cold * mechanistic * rigid *Evaluation* * closed minded * power and status conscious * argumentative * useful when seeking to move towards a communitarian worldview	*Character* * picky * frightened * conformist *Evaluation* * resistant to change * mired in detail * incapable of sharing ideas * useful when willing to participate, with few strings attached, in a network

Figure 3.3   Bureaucratic leader: portraits

and wasteful creature. The buccaneer measures intelligence by speed to action. Those who act swiftly are smart. Bureaucrats are not. But what is more appalling to the buccaneers is that bureaucrats demand that others follow their rules and play the game as they do. If, argue buccaneers in a strident voice, one seeks to do business with bureaucratic leaders, they will flail you with red tape, banish you to a waiting room and refuse to deal with you until you have developed a plan which meets with their approval. When push comes to shove, the buccaneers do not see the bureaucrat as impartial at all. They have, buccaneers insist, a hidden agenda. They do not treat all equally. They are not nearly as fair as they seem to want to be seen. They are out to get the little guy or gal who is trying to make it. The only time bureaucratic leaders are useful is when they go or are pushed to the sidelines and stay out of the game.

The participative leader in the communitarian worldview frames the head of the hierarchical system as cold, mechanistic and rigid (see Figure 3.3). In simple terms, feelers are often perturbed by thinkers' need for distance and control. Participative leaders view the bureaucratic leader as closed minded. Rather than enter discussions with a desire to dialogue, they prefer to come in with debating tools. They use rules to control and guide discussions. They take a position and claim that they have proof that this is best for the collective, but they do not attend to feedback, especially from lower participants. They do not empower. In adhering to norms of objectivity they discourage emotional involvement and passion. They relish a top-down mode of communication. This, communitarians argue, results in subordinates complying with rather than actively engaging in the community. This destroys trust.[24] In flattening the system and opening it to the influence of grassroots or lower participants, the communitarians feel that systems can, when tuned into communities, accelerate learning and more flexibly deal with change. To make this transition possible, bureaucratic leaders must be replaced or learn to become more participative.

Knowledge leaders view the bureaucratic leader as a strong force in society impeding innovation, change and the development of curiosity in instrumental action and reasoning (see Figure 3.3). The bureaucratic leader is characterized as unimaginative, controlling and simplistic. The three can be rolled into one image – the bureaucratic leader is afraid of his or her shadow. In attending to tradition, they resort to conformity. They stick with what can be most easily proven. In seeking to reduce uncertainty, they avoid error – even the possibility of it. In this way, innovation is outlawed. While they do support research, it is of the painstaking variety. They get mired in the details. They need to get things perfect. Worse, they do not share ideas in a way that stimulates generative thinking. Bureaucratic leaders reinforce specialization, a condition in which ideas ought best be shared with other specialists. The difficulty here is that new ideas, insights and innovative potential – a growing language between and among the specialists – is lost. Knowledge leaders see bureaucrats as useful when, with few strings attached, they join networks which are willing to genuinely invest in exploratory options. Knowledge leaders, however, note that despite their best intentions bureaucrats get cold feet and resort to the quest for rules, clarity and objective criteria as soon as the network heats up with highly ambiguous and often controversial options. Knowledge, insist network champions, grows in ambiguity and controversy. This is a foreign land to the head of a hierarchical system hell-bent on reducing uncertainty.

The built to last story celebrates enduring structure. The bureaucratic leader monitors a stable, reliable system. The genre here focuses upon this stability. Let us turn to the genre of the bureaucratic leader's story.

GENRE: BUREAUCRATIC LEADER

Structure permeates the story genre of the leader in the regulatory worldview (see Figure 3.4). Genres carry information.[25] The genre of the bureaucratic leader's story is a highly scripted play. In Chapter 2 we briefly discussed how this genre infringes upon the buccaneer leader's quest for freedom.

The highly scripted play marries control with systems maintenance. Control which rests in the script and the actors' interpretation of it is limited to minor variations in routine. Experts are assembled – costume designers, voice coaches, programme designers, make-up artists, marketers, stage hands and the like – under the control of the head. Experts work within their specialties, adhere to the rules, follow the script and produce an event. The highly scripted play is a complex event. It is replicable. Should one of the main actors come down with flu, the redundancy in the system kicks in. There are understudies and standbys. Contingencies are planned. All the parts in both the play and those supporting it, including the leader at the head of the system, are replaceable. The same play can be done in a new theatre with an entirely different cast and still be the same play. It is the script, the very structure of the repetitive routine, that both defines its essence and makes it a built to last story. The leader both follows the script and adapts it as the need arises.

All genres have the ability to suppress aspects of reality. In the bureaucratic leader's story, we as the audience are enveloped in a preconfigured world wherein the didactic or entertainment value of the story has been worked out beforehand. Despite the play being live, it is well rehearsed (see Figure 3.4). Efforts to adhere to a tradition within the genre have taken place. It is self-consciously aware of its genre and uses this to create the very notion of stability it seeks. It aligns public expectations with an understanding of the play as an entity that over time can and will be perfected. The play, as it is repeated, has had the bugs and glitches taken out. Audiences who prefer the classics, those riveted by the built to last story, bring high expectations with them. They are familiar with the genre; they have often

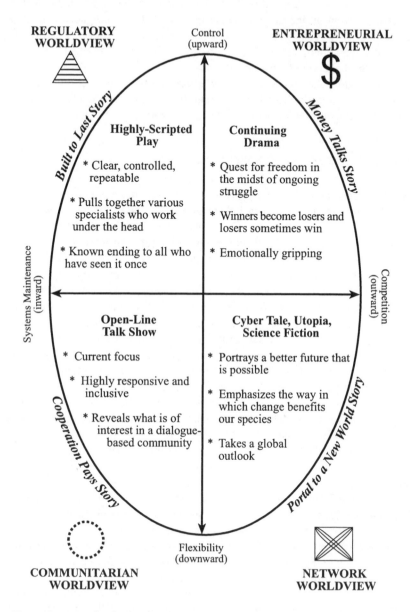

Figure 3.4   Leadership stories: genre

observed other versions of the play. There are standards. There is a base line. Measurement is possible. Errors can be detected and reduced. This is the essential tale of uncertainty reduction. It is the story of how over time we build things and ideas to last.

In this uncertainty-reducing genre, the ending is known. Anyone who has seen one version, at one level of understanding, has seen all future versions. The script is a structure that does not easily alter. It is set. Improvisers, so prized in the knowledge leader cybertale or utopian science fiction story, are seen by bureaucrats as impatient dreamers. The science fiction story is open ended. It is too promissory. It is wild, not under control and, if confused with fact, will lead impressionable people astray. The script or regulatory core is necessary lest the genre lose its hold on reality and, in the view of bureaucrats, cause damage – the damage of the rash experimenter, the mad scientist or the genius unrestrained by history. Advocates of the highly scripted play see genius as intelligence under control and tied to a known and accepted fact base. Those who admire the cybertale in the portal to a new world cringe at this failure to capture the revolutionary change potentially bottled up in the genius.

Communitarians are made uncomfortable by the highly scripted play of the bureaucratic leader (see Figure 3.4). As we shall see in far more detail in the next chapter, the participative leader prefers the genre of the open-line talk show. It is focused upon what is current and on the minds of community members. It is highly responsive to members' views of what is and is not important. It is inclusive. The leader facilitates dialogue which rouses controversy and this gives rise to opportunities to hear others. These others' views often differ from one's own. They stimulate. The community must learn how to abandon its dependence upon the highly scripted play and the role-playing that accompanies it. The call is plain and clear in the participative leader's reaction to the highly scripted play in the regulatory worldview – we are not actors, we are people who must express our authentic feelings and heartfelt emotions if we are to learn and grow. In populist terms, the communitarian speaks to the virtues of the everyday person as genuine and reveals a deep distrust of the role-playing expert – those who act as if they know when they often do not.

The parry and thrust against the apparent elitism of the bureaucrat's genre is framed in a political fashion by buccaneers in the money talks story. Rather than argue against the bureaucratic leader's inability to feel comfortable in his or her own skin, as do communitarians, the buccaneers portray the genre of the bureaucrat's story as a highbrow inaccessible form of culture that is out of touch with the everyday actors on Main Street. It is an establishment genre which presents itself as the legitimate thing – the height of sophistication – but it is just the remnant of the old cronies' network attempting to assert itself. While the communitarian's critique of the bureaucratic leader's genre is driven inward towards a failure of authority, the buccaneer's critique pushes outward. The scripted genre is a dying breed. It requires subsidies in order to compete with more engaging and popular genres. Once these subsidies are removed, the genre will be unable to compete with those that are far more accessible. However, supporters of this genre have been convinced that if and when subsidies are removed, something important will be lost. The buccaneers argue that what you will not voluntarily pay for cannot be so important.

The genre of the bureaucratic leader's story, however, is reassuring to those who seek stability in a confusing world. It is far from a dying breed. One can argue that it is the very success of the built to last story that makes it so easy to attack. We actually believe in the system. We obey the carefully timed traffic lights and adhere to the signs posted on the expressway. It is credible to purchase insurance policies and to believe that when we retire both our workplace and government pensions await. But in raising expectations regarding the reduction of uncertainty, the bureaucratic leaders in the regulatory worldview set themselves up for failure. Uncertainty happens. Master bureaucratic leaders who successfully reduce uncertainty are caught in a paradox. Let us use airplane safety as an example. In reducing lives lost in aviation accidents, over time the public expects fewer and fewer. Fewer actually happen, but when a crisis in which lives are lost occurs, it is the lead item on the news. The public rails at the ineptitude of those in charge.

The paradox of success in the bureaucratic leader's story is central to understanding our deep and abiding interest in it when we believe that the system as a whole is being attacked. It is then that we turn, each still within our preferred story, to the security of the well-designed, maintained and finely tuned system.

LESSON: BUREAUCRATIC LEADER

The bureaucratic leader is an embodiment of the call to duty – the call to serve at the head of a system that aims to attain the greatest good for the largest number. In the pull inward, the lessons in the built to last story are clear. Here, prudence prevails and the bureaucratic leader succeeds by maintaining and finely tuning a smooth, reliable, steady state that, like a humming motor, not only gets the job done, but over time with fewer and fewer glitches. This is portrayed in Figure 2.4 in the previous chapter. One might say that instead of getting into the "zone" as does the buccaneer leader, the bureaucratic leader oversees a system and monitors it so as to make sure it is in the zone. The two zones differ. The buccaneer's is a peak state; the bureaucrat's is a steady state. This steady state suits the tone and tenor of the regulatory worldview focus on systems maintenance. However, when the built to last story is pulled outward toward competition, it experiences a crisis. The lesson to be learned from the built to last story when it is confronted and threatened by those who neither play by its rules nor recognize its legitimacy instructs us on how bureaucratic leaders protect and defend when attacked.

When, as true believers see it, the built to last story is attacked by outsiders, it reacts by calling those in the system to their duty. Interestingly, bureaucratic leaders, when their back is up against the wall, are fighters. They invest heavily in fortifying and protecting the core routines of the system. They press the security button and quickly identify the attacker as an enemy. Enemies are those who not only fail to recognize the legitimacy of the system, but seek to confront rather than engage it. Activists, terrorists, and all those who come from stories not on the system's map, must be discredited. Recall that the system wards off attack by reinforcing its legitimacy in the eyes of its stakeholders. In dealing with the enemy, it engages in framing tactics that play upon their illegitimate motives, their base passions, and evil intent. The enemy is vilified both for the psycho-social reasons of pumping up true believers and for guaranteeing that neutrals do not flock to or sympathize with the enemy.

From a behavioural perspective, bureaucratic leaders are interesting to examine in the midst of crisis.[26] This is because they shift from monitoring the rules to fire fighting. In fire fighting the bureaucratic leader, like the buccaneer, emphasizes getting results. The position that the ends justify the means, one usually disowned by the bureaucratic leader when the system is in its steady state, increases in attractiveness as uncertainty rises. It becomes an obsession as the hierarchical system believes it is struggling for its survival. Bureaucratic leaders justify embracing a position where "the ends justify the means". They point out that systems, unlike competitive firms, are not easily replaced. They are symbols of a way of life. Their destruction is far more than a mere economic event. It signals a sea change in the economy. For example, in my country (Canada), talk of privatizing state-funded medicine is viewed as the desecration of a symbol. I am sure that the wanton destruction of the World Trade Center in New York City is seen as a tragedy that should not be framed solely in economic terms. Bureaucratic leaders defend their turf by arguing that it is significant – indeed, monumental.

This is not the position taken by buccaneer leaders. To them crisis is framed in economic terms and those terms alone (see Figure 3.5). Crisis is seen as both positive and negative. Just as the Chinese point to the ambiva-lence in the statement "may you live in interesting times", by employing it as both a curse and a blessing, so too buccaneers frame crisis. In its positive guise crisis signals an opportunity to engage in risk taking during times of uncertainty. Buccaneer leaders realize that the greater the certainty, the more likely it is that bureaucratic leaders with their prudent decision-making, adequate capital and desire for stability will prevail. Crisis, to the buccaneer, presents as an opportunity to mobilize swift reactions and direct results-oriented action. However, the negative framing of crises clearly indicates that a great deal of money can be lost. In the face of crises which spell loss, buccaneer leaders are unequivocal. Exit. Do not throw good money after bad. Cut your losses. Move on. Start afresh. In the face of crises, buccaneers are optimistic. Crisis provides an opportunity to regroup and try new tactics. Those who do not rise to the challenge will, and in the eyes of buccaneers should, be swept under. It is crisis and how leaders rise to this occasion that separates the leaders from those who are still learning the ropes.

In the communitarian worldview, you do not exit or remain loyal in the midst of crisis – you give voice (see Figure 3.5). You speak up. The buccaneer notion of strategic exit entails, so communitarians insist, abandoning those you love and trust. It is a form of self-exile when done voluntarily; banishment or excommunication when imposed. The bureaucrats' loyalty response is seen as blind and unquestioning. In crisis, voice is the means of making clear, in public, what you feel regarding those whose views and values are seen as incompatible with yours. Voice gives rise to dialogue. Dialogue reduces tensions. It lowers incompatibility. It turns combatants, over time, into lovers. While bureaucrats are rule makers and true believers in systems and buccaneers are tactically minded escape artists, communitarians are lovers. The irksome other must be embraced in a process of dialogue and mediation. Healthy communities are open to all – even disagreeable – voices. Crises are rifts in the community. Rifts are sutured and heal through compromise, accommodation and the search for common interests. It is in the idea of a truly shared destiny that organic communities, insist communitarians, achieve genuine inclusiveness. As we shall see in the next chapter, those embedded in other stories cringe at the application of the religious and moral doctrine "love thine enemy as thyself" when applied in the secular context. Not surprisingly, it is communitarians who seek to probe the spirituality and moral integrity of leaders.

Finally, the knowledge leader in the network worldview rises to the challenge of crisis by reinforcing the quest for thinking outside the box and arriving at new options to reduce the crisis (see Figure 3.5). These are not lovers as are the communitarians under crisis, but clever creators and inventors. Their call is to create and operate collaborative networks of best minds and practices determined to come up with original solutions in order to diminish the crisis. Creativity diminishes crisis. The network is neither a

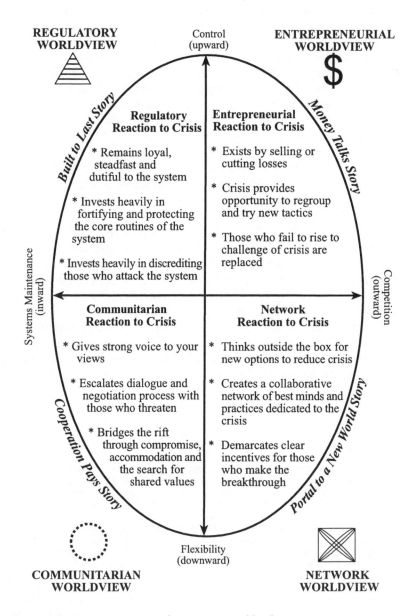

Figure 3.5 Reaction to crisis: four instrumental leaders

permanent, ongoing community as envisioned by the participative leader, nor the hierarchical system of the bureaucratic leader. It is a loosely structured coalition of knowledge workers willing to put their minds to a problem. The motives of those would-be problem solvers vary. Some are in it for the money, others are meaningfully engaged in contributing to a community of practice, and still others are attempting to self-consciously alter the known paradigms prevalent in and borrowed from the regulatory worldview. In the network worldview, new knowledge is not only a portal to a new world, it averts the crisis festering in the old world.

In emphasizing the reaction to crisis as a means of conveying the lessons to be learned in the built to last story, I am trying to convey the complexity and depth of the bureaucratic leader. This is not simple. We tend, on hearing the terms bureaucracy and system, to wrap this leader up too easily within a stereotype. This stereotype is too tied down with images taken from the other worldviews to clearly convey its hero. The bureaucratic leader is, as the buccaneer reminds us, wasteful and inefficient. The bureaucratic leader is too distant, aloof and detached. He or she is hardly the beloved friend and mentor sought after by communitarians, nor is the bureaucratic leader an innovator or champion of change. However, what the bureaucratic leader does is defend the very reality we take for granted. When crisis becomes pervasive, it strikes at our core routines – those unstated views that are so ubiquitous that they define us without our knowledge or permission. When the system is attacked, it is the monitor-turned-fire fighter who, in a counter-intuitive manner, legitimizes struggle and simultaneously calls us to duty. Not all heed the call. However, all who do, hear the built to last story.

NOTES

1. See Kenneth R. Thompson (2002), "Conversation with George Warrington: Leadership at Amtrack," *Organizational Dynamics*, **31**(1), pp. 85–98. In this interview, Warrington portrays the skills required to be an effective leader in the built to last story.
2. Paul C. Nutt (2002), *Why Decisions Fail: Avoiding the Blunders and Traps that Lead to Debacles*, San Francisco: Berrett-Koehler, points towards the traps to which an attentive decision-maker must attend. Jacques Frank Yates (2003), *Decision Management: How to Assure Better Decisions in Your Company*, San Francisco: Jossey-Bass, addresses the implementation and smooth sailing issue required to work with standard operating systems.
3. To get a broad overview of the bureaucratic leader as agent, peruse Christian Knudsen (2003), "The agency structure dilemma in organizations," in Haridimos Tsoukas and Christian Knudsen (eds), *The Oxford Handbook of Organizational Theory*, Oxford: Oxford University Press. The complications of the leader as agent in public sector organizations are effectively portrayed by George A. Boyne, Julian S. Gould-Williams, Jennifer Law and Richard M. Walker (2004), "Problems of rational planning in public organizations: An empirical assessment of conventional wisdom," *Administration and Society*, **36**(3), pp. 328–50.
4. Victor Alexander Thompson (1967), *Modern Organization*, New York: Knopf, opens up

the contemporary discussion of what has been euphemistically called bureau pathologies or the failings of bureaucracies. For an updating of this view, see Barry Bozeman (2000), *Bureaucracy and Red Tape*, Upper Saddle River, NJ: Prentice Hall.

5. These baseline, recurrent routines are portrayed by Martha S. Feldman (2004), "Resources in emerging structures and process of change, organization science," *Organization Science*, **15**(3), pp. 295–314. Feldman discusses how organizational routines set the boundaries in social practice for change in most bureaucratically structured organizations. Jannis Kallinikas (2004), "The social foundations of the bureaucratic order, organization," *Organization*, **11**(1), pp. 13–36, points out that, while the standard operating procedures in bureaucracies seem immovable, they are both flexible and open to change.

6. Ian Wilson (2000), *The New Rules of Corporate Conduct: Rewriting the Social Charter*, Westport, CT: Quorum, successfully explores the way bureaucracies in pursuit of legitimacy seek to engage in or be perceived as engaging in corporate social responsibility. John Elkington (2001), *The Chrysalis Economy: How Citizen CEOs and Corporations Can Fuse Values and Value Creation*, Oxford: Capstone, the founder of the triple bottom line takes this quest for legitimacy to a communitarian conclusion.

7. John G. Sifonis and Beverly Goldberg (1996), *Corporations on a Tightrope: Balancing Leadership, Governance and Technology in an Age of Complexity*, Oxford: Oxford University Press, capture the intricate balance needed to achieve this orderly equilibrium. Jan Thornbury (2003), "Creating a living culture: The challenges for business leaders," *Corporate Governance: The International Journal of Board Performance*, **2**(2), pp. 68–80, portrays the bureaucratic organizational culture as one that has difficulty in developing a living culture.

8. The term kleptocracy refers to a state of affairs where, in the regulatory world, thieves and self-interested scoundrels take up top positions in determining and/or skirting the rules of hierarchical systems. Jared M. Diamond (1997), *Guns, Germs and Steel: The Fates of Human Societies*, London: W.W. Norton and Company, explores the origins of corrupt kleptocratic elites. In an instrumental leadership context, Daniel Quinn Mills (2003), *Wheel, Deal and Steal: Deceptive Accounting, Deceitful CEOs and Ineffective Reforms*, Upper Saddle River, NJ: Prentice Hall/Financial Times, captures the motivational dynamics of corrupting systems from the top.

9. Willis Emmons (2000), *The Evolving Bargain: Strategic Implications of Deregulation and Privatization*, Cambridge, MA: Harvard Business School Press, provides insight into the dynamics of privatization in the built to last story. J. Brian Heywood (2001), *The Outsourcing Dilemma: The Search for Competitiveness*, London: Financial Times/Prentice Hall, draws out the implications of bureaucratic leaders seeking to simultaneously pursue systems maintenance and control while outsourcing.

10. George Ritzer (ed.) (2002), *McDonaldization: The Reader*, Thousand Oaks, CA: Pine Forge Press, compiles a first-rate set of insightful readings probing communitarians' dissatisfaction with standardization and the bureaucratization of consumption addressed in the global success of McDonalds. See Gregory A. Gull and Jonathan Dohn (2004), "The transmutation of the organization: Toward a more spiritual workplace," *Journal of Management Inquiry*, **13**(2), pp. 128–39 for good examples of the communitarians' call to end workplace disenchantment by focusing upon spirituality in the workplace.

11. The inability of hierarchically structured systems to innovate is creatively probed by Ian Palmer and Richard Danford (2002), "Out with the old and in with the new? The relationship between traditional and new organizational practices," *International Journal of Organizational Analysis*, **10**(3), pp. 209–25. See Gary S. Lynn and Richard R. Reilly (2002), *Blockbusters: The Five Keys to Developing New Products*, New York: Harper Collins, for their discussion in Chapter 10 on breaking through bureaucracy at NASA in order to innovate.

12. William Hollingsworth Whyte (1957), *The Organization Man*, Garden City, NJ: Doubleday, first portrayed the conformist individual in the hierarchical system. More contemporary efforts by Paul Leinberger and Bruce Tucker (1991), *The New Individualists: The Generation After the Organization Man*, New York: Harper Collins, show that, despite surface changes towards individuality, loyalty to the system by bureaucratic leaders still

prevails. Michael Roper (1994), *Masculinity and the British Organization Man Since 1945*, Oxford: Oxford University Press, examines the life histories of 25 British men and women bureaucratic leaders and shows where the myth of the rational organization man still holds and where it is wearing thin.

13. Adam Bodwai (2003), "Unceasing animosities and the public tranquility: Political market failure and the scope of commercial power," *California Law Review*, **91**(5), pp. 1331–74 uses a discussion in common law to draw out the public choice implications of the bureaucratic leader's view on the limits of commercial markets. For a good set of readings on this topic grounded in the recent economic literature on market failures, see Tyler Cowan and Eric Crampton (eds) (2002), *Market Failure or Success: The New Debate*, Cheltenham, UK and Northampton, MA, USA: Edward Elgar Publishing.

14. Bureaucratic leaders discern a cult-like quality and worry about the growing distortion of reality that is possible in a therapy culture. See Frank Füredi (2004), *Therapy Culture: Cultivating Vulnerability in an Uncertain Age*, London: Routledge, for the critique of the therapy culture. Nicholas Rescher (1993), *Pluralism: Against the Demand for Consensus*, Oxford: Clarendon Press, employs Jürgen Habermas' notion of consensus to argue how communitarians over time exclude the views of those who challenge their values in a fundamental manner.

15. The metaphor of the "iron cage" to depict the disenchanted state of modern bureaucracy was coined by Max Weber. See Lawrence A. Scaff (1989), *Fleeing the Iron Cage: Culture, Politics and Modernity in the Thought of Max Weber*, Berkeley, CA: University of California Press, for an insight into Weber's views. Martin Parker (2002), *Against Management: Organization in the Age of Managerialism*, Oxford: Blackwell, picks up the iron cage metaphor in his discussion of the demonization of big organizations in contemporary culture.

16. For a substantial discussion of the tie between creativity and spirituality in the network worldview, see William Cox Miller (1996), *Flash of Brilliance: Inspiring Creativity Where You Work*, Reading, MA: Perseus. Jeff Mauzy (2003), *Creativity Inc.: Building the Inventive Organization*, Cambridge, MA: Harvard Business School Press, outlines how the network organization creates a culture requiring creative skills. Ken Wilber (1997), *The Eye of Spirit: An Integral Vision for a World Gone Slightly Mad*, Boston, MA: Shambhala Press, using transpersonal psychology and a model tying eastern and western perspectives on spirituality outlines a very intelligent programme for aspiring creatives.

17. Whistleblowers often find the regulatory worldview one which prizes loyalty to the system and becomes confused when insiders appeal to the "good" of a larger system. See Fred C. Alford (2003), *Whistleblowers: Broken Lives and Organizational Power*, Ithaca, NY: Cornell University Press, for an in-depth discussion of the psycho-social tensions of whistleblowers. Roberta Ann Johnson (2003), *Whistleblowing: When it Works and Why*, Boulder, CO: Lynne Rienner, especially in the last two chapters, provides a good up-to-date discussion of the state of whistleblowing protection legislation in an international context.

18. Eran Vigoda (2003), *Developments in Organization Politics: How Political Dynamics Affect Employee Performance in Modern Worksites*, Cheltenham, UK and Northampton, MA, USA: Edward Elgar, provides an excellent review of the impact of office politics in bureaucratic contexts. Lyle Sussman, Arthur Adams, Frank Kuzmits and Louis Raho (2002), "Organizational politics: Tactics, channels and hierarchical roles," *Journal of Business Ethics*, **40**(4), pp. 313–29, point out the ethical tensions that emerge in politicized systems.

19. Kevin O'Connor (2003), *The Map of Innovation: Creating Something Out of Nothing*, New York: Crown Business, explores the careful preparation needed to innovate. Ralph H. Kilman (1989), *Managing Beyond the Quick Fix: A Completely Integrated Program for Creating and Maintaining Organizational Success*, San Francisco: Jossey-Bass, probes the care required to create sustainable change. Manfred F.R. Kets De Vries and Kathrina Balazs (1998) "Beyond the quick fix: The psychodynamics of organizational transformations and change," *European Management Journal*, **16**(5), pp. 611–22 emphasize the psychological dimensions of preparing for innovation.

20. See Martha S. Feldman, "A performative perspective on stability and change in organizational routines," *Industrial and Corporate Change*, **12**(4), pp. 727–51, for a discussion of the mindlessness that bolsters organizational routine. For a psychologist's insight attend to Ellen J. Langer (1998), *Mindfulness*, Reading, MA: Perseus.

21. Peter Schwartz (1996), *The Art of the Long View: Paths to Strategic Insight for Yourself and Your Company*, New York: Currency/Doubleday discusses the implications of responsible planning when one raises one's time horizon as a leader. Max Brand (1999), *The Clock of the Long Now: Time and Responsibility*, New York: Basic Books, pushes the envelope in his discussion of taking the long view.

22. In their notion of the knowledge life cycle, Joseph M. Firestone and Mark W. McElroy (2003), *Key Issues in the New Knowledge Management*, Amsterdam: Butterworth-Heinemann, make sense of how knowledge leaders push tacit into explicit knowledge. Thomas H. Davenport and Lawrence Prusack (1998), *Working Knowledge: How Organizations Manage What They Know*, Cambridge, MA: Harvard Business School Press, use a market metaphor of knowledge sellers, buyers and intermediaries to establish the importance for organizations of making their employees' tacit knowledge explicit.

23. The classic interpretation of the central role of organizational routines has been worked out by Richard R. Nelson and Sidney G. Winter, *An Evolutionary Theory of Economic Change*, Cambridge, MA: Belknap Press of Harvard University. For a recent application of this position, see Martha S. Feldman and Brian T. Pentland (2003), "Reconceptualizing organizational routines as a source of flexibility and change," *Administrative Science Quarterly*, **48**(1), pp. 94–118.

24. Communitarians frame the control and command system of the bureaucrats as destroying the basis for trust. See the compilation of readings by Roderick M. Kramer and Karen S. Cook (eds) (2004), *Trust and Distrust in Organizations: Dilemmas and Approaches*, New York: Russell Sage Foundation. Dan Cohen and Laurence Prusak (2001), *In Good Company: How Social Capital Makes Organizations Work*, Cambridge, MA: Harvard Business School Press, focus upon how the lack of an expressive community in the regulatory worldview diminishes interpersonal trust.

25. Clay Spinuzzi (2003), *Tracing Genres Through Organizations: A Sociocultural Approach to Information Design*, Cambridge, MA: MIT Press, uses the genre ecology approach to fruitfully examine the evolution of genres and their instability over time. For a very different approach see Pete Thomas (2003), "The recontextualization of management: A discourse-based approach to analyzing the development of management thinking," *Journal of Management Studies*, **40**(4), pp. 775–801.

26. Crisis is a prime test of the resilience of the bureaucratic leader since it pushes the regulatory worldview to recognize and focus upon rising uncertainty. Otto Lerbinger (1997), *Crisis Manager: Facing Risk and Responsibility*, Mahwah, NJ: Lawrence Erlbaum, focuses on the bureaucratic leader's tendency to have his or her values tested during crises. Karl Weick and Kathleen M. Sutcliffe (2001), *Managing the Unexpected: Assuring High Performance in an Age of Complexity*, San Francisco: Jossey-Bass, look at how high reliability systems make sense and, in time, manage the unexpected.

4. Participative leaders: the cooperation pays story

"We are not destined to be empty raincoats, nameless numbers on a payroll, role occupants, the raw material of economics of sociology, statistics in a government report. If that is to be its price, economics is an empty promise. There must be more to life than being a cog in someone else's great machine, hurtling God knows where."

Charles Handy[1]

There indeed must be more to life than being a cog in someone else's great machine, hurtling God knows where. Handy, with splendid literary ability, captures how communitarians wedge themselves between bureaucratic leaders, those who would have us as cogs in someone else's machine or system, and knowledge leaders, those whose portal to a new world story projects diverse futures, many of which even God has yet to imagine. Participative leaders provide those who hear the cooperation pays story with a sense of meaning, purpose and belonging. This story addresses the quality of life of those who become active and committed members in a vital, trusting community. In the experience of a shared destiny within a common culture, members need not feel either alone and suspicious of others, as is the case in the dog-eat-dog world of the buccaneer, or claustrophobically cosseted, yet secure, within a closely monitored hierarchical system. After all, the participative leader's story is neither the tale of liberty made possible by free markets nor the pursuit of routine and security ensuing from a well-managed, planned, and finely tuned system. It is the story of the quest for meaning and purpose. This results from membership and active commitment to a clan.[2]

The symbol of a circle bound by a circumference open to external influences and tolerant of diversity denotes the communitarian worldview. In this worldview which marries systems maintenance with flexibility, the participative leader is drawn inward by the clan or community towards the centre of the circle. The clan stresses system maintenance in its ongoing perpetuation of identity and nurturing of the values of members of the community. Flexibility within the community is encouraged. Participative leaders empower members of the clan to use discretion, question rules and remain open to and tolerant of different points of view.[3] The circle provides members with a strong "we" feeling, enhances trust-based exchanges, and generates a sense of purpose and meaning for members. The partial opening in the circle indicates flexibility and highlights a tolerance for diverse views and a willingness to engage these in an ongoing dialogue. The safety of the "we" feeling and sense of commitment to the community give rise to the potential of the clan to adapt via learning.[4]

The participative leader leads from the centre of the clan. He or she is selected by community members. There is a grassroots, consensus-based ideology in clan governance that prohibits the strategies used by *bona fide* leaders in other stories. Thus the participative leader who is seen as aggressively pushing him or herself to the front of the pack violates the grassroots premise of communitarian leadership. Leadership is a form of "stewardship". One is a servant of the community.[5] In the communitarian worldview, information flows in two ways – from the bottom upward and with consultation from the top downward. Tall hierarchies are flattened by participatory leaders. Status differences are reduced. Open dialogue with member participants replaces the specialized rule-based debate of experts. Participative leaders need not represent a leading or bleeding edge of knowledge as is the case in the network worldview. The participative leader fosters a community in which intelligence emerges from the centre. It is a social or emotional intelligence – an intelligence that harmonizes community and enhances learning.[6]

The leader in the cooperation pays story is a mentor, facilitator, advocate and diplomat. In a practical sense, the communitarian worldview flourishes in four key contexts: non-profit organizations highly dependent upon the ideological commitment of volunteers and donors; professional associations where peer relations, a common occupational history and culture prevail; social movement developments wherein groups seek to throw off the yoke of a common oppression; and lastly, business organizations which seek to either benefit from the implementation of high involvement management practices or niche market their goods and services to communitarians.[7] The communitarian worldview pervades discussions of values and ethics in applied contexts. It speaks to the kinder, gentler leader who, in an outgrowth of earlier management theories like the human relations school, heralded the socially skilled and compassionate leader. The participative leader is still put forward in many leadership courses as the solution to the greed of the corruptible buccaneer, the grey flannel-suited conformity of the detached and uncaring bureaucrat, and the rash experimentation of those who promise to solve our problems by virtualizing, globalizing and/or digitalizing our communities.

The hero in the cooperation pays story is the quiet leader who uses courage and personal integrity to demonstrate that talk is more than mere talk. To walk the talk, the participative leader is a teacher/mentor. He or she highlights not only the cherished values to be taught to new members as they are socialized into the community, but also imports ideas and enlivens discussions with new members or those outside the community. In the participative leader's story, the community is not merely a medium for executing exchanges required to get food on the table or stay out of danger; it is a classroom in which we learn new lessons. It is we who differentiate between the lessons worth passing on to our children and those best tossed aside. As a facilitator, the participative leader is empathic – an individual sensitized to the psycho-emotional needs of others. The task of the facilitator is to provide the community with the balance to turn conflict, with all its disruptive potential, into creative controversy. In the facilitator's role, the participative leader is a matchmaker bringing disparate members of the community into beneficial contact with one another. As an advocate, the participative leader champions positions which, if left to their own, might fly below the radar of the community. The participative leader scans the environment both within and beyond the community in search of what will, when mulled over by the community, add to the quality of life of its members. Lastly, in his or her diplomatic capacity, the participative leader represents the community to outsiders. In this diplomatic capacity, the participative leader takes on a symbolic function, embodying the community and its values to those who know little of its workings.

The cooperation pays story is often dismissed, especially when applied in business and political circles. Its critics contend that it is too idealistic or too sanctimoniously grounded as an altruistic model of our species. This is not at all how communitarians see it. Theirs is not a story rife with mere bromides, but a realistic model of how to create a caring, loving, healthy, humane environment in which to work and grow. Their leader is neither a touchy-feely flake nor a quick weeper. The participative leader is a courageous toxic handler, a sage with the capacity to create the conditions for a renaissance in personal integrity, social responsibility and the building of bonds of trust and intimacy.[8] We are all, communitarians insist, far better off when we are surrounded by people we care for and who, in our time of need, will reciprocate and tend to us. Leaders, so the cooperation pays story goes, are at their best when they bring out the best in us. They have the ability to reduce anxiety and get people to work together in harmony. Participative leaders create the conditions which give rise to a shared culture. In its reflection, we no longer see one another as the means to an end, cogs in a great wheel, or as supplicants riveted to the just-in-time promise that an innovation will provide a portal to a new world.

The cooperation pays story, told in its six-point story template – origin, plot, audience, protagonist, genre and lesson – unfolds around the basic and rarely outgrown fear of abandonment. It weaves its way into discussions of how, why and where to build, sustain and nurture a form of humanism within instrumental ventures as an antidote to this pervasive, all too human fear. The participative leader is at the centre of a version of capitalism which affirms the centrality of the family and the intimacy of open, trusting and morally grounded relationships as the procrustean bed for solving our problems. This story is a foil to living as a wealthy individual and buying the favours of others. It reminds us of the dangers of blind duty to a system that treats one as a subordinate and childlike even as one climbs upward within the hierarchy. It asks us to have faith in our collective wisdom rather than wildly experiment with options that may be detrimental to a healthy and sustainable community. Let us turn to the origins of the cooperation pays story and its centre, the participative leader.

ORIGINS: PARTICIPATIVE LEADER

The beginning of instrumental or goal-directed behaviour is accompanied by the feeling of anxiety as problems arise. All four worldviews or faces of capitalism are secular stories that start in a world rife with problems and in which rational men and women seek to reduce this pervasive experience of anxiety. These are secular stories because the attainment of paradise – a state without anxiety, without the anticipation or perception of problems – is not viewed as a viable option. We look to the four worldviews or faces of capitalism as a means, hearing one as dominant, to help inform us as to how, when, why, where and with whom to attempt to reduce our experience of anxiety. Leaders concretize and embody stories. They make them real. They are the basis for our rich understanding of our preferred story and the stereotypical view we hold of those we have trouble hearing. Each story suggests a different origin to the problems giving rise to our anxiety. Each posits that we solve our rising anxieties in different manners.

The participative leader seeks to reduce a persuasive sense of meaninglessness or the feeling of a lack of purpose experienced when men and women reach out for others, but find themselves psychologically alone, without intimacy, and all too aware that they are playing a role rather than feeling authentic or fully alive. Anxiety pervades one's sense of identity. In the communitarian worldview, anxiety is alleviated in a trusting, open and responsive community. Members increase their involvement and commitment as they begin to experience the community as a safe place where, in tanem with significant others, they can explore options, develop as individuals and learn. The participative leader removes the aggressive competition and strong demarcation between winners and losers in the buccaneer story. In the communitarian worldview, the leader reduces the top-down communication emphasis prevalent in the bureaucratic leader's story. Status differences are lessened, but differences between individuals with varying points of view are retained. Diversity, communitarians insist, when married to trust in a common culture does not increase anxiety of members.[9] Rather, diversity aids in avoiding groupthink and the complacency, even smug superiority, that may result when a community becomes too inward-looking, conformist, or cult-like.

The communitarian strategy for alleviating anxiety does not turn its back on losers (buccaneers), reduce uncertainty (bureaucrats) and innovate (knowledge) (see Figure 4.1). Rather, it appropriates each of these as best accomplished when done in and through communities of trust. Communitarians argue that the family-like clan will bolster a firm's profits when workers are empowered, participation is enhanced, and decision making is decentralized. Here, profits are best understood in the long term. Ultimately the ability of a firm to consistently generate profits rests on the satisfaction and commitment of employees to the firm and the reputation of the firm in the eyes of stakeholders. Communitarians insist that firms which act in a questionable manner and/or insist that followers simply heed the buccaneer will stumble. Uncertainty is best reduced, not by creating rules and one-size-fits-all policies, but by enhancing the capacity of members to use discretion – to think for themselves. The inability of many in hierarchical systems to cope with change is a function of the inability of silo-like subsystems to customize solutions to ongoing and altering problems. The rigidity of rule adherence essential to standardization inhibits the very diversity which is the bread and butter of the way communitarians think systems learn best. Innovation is handled most appropriately, argue communitarians, when it is the users that assess whether an innovation is good for the community and not the originators of the innovations. It is the grassroots users embedded in a community who can best assess whether or not this or that technology, this or that genetic modification, is appropriate.

The wisdom of community is seen neither as an anxiety reducer nor as a solution to very many problems by those who hear other stories. Buccaneers, as outlined in Figure 4.1, are made anxious by the call to community. It slows down actions. It increases cost. Most worryingly, buccaneers believe that communities dumb down rather than increase the intelligence of individuals. Those who resonate with the entrepreneurial worldview do not see two heads as better than one. Rather, they view the group as requiring the individual to compromise, to conform and, in the end, to settle with a result which is far from optimal. Rather than feel comforted by a decision made by the public,

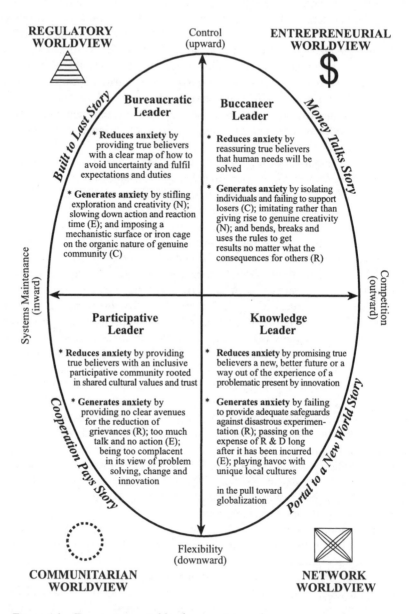

Figure 4.1   Four instrumental leaders: anxiety cycle

the buccaneer sees it as tainted with political correctness and fraught with rose-coloured glasses. The reason for this is that participative leaders stress process, emphasizing fairness, inclusivity and the consensus-based nature of implementable outcomes. Buccaneers look solely at short-term results. They care little about who did not buy in or who resents the processes. Good processes, communitarians insist, assure good long-term outcomes; bold actions taken decisively, buccaneers argue, result in a big win.

Bureaucratic leaders (see Figure 4.1) are not comforted by the communitarian solution. Rather than alleviate their anxieties, it exacerbates them. Clans are unabashedly value-based. To bureaucrats, they lack objectivity, possess little rigour, and often bypass careful analysis in favour of what seems to be the trend of the month. Clans have an oral tradition which enables attention to move quickly from one topic to others. But by downplaying the written tradition with its accompanying emphasis upon memory, there is a lack of depth, a strong hold upon the facts, and a tendency to follow rumour and get easily distracted. Bureaucrats worry that hearsay passes as fact. Character perception rooted in the organizational grapevine, takes on the status of evidence. What ensues, insist bureaucrats, is that in the name of trust clans can become rife with nepotism. Worse, this is not seen by either outsiders or true believers in the cooperation pays story. Insiders buy into the community and they recognize that membership has its privileges. Despite calls for transparency by communitarians, much of what occurs in the informal but powerful culture of the clan is for members' eyes only. Bureaucrats worry. What grievance procedures are forfeited in the name of trust? What facts are overridden by the need to retain the solidarity of members? Bureaucrats are curious. Clans turn bad when they fall into the wrong hands and once this occurs they are difficult to set right. Those with a regulatory temperament are made uneasy with the loose informality, poor systems of accountability and value-based premises that substitute for fact in the reasoning of communitarians.

The knowledge leader in the network worldview is not relieved by the problem-solving acumen of participative leaders. In the portal to a new world story, cooperation is necessary, but not sufficient. The knowledge leader, like the participative leader, employs collaboration. The knowledge leader believes that flexibility, when married to competition, keeps participants alert and poised for the future and its challenges. Competition tied to flexibility reduces the complacency, smugness and "we are the best" thinking that can prevail when flexibility is tied to system management. Rather than rising to challenges and facing constraints, scarcities, and hard problems, clans turn inward celebrating past success or idealizing positions which they seem unwilling to put to the test. Via the shared culture and legends, they reinforce untested premises. This apparently safe psychological territory, insist knowledge leaders, is only safe if it is tied to working knowledge. Network champions become anxious in communitarian settings. They are too easily blindsided. They fail to benchmark external sources and view change in value-laden terms. They do not engage in active experimentation. They confuse social movement development with genuine innovation. Thus knowledge leaders worry about the communitarians' distinction between, for example, appropriate and inappropriate experimentation. The former is experimentation approved of by the community. The latter is championed by leading edge thinkers, but framed as "risky" by the community. In this manner, those who resonate with the knowledge leader's story are made anxious by the communitarians' resistance to globalization, genetically modified foods, and cloning. In the network worldview, it is the knowledge leaders who determine whether or not experimentation should be curtailed.

The anxiety cycle (Figure 4.1) of the four instrumental leaders reveals that each of us has our anxieties reduced in the story we most easily hear, but feel uncomfortable with the origins and solutions offered in other stories. They do not seem to calm us. Those who hear the cooperation pays story are comforted by the sense of purpose, meaning and belonging that is possible in the midst of a viable, full-bodied clan experience. This is a safe territory wherein one can develop, grow and learn in a trusting and nurturing environment. Yet others who hear this story shudder. It does away with the clarity of rules and the objective and careful scrutiny of the hard, cold facts. It confuses talk and the psychology of well-being with action and the very real economics of competitive markets. It successfully creates a safe territory, but this enables clan members to complacently settle down, become nostalgic for the good old days, and too easily shy away from the challenge of coping with the future.

While the cooperation pays story originates in the quest for meaning, purpose or belonging, the plot hinges upon a form of rationality not easily embraced in the other stories. As discussed in Chapter 2 (Figure 2.2), the participative leader's story follows a psycho-social form of rationality. This plot seeks emotionally intelligent participants within clans or communities of peers to realize their full potential by becoming authentic, then using this in dialogue with others to learn and adapt to change. Emotional intelligence is depicted as superior to the buccaneer's tactical intelligence, the bureaucratic leader's strategic intelligence and the knowledge leader's creative intelligence. In the participative leader's plot line, psycho-social rationality trumps the others. It provides a means of knowing oneself and thereby entering into dialogue with trusting others. This dialogue facilitates team or collective learning and adaptation. Taken to its logical end, communitarians insist that psycho-social rationality applied in the long run will be profitable, reduce uncertainty and stimulate innovation.

PLOT: PARTICIPATIVE LEADER

The psycho-social rationality at the heart of the participative leader's plot entails a three-step process. Each step is necessary. First, the participative leader and all who aspire to centrality in the communitarian worldview must develop self-knowledge. The initial tension and conflict in the plot are taken inward towards the psychological territory of the self. The participative leader must develop, be able to enact and articulate a sense of authenticity in the self.[10] The authentic self is an achievement. To accomplish this, participative leaders must work through their personal anxiety, wrestle with their shadow and find the calm at the heart of the authentic self. It is the location of this calm at the centre of the community that gives rise to the second stage. This stage is driven outward, but not towards competition. Trust, which gives rise to sharing and cooperation, is the glue that holds others in relationship to both the authentic participative leader and others who are drawn to the shared values that ensue.[11] In stage two the social is added to the psychological. The self–other relationship is nested in the trust and reciprocity born of the clan. It is the pervasiveness of trust that leads to stage three. In stage three, people in the clan say what they think. They do not kowtow to the buccaneer, blindly conform to the rules of the hierarchical system, or rashly chase after the new. The community expresses diverse points of view in an atmosphere of trust, inclusion and empowerment. In the third stage, learning ensues. The community becomes, as communitarians feel, open, adaptive and smart.[12]

   This three-step process in the participative leader's plot – authentic self, interpersonal trust and learning through dialogue – is made possible by a radical departure in the leader–other relationship in the communitarian worldview from those found in both the entrepreneurial and the regulatory worldviews. In the cooperation pays story, the leader closes the distance, both psychological and economic, between leaders and followers. In fact, the term "follower" is not used in the communitarian worldview. If it is used, "follower" has a pejorative connotation and is used to refer to one who has bought into the get-rich-quick schemes of the buccaneer leader, The "other" in the leader–other relationship is called a member (see Figure 4.2). The participative leader and members in the clan seek to reduce status differences. This is not necessarily a call to egalitarianism, but recognition that in a trusting relationship all parties must feel that they can both speak up and openly voice their opinions. This is a far cry from the superordinate/subordinate relationship in the regulatory worldview. In the cooperation pays story, members must not fear either retaliation or censure. Peer relationships between the participatory leader and members prevail. The participative leader is the steward of the community. In the heartland of the communitarian

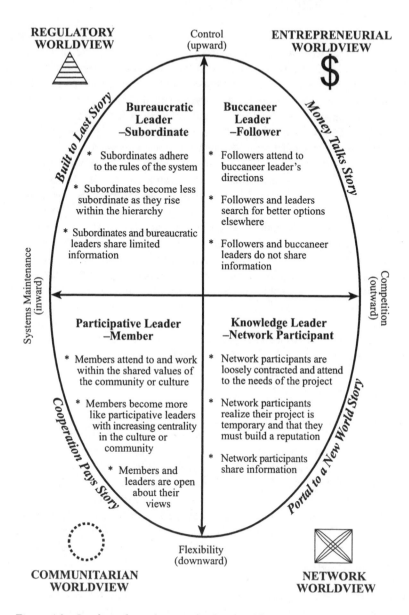

Figure 4.2   Leader–other relations: the four worldviews

worldview, the participative leader is a servant leader, enacting, facilitating and helping to bring into life the views of the clan members.

Due to the closing of the distance between leader and the other in the cooperation pays story, the irksome other becomes a major complication in the plot of the participative leader's story.[13] The irksome other, as seen within each worldview, violates the plot of the story. In the entrepreneurial worldview, the irksome other is the follower who squanders capital, dissipates opportunities and assists the buccaneer in losing rather than making profits. Given the follower–leader relationship here and the economic and psychological distance fostered by competitive markets, buccaneers can fire followers who they view as irksome. In a story which licences exit, followers who view their boss as irksome can leave for other jobs. Those who are uncomfortable with the buccaneer leader's solution to the irksome other view buccaneers as rather cavalier in their impulse to dismiss followers and point out that followers who view their boss as irksome often must stay with a bad job as others are not easily found. Ideally, a libertarian or just desserts perspective flourishes when one can, upon exit, start afresh or put the past behind.

Putting the past behind or starting afresh is not highlighted in the built to last story. Here the leader–other relationship is between the leader as superordinate and the other as subordinate (see Figure 4.2). Loyalty, not exit, mark this treatment of the irksome other. The problem of the irksome other is handled by the use of position power. Superordinates or bureaucratic leaders can formally block, slow down, demote or tarnish the aspirations of subordinates who do not attain the performance evaluation required to credibly establish that one is contributing to the ongoing stability of the system. Note that the hierarchical nature of the system enables most members to be both superordinate to some and subordinate to others. This fosters the checks and balances, the very prudence that is the earmark of procedural rationality. The irksome other is perceived as the internal source of system instability. They are held accountable for errors and lapses in procedures. The system acts in the best interest of the largest number of system actors when it acts rationally to slow down or sideline subordinates who fail to contribute to system stability. Buccaneer leaders sneer at the retention of the inept in hierarchical systems. Knowledge leaders view measures of stability as potentially penalizing the innovator in the hierarchical system as an irksome other. Participative leaders see subordination itself as a failure to address the problem of motivating members to increase their commitment and take on greater challenges.

In the network worldview which we will examine more fully in the next chapter, the irksome other is handled contractually. The knowledge leader creates a loose coalition or network of participants. These participants are linked by contracts which stipulate the relations between and among them. The temporary nature of these collaborative and creative communities of practice and "hot" groups necessitates that the knowledge leaders protect the network from dominance by a sole source of ideas and allow those who are no longer contributing useful knowledge to the network to lapse.[14] The irksome other in the portal to a new world impedes the growth, transfer and application of knowledge both within the network and between the network and final users of the innovative product, technique or service. Those who are uncomfortable with the manner in which the knowledge leader deals with the irksome other point out how these networks suck up the knowledge of network participants, use it and then abandon them. The network gets smart by taking the tacit knowledge of network participants, transforming it to explicit knowledge, then converting it into intellectual capital.

The participative leader feels uncomfortable with fire and demote strategies and deploys them only when they are the only useful means of handling the irksome other. In the cooperation pays story, those who are viewed as violating community values – trust, authenticity and dialogue – are labelled as irksome. The irksome other is seen as putting their needs before those of the community; they foster and benefit from non-constructive conflict, engage in efforts to politicize and factionalize discussions and partake in deceptive practices which reduce trust and impair the reputation of the community in the eyes of outsiders. To rein in the irksome other, the participative leader relies on three techniques – socialization, resocialization and ostracism. The first is employed on all new members to the community. It is a process that assumes that the norms of the community are understood. The participative leader socializes by acting as a mentor. Resocialization entails the use of moral persuasion and the gradual denial of attention to members who are seen as knowingly violating the community norms. If this continues, the community threatens, then ostracizes or treats the member with both distance and/or silence.[15]

In a plot which extols authenticity, builds trust and creates new options through dialogue, distancing and silencing take on special significance. Ostracism entails a complex form of expunging the non-rehabilitated irksome other by marginalizing them and then failing to recognize their voice. The community justifies this by pointing not only to the irksome other's violation of community norms, but their failure, upon warning, to express contrition or provide indications of altering their behaviour. In the eyes of the community, the ostracized are viewed as engaging in a self-selected form of exile. This is not a story which hinges on the promise of new beginnings as told by the buccaneer, the demoted subordinates unable to get it right, or the brazen creator setting off to discover new territory. It is a plot in which the community mourns the loss of one of its own. Leadership in the cooperation pays story frames the ostracized, not as one lured away by the appeal of other stories or other value systems, but as a moral lapse on behalf of the ostracized. At the heart of the communitarian plot is a moral tale. To be good and virtuous is to be socially responsible to the clan.[16] The notions of integrity and virtue in the communitarian worldview are value-laden terms that tell members where in the community the boundaries exist. While the circumference of the circle in the symbol denoting the cooperation story is open, all insiders know the boundary.

The participative leader's story draws an audience that sees the social contracts of healthy relationships as vital in establishing responsible behaviour which need not be driven by short-term market signals, long-term planning designs of rule-based hierarchies, or the visions of charismatic innovators and self-proclaimed masters of the next new thing. Social contracts are open to discussion. They require voluntary, informed assent. They are, when due consideration is given to the other, amendable. They are public and inclusionary. Moreover, in making social contracts primary, participative leaders are held up to high standards. They must walk their talk.

AUDIENCE: PARTICIPATIVE LEADER

Those drawn to the story of the participative leader possess a spiritual hunger for a life in which work and domesticity take on substance and which involves a quest for meaning. In this story, meaning is a psycho-social construction grounded in an idealized view of the authentic self, fully realized in the midst of an open and trusting community. This audience is dissatisfied with the solutions to anxiety offered in other leadership stories. Theirs is a "feeling" story and they know that they feel good when they are both comfortable within their own skins (authentic) and at home in their surroundings (community). To feel comfortable in their skins, true believers in the communitarian worldview seek to know or understand themselves. This, while framed as narcissistic by those outside the participative leader's story, is viewed as the basis for reaching out and understanding how and with whom to develop genuine caring relations.

The audience attracted to the cooperation pays story seeks the warmth and sense of purpose reflected in developing a meaningful and significant set of trusting relationships. These relationships serve as an antidote to the communitarian apprehension and fear of isolation, abandonment and meaninglessness. When heard in their own terms, communitarians want to be winners, to be secure and to be on the cusp of the next new thing. However, they frame winning, security and innovation quite differently from buccaneer, bureaucratic or knowledge leaders. Those who hear the cooperation pays story are uncomfortable with the rugged individualism and the "win, baby, win" dictum of the self-made buccaneer, ambivalent regarding what they see as the blind adherence to rules required in hierarchical systems and alarmed at the manner in which a spate of rash innovations endangers healthy communities.

Communitarians frame winning in quality of life terms. One wins when one can call upon authentic, trusting others in time of need and they will be there without qualms – freely, lovingly and attentively. This, contend those who resonate with the participative leader's story, is genuine winning. One has taken the time to build and integrate one's values with others. Communitarians shudder at the wealthy and self-important who, with a dearth of significant relations, must, to use an example, hire others to hear their views and escort them in times of need. Wealth, insist communitarians, is the social support, love and esteem that is freely given by those who choose to form meaningful relations with us. It is rooted in reciprocity and trust. Those who give loving kindness in both the small gestures of daily life and the vital moments when others find themselves in need, will, in time, receive it back with compounding interest. Communitarians are not so much anti-materialists as they are pro-community. The small but significant face-to-face interaction, or its electronic equivalent in a more modern and technologically adjusted virtual community, stands for that which opposes the anonymity of cold, sterile systems and the pull of mercenary markets. With membership in the community or clan comes privileges. The privileges include feeling important, significant and part of something that will live on long beyond the lifespan of the member.

Security, in the lexicon of the audience drawn to the participative leader's story, is not dependent on the existence of or deference to a code of rules or a formal plan – even a good one – intended to reduce uncertainty. Hearing the call of flexibility, communitarians envision the future as robust and uncertain. It foils the best efforts of even the most cerebral analysts and well-trained specialists working in the most effectively designed hierarchies. Communitarians insist that one is never genuinely secure when deferring to the cerebrality of top-down experts or blindly placing one's faith in systems. Rather, one is secure when one is sufficiently aware and an integral part of one's community so as to question and probe. In addition, one is secure if one can use discretion in revising and interpreting the rules, enter into dialogue with others in order to work through problems, and learn how to adapt to emerging issues. One is secure when empowered. Dependence, argue communitarians, increases one's vulnerability. It is the redistribution of power from the top in the bureaucratic leader's story to the centre and members in the participative leader's story that fosters genuine security. The many, with differing views, partake in communal or social intelligence; the few, in procedural rationality. This attenuates diversity. It accelerates learning. The hierarchical system with all or most of its eggs in one basket (even a well-designed one) is much more vulnerable, communitarians reckon, than a community with open dialogue, diverse points of view and options.

The audience to the cooperation pays story desires innovation, but feels uncomfortable with the manner in which it is framed within the knowledge leader's story. Here innovation is extolled as a positive force, an experiment with benefits that stimulates competitive advantage and opens up new opportunities. Innovation is a driver of globalization and a force which increases the wealth of nations and unburdens large numbers of people. Communitarians, on the other hand, are much more ambivalent regarding innovation, globalization and the blessing of experimentation from a network point of view. They see innovation as appropriate when it fosters community, empowers community members, generates inclusiveness and is sustainable. The position is simple but powerful. Small is beautiful. Local is liveable. Sustainable is healthy. This set of positions does not hold for all innovations. Inappropriate innovations foster dependence, homogenize and diminish the uniqueness of communities, concentrate power in the hands of a few and waste or deplete non-renewable resources. In the cooperation pays story, the participative leader must mobilize the collective wisdom of the community in order to steer clear of inappropriate but luring innovations. These innovations, insist audiences drawn to the participative leader's story, tinker with the basic fabric of life and community and turn neighbourhoods into high-rise canyons and haunts for the lonely. They warp liveable communities, quickly morphing them into edge cities feeding off turnpikes and super-highways.

The audience drawn to the participative community cherishes communal wisdom as a virtue and worries about those whose thought and actions are viewed as violating clan values. The communitarian worldview tiptoes along a tightrope which licenses dissent, encourages dialogue and respects diverse points of view. It insists on principled, value-based behaviour, encourages consensus and shies away from conflict and other activities which might fragment the community. The protagonist in the cooperation pays story must aid the community in walking this tightrope. The hero in the communitarian worldview is attuned to the values of the community and able to mediate among diverse points of view so that, as a result of dialogue, learning and trust, fractiousness is kept to a minimum. However, if communities become fragmented and politicized, the participative leader's work grows more difficult. With the use of exit, community values are threatened. The participative leader succeeds when community members remain open, trusting and truthful. The leader puts these values into practice.

Those who hear the participative leaders see themselves as worldly realists. This, as we shall see in the next section, is not how those imbued with other stories frame this audience. They do not, like network advocates, embrace innovation as a silver bullet. They insist upon the hard work of assessing and slowly separating that which bolsters community from that which endangers it. This takes time, talk and grassroots involvement. It is the very nature of civil discourse that humanizes the rule-based, austere and impersonal systems of those in the regulatory worldview. Communitarians honour the educator before the legislator. It is the educator who creates the values which serve as the basis for living in an ethical community, not relying solely upon the legislator's notion of a rule-based, code-adhering system. Lastly, the audience to the participative leader's story does not view money, even fortune-getting, as the royal road to personal happiness. Communitarians do not advocate poverty, but are made uneasy by what they see as "unfair" inequities. They champion the idea that the pursuit of quality of life issues, not wealth as an end in itself, is the way to live happily, respectful of acts of kindness, charity and sharing.

PROTAGONIST: PARTICIPATIVE LEADER

The hero is the team. Participative leaders are individuals who bring out the best in themselves and others. The protagonist in the cooperation pays story occupies a central role in the community. He or she is not selected as the leader on the basis of more wealth, better credentials or more creativity, but because members see them as exemplifying the values of the clan, team or community. As such, the participative leader is trusted. He or she, as will become more apparent in Chapter 6, is a mentor, facilitator, advocate and diplomat. Through each of these skills, the participative leader seeks to enhance the quality of life of members within the team, clan or community. This is not accidental. The community thrives and is resilient when new members with new blood, energy and ideas are eager to join. Veteran members are willing to escalate their commitment and the values of the community are seen by members as reducing anxiety. As a facilitator, the participative leader enhances and reinforces the community by transforming destructive conflict and animosities which may fragment the community into useful dialogue. The leader in the cooperation story advocates for a position which needs hearing within a principled community. Lastly, the hero serves as a diplomat, symbolically representing the community and its values to outsiders and others with whom, over time, the community must enter into relations if it is to remain resilient.

True believers in the cooperation pays story see the participative leader as compassionate, appreciative and open (see Figure 4.3). He or she is like a midwife assisting others in bringing new ideas, events and products which contribute to the community into the light of day. The hero in the cooperation

Bureaucratic Leader's View of Participative Leader	Buccaneer Leader's View of Participative Leader
Character * new age (touchy-feely) * inclusive * informal *Evaluation* * focuses on personal relationships, not data * too team or group oriented * unable to separate work from private affairs * useful when bureaucrats seek to increase subordinates' involvement or satisfaction in the system	*Character* * idealistic * indecisive * politically correct *Evaluation* * all talk, no action * unable to act independently * uncomfortable with conflict * useful when buccaneers must deal with slow-moving consensus types
Participative Leader's Self-Portrait	**Knowledge Leader's View of Participative Leader**
Character * compassionate * appreciative * open *Evaluation* * fosters organizational culture in which learning thrives * challenges members to self-actualize * opens dialogue and builds trust * useful in all situations which require adaptation and learning	*Character* * collaborative * hesitant * normative *Evaluation* * fails to disrupt uncreative teams * uncomfortable with globalization * change must bolster community * useful when knowledge leaders must blend collaboration with competition

Figure 4.3   Participative leader: portraits

pays story challenges him or herself and then members to both self-actualize and to realize their potential within a dynamic changing community. The participative leader is not in control; rather, he or she helps to foster a culture in which members are empowered to escalate their involvement, speak their minds and develop themselves and their community.[17] This, communitarians assert, opens up dialogue, fuels curiosity and reinforces the pursuit of alternatives. Learning, with the participative leader as the mentor, ensues. Learning in this story entails not only confronting new ideas, but working with diverse points of view to negotiate and/or mediate common interests.[18] In this sense, as individuals learn, community adapts. It evolves. Communitarians see the participative leader's story as applicable in all contexts requiring organizations, adaptation and learning. Theirs, they insist, is the most resilient of worldviews. To claim sustainability as theirs, they emphasize how communities can, when their values are intact and healthy, remake themselves after even the deepest crisis or most devastating trauma.

Those in the regulatory worldview attuned to the bureaucratic leader and measured cadence and preference for objective dispassionate analysis do not share in this heroic depiction of the participative leader. In lieu, the participative leader, argue bureaucrats, fails to adhere to formal policy, reporting lines and clear rules of accountability. They conduct serious decisions with important consequences as if they were seated around the kitchen table. Bureaucratic leaders chide communitarians for being too touchy-feely, informal and simpleminded regarding both the educative capacity of grassroots dialogue and the stability and resilience of communities. The cooperation pays story is useful, but only when bureaucrats seek to increase subordinates' involvement in and satisfaction with the system. Rather, in most circumstances, it is the committee structure and the clarity of the distinction between subordinates and superordinates that make it apparent who does what, where, when and why. Equally important, the structure and rules of the system hold those who make errors accountable. Clear measures and policies are provided so that errors can be reduced. Structure stands the test of time. With the diminished reliance on structure, communitarians are, despite their best intentions and shared values, unable to make the corrections necessary to learn or to lay claim to theirs as the story most poised to generate sustainability. Bureaucratic leaders believe that the communitarian's worldview is revised too frequently to truly stand the test of time.

The knowledge leader applauds the participative leader's departure from the structured hierarchical preferences of the bureaucratic leader. However, they insist that participative leaders have not gone far enough in dealing with and championing change (see Figure 4.3). The knowledge leader characterizes the hero in the cooperation pays story as too hesitant, bound up in the pursuit of consensus. He or she is unable to recognize that community is not an end in itself. To the knowledge leader, community is a tool. It is most useful in stimulating creativity and motivating participants to innovate. The knowledge leader views the participative leader as a lame duck leader when it comes to dealing with change. The participative leader fails to focus on key problems early, reinforce out of the box thinking and reward those who make breakthroughs. What is worse, the participative leader actually believes he or she is an agent of change. This is less a function of wilful deception, but more that the communitarians continually compare their position on change with that of the static, uncertainty-reducing bureaucratic leader. To embrace radical change, the participative leader must, insist knowledge leaders, bring together the best minds from throughout the world, form communities of practice or project-based hot groups and reward those who genuinely question the values and norms of the community. The participative leader is seen by champions of the network worldview as relatively passive and inward-looking despite their bold talk of openness, learning and adaptation. They are seen as servant leaders protecting the local, unique community and its clan-like values. The knowledge leader's vision is global. In this vision, communities converge as they move into the future. In time, communities will adopt the best of the new and, in so doing, become an integral part of a global knowledge community.

The buccaneer leader in the entrepreneurial worldview, as outlined in Figure 4.3, maintains the least flattering portrait of the participative leader. To the hard-nosed self-made hero in the money talks story, the participative leader is a poor leader. The participative leader is depicted as a politically correct, indecisive idealist who confuses therapy and mental health issues with bottom-line economic ones. The buccaneer leader glibly but effectively puts down the participative leader as all talk and no action. Pushed even further in this direction, the buccaneer leader denies that the participative leader deserves the right to be called a leader. The buccaneer frames the participative leader as failing to impart precisely what it is that genuine leaders provide – direction. The participative leader, buccaneers insist, solicits the group or community's view. Rather than assert control and push in a particular direction, the participative leader is seen as seeking to satisfy the group's needs. In the lexicon of buccaneers, giving into what followers want avoids the hard problems that accompany decisive leadership. The only time the buccaneer leader sees utility in the communitarian worldview is when he or she must engage, albeit in a token manner, in a slow moving consensus-like process in order to acquire strategic entry into a potential gold mine of future profits.

Taken as a whole, the portraits of the participative leader suggest that this form of leadership is not always prized in other worldviews. Within the communitarian worldview, the marriage of flexibility and systems maintenance highlights the participation leader as a genuine hero – a quiet, courageous leader who leads with decency, openness and integrity. Other stories, while disparaging the character of the participative leader as "the" leader in their story, see possible ways to meld parts of this story to their own. This, I believe, is more possible with the cooperation pays story since it licenses subjectivity, acknowledges feelings and places the emphasis upon finding purpose of meaning. At its core, communitarianism addresses talk and dialogue that are malleable. Others from other stories use it. Entrepreneurs utilize token forms of communitarianism, as we have learned, to bolster profits. Bureaucrats employ teamwork, culture building and dialogue to enhance the stability of systems. Network advocates mobilize parts of this story to enhance collaboration in temporary knowledge-based projects. None, however, see the communitarian leader as hero. Each sutures the search for dialogue and collaboration to fit the tone and tenor of their story. As a result, communitarians often balk at what they see as the usurpation of the principled talk that affirms their chosen worldview.

To set things right, true believers in the cooperation pays story seek to open their airwaves or chat groups to educate all who will listen to and partake in the conversation. The community establishes and affirms its values by signalling these in everyday dialogues and drawing in those who show interest. The genre which best addresses this story is, as was discussed in Chapter 3 (see Figure 3.4), the open-line talk show. Whether highbrow or lowbrow, this format provides those who seek involvement with a sense of community. It enhances involvement. It promotes a tolerance for points of view at variance with one's own, yet still generates a sense of membership in an open-minded discussion.

GENRE: PARTICIPATIVE LEADER

The open-line talk show with the moderator on radio, the Internet, or even television fielding calls and enabling interaction between and among participants eager to express their views, provides a fair sense of the genre binding the cooperation pays story. Readers who feel more comfortable with highbrow conversation formulated on public radio or in chat groups focusing upon public policy issues or matters under the domain of a professional group are encouraged to employ this as the basis for sense-making in this section. Those who are more at home with commercialized forms of the talk show genre or the Internet chat room – running the gamut from alien abduction, to sports, to child-rearing practices – can employ this as their image. Regardless of which one is selected, the talk show genre is open, highly responsive, inclusive and dialogue-based. Those who participate genuinely believe that, as a consequence of their involvement, they are both learning and, in many cases, adding meaning to their lives. Involvement in this genre, even in its highbrow format, does not require expertise, wealth or proof of one's creative powers.

Those who join in the ongoing and alterable conversation feel strongly about the topics raised. Old-style communitarians urged on by mentor/ facilitator leaders, prefer the clan-like, face-to-face nature of conversation as dialogue. Newer, technology-friendly communitarians expand the format to include virtual communities in which the leader plays the role of a diplomat and advocate.[19] The participative leader in the cooperation pays story succeeds when people increase their involvement, develop an openness to one another and feel free not only to speak their minds, but to do so publicly. The genre is less interested in getting to a correct or definitive answer than it is in exploring diverse viewpoints, stimulating thought, building community and raising constructive controversy. The genre's claim to learning is not established by objective measures, the creation of new products or ideas, or even by the generation of profit. It is assumed that the more interest and satisfaction in increasing a divergent public's involvement with sharing ideas, finding common interests, building trust and establishing a culture of cooperation, the greater the learning potential that ensues. Those who feel at home with these assumptions buy into the cooperation pays story and the dialogue genre at its centre. They are, they believe, not only involved in community making, but in making community better by helping it adapt to change (see Figure 4.4).

The open-line talk show genre, as framed by true believers in the communitarian worldview, trumpets theirs as a genre worthy of emulation since it handles change as a positive form of community adaptation. The participative leader, at the centre of the community and entrusted with dialogue building, is viewed as a change agent helping the community handle new and emergent ideas and rise to challenges.[20] When pressed on the topic, communitarians express disappointment in the views on change taken by others. Those in the regulatory worldview are depicted as ritualizers, afraid of their own shadow and embracing change only if it is planned or as an exercise in fine-tuning the system. As a champion of reliability and stability, the bureaucratic leader views unplanned change as that which destabilizes the system and unleashes uncertainty. Those in the network worldview are seen by communitarians as suffering from hubris – the very sort which comes before a fall. Knowledge leaders champion change, but do so without regard to which among alternative innovations is best suited to the community and its needs. The hubris of the knowledge leader, insist communitarians, stems from their conviction that they, not the community, know what is best. They, after all, are the creators and makers of the new world. Finally, those in the

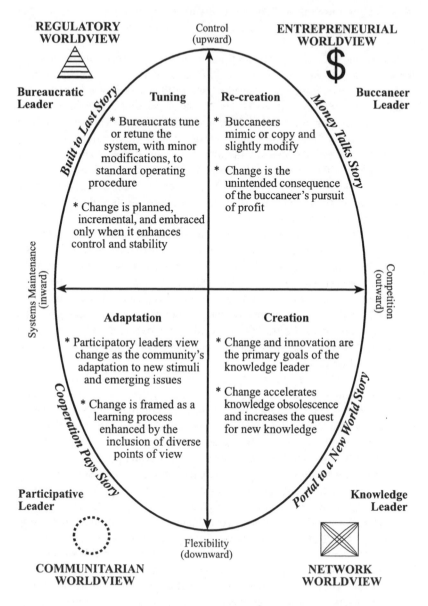

Figure 4.4   Change: the four leadership stories

entrepreneurial worldview are depicted as pirates, mimics and mercenaries. They re-create. They place old wine in new bottles and trumpet, in hyperbole, their product or service as state of the art. Change in the entrepreneurial worldview is the unintended consequence of the buccaneer's quest for profits.

The buccaneer leader strongly disagrees with the participative leader's characterization (see Figure 4.4). In the genre of the entrepreneurial worldview – the continuing drama – the quest is for freedom in the midst of an ongoing struggle. Change is the outcome of contests in which the spoils go to those who are swift, bold and capable. The act of re-creation is the central element in change. It brings goods and services to markets faster, cheaper and with better quality. Change is a process of creative destruction. From the ashes of the old, new demands are skilfully met by those who deserve to be treated as winners. The winner is not a change agent but a profit maker. Buccaneers insist that when the old processes of production reap satisfactory profits, they should be continued. The buccaneer believes strongly that all actors in the continuing drama should be free to mimic, copy or emulate others with whom they compete. The goal of the process, that which pushes us forward, is not guarding our intellectual capital from others but using what is clearly in the public domain to lower prices and ease the access to consumers.

The knowledge leader, as depicted in Figure 4.4, takes umbrage with the views of the buccaneer leader in regard to change. The genre of the knowledge leader's story is the cybertale or the utopian science fiction novel. In it, change is conceptualized as the process of creation wherein radical innovations or paradigm changes originate. This is a concerted process of making or creating something new and/or original and it requires exploration. Time and money need to be invested in research and development. Those who succeed in pushing the envelope, after much costly trial and error should possess the intellectual property rights to their creations. This motivates innovators and encourages investment in the speculative processes that pervade the creative aspects of the network worldview. Buccaneer leaders who pirate or backward engineer and emulate the innovation are seen as interlopers, thieves and bottom feeders by advocates of the network worldview. Knowledge leaders see change and visionary exploration as the primary skill of the effective leader. Change accelerates the quest for new knowledge. It is the motor of progress. Its driver is the knowledge leader.

The bureaucratic leader does not see radical innovation as the motor of progress. In the built to last story, as we have seen in Chapter 3, the genre is that of the highly scripted and rehearsed play. The bureaucratic leader views change as a form of fine-tuning or introducing new plans into a hierarchal system. Change in the built to last story is planned, incremental and embraced only when it enhances control and stability within the system. The motor of progress entails possessing the discipline of not rashly leaping into the future in search of solutions when many of these are found in the tried, tested and true. Change is not a panacea. It is one of the options available to decision-makers and problem solvers. This fine-tuning of the bureaucratic leader is also quite at odds with the view of change as adaptation by the participative leader. In the adaptive open-line show, change is rooted in the empowering of community members to use discretion in their efforts to learn and make sense of emergent issues. In the highly scripted play, change is a top-down revision to the script or schedule.

What we learn in the midst of the communitarian open-line show is that we are not alone. Others in our midst are also troubled. However, by giving voice, listening deeply and seeking out others with shared values and common interests, it is possible not only to learn new things but to attain a sense of membership, meaning and purpose. The talk of the participative leader as mentor, facilitator, advocate and diplomat is to create a culture in which trust flourishes, members escalate their involvement and commitment and, as a consequence, the community adapts. It changes. These lessons are played out in a safe place – a place wherein, with the help of the participative leaders, members not only feel empowered but also imbued with a sense of the virtue, if not wisdom, of the community.

LESSON: THE PARTICIPATIVE LEADER

The communitarian worldview provides those who adhere to it with a sense of meaning and purpose. Values are at the core of the cooperation pays story. It is the quality of life and a genuine sense of membership in a community with integrity that motivates the true believer in the communitarian worldview. The participative leader exemplifies the values, aspirations, quest for meaning and integrity sought by members within the community. When one attends to the dialogue between and among divergent points of view within the community, one continually hears about the need to find life–work balance, walk one's talk and act with principle and integrity. Finding meaning is not treated as an easy accomplishment in the communitarian worldview. It takes hard work and effort.

Ethics and a concern for the integration of one's morals into one's public persona are lessons that emerge from attending to the cooperation pays story. Each leadership story (see Figure 4.5) deals with ethics, but it is only in the communitarian worldview that ethics is framed as the glue, the very social capital, that binds a community.[21] In the cooperation pays story, the focus upon social contract ethics is the basis for acting with integrity. In social contract ethics, participants ought not only to uphold the written legal

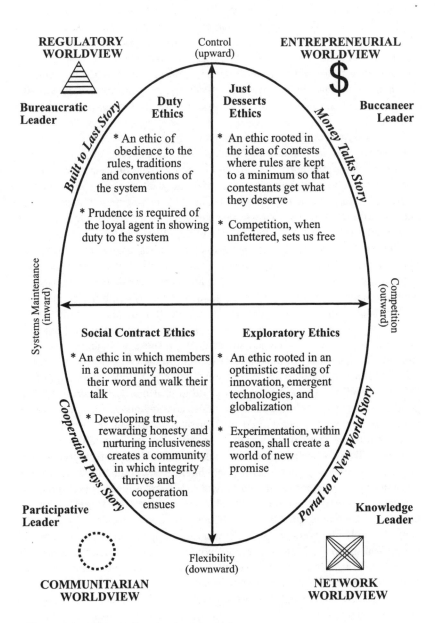

Figure 4.5   Ethics in four leadership stories

contracts recognized by buccaneers, but to attend as well to the tacit or implicit word-of-mouth exchanges that bind exchanges in a primary group or clan.[22] To be a member in good standing in the communitarian worldview, one must walk one's talk. Talk is not cheap in this worldview. It is the basis for dialogue. Those who engage in strategic, deceptive or hyperbolic talk are frowned upon. One cannot arrive at consensus, generate trust and live with open boundaries when members do not, for varying motives, speak with authenticity.

The participative leader is an embodiment of the social contract ethics generated in the cooperation pays story. It is not possible to develop trust, reward honesty and nurture inclusion when the central figures within the community are viewed with suspicion, when they are seen as engaged in self-interested behaviour or engaged in conflicts of interest and/or misrepresentations of the community's views. The participative leader, as selected by the community to steward its values, is held to the ideals and principles espoused by the community. The swift, tactical opportunism of the buccaneer, the obedience in all circumstances to the rules by bureaucratic leaders, and the touting of often-risky or frivolous innovations by knowledge leaders as the next new panacea are all given a clear thumbs down by communitarians.

The claim to integrity and ethics as central to the communitarian worldview, while rising in popularity in many communitarian books on business ethics, is not seen as self-evident by those who adhere to other stories. The lesson of an authentic voice and integrity as told in the social contract ethics of participative leaders is scoffed at by buccaneer leaders. In the money talks story, a "just desserts" ethic prevails (see Figure 4.5). The good is to increase one's wealth by winning and therefore contributing to the public in fair, open contests. To be ethical is to follow or, perhaps more descriptively, not get caught violating the law. Those who win deserve their winnings. Those who fare poorly in these contests deserve their losses. The buccaneer emphasis is upon action, self-interest and competition. It is up to the individual to determine their life–work balance, principles and integrity. Buccaneers worry about the political correctness of the so-called ethical principles. They argue that these are being foisted upon the individual by the community. Doing good, insist buccaneers, is the unintended consequence of the pursuit of profit. Men and women with integrity work hard and provide employment for others; those that seek to go above and beyond the call of the market can give philanthropy to causes in which they believe.

Those drawn to the built to last story prefer a duty-based ethic rooted in clear absolute rules, measurable conventions and universal applications. Reducing uncertainty requires clarity and structure (see Figure 4.5). Bureaucratic leaders recognize that the rules of the hierarchical system, while necessarily compatible with the laws of the land, can require standards above those required by law. The short-term focus of buccaneers circumvents this position. The built to last story concerns itself with the long term. It seeks wherever possible to generate a procedurally rational approach to dealing with ethical quandaries. The bureaucratic leader prefers to employ codes of conduct, tribunals, commissions, ombudspersons and ethics audits as techniques for dealing with the uncertainty that ensues from unmanaged ethical problems. Those drawn to the regulatory worldview frame social contract ethics as idealistic and impractical. Social contract ethics are dialogue-based. There are no clear sanctions for ethics violators. There are no solid lines of accountability, no rules for amending, revising or modifying codes of ethics. The very flexibility which provides communitarians with a sense of adaptability is viewed as problematic when applied to ethics by bureaucrats. Bureaucratic leaders see social contract ethics as an ideological position rather than as a series of explicit policies to be implemented in order to decrease the probability of future ethical lapses in well-managed hierarchical systems.

The knowledge leader in the network worldview lauds the communitarians' social contract ethic for its ability to foster collaboration and flexibility, but openly chides them for their failure to push the envelope and embrace an ethic of exploration (see Figure 4.5). The network draws together leading-edge participants in loosely structured or *ad hoc* temporary coalitions in order to generate creative new options. The social contract ethic, insist those drawn to the knowledge leader's story, stresses the status quo. It is a "walk the talk" ethic premised on the assumption that the community has an agreed-upon understanding of what is and what is not authentic. Much can be made, insist knowledge leaders, about how much more flexible social contract ethics is when compared to the duty ethics of the bureaucratic leader. This is the usual foil used by communitarians, insist network champions, to assure themselves that they are powerfully aligned with the forces of change. They are not. Communitarians fear exploration without the consent of the community. They worry about technologies they do not understand. Knowledge leaders argue that many communitarians are openly hostile to globalization since it is viewed as obliterating the integrity of the local community. Those advocating exploratory ethics, as we shall see in the next chapter, treat ethical citizens as informed and willing to explore genetically modified foods, cloning, and the like as means of attempting to do the greatest good for the largest number.

What is important in the lesson we learn from the cooperation pays story is that, in pushing ethics, integrity and morals to the forefront in the vocabulary of many students of leadership, they remind us that all the four faces of capitalism ground their ethics in a utilitarian claim.[23] The rising tide of wealth, insist buccaneers, raises all – even the poorest. Firms, systems, communities and networks are enriched when, via "just desserts", winners are motivated to increase their efforts. In the built to last story, bureaucratic leaders insist that, with an ethic of duty, all in and dependent on the system will experience stability – making it more possible for those on even the lowest rung in the hierarchy to plan and make rational decisions. The participative leaders trumpet social contract ethics as a means of knitting together adaptive communities which can hear the poor, the lame and the troubled. Moreover, communitarians insist that over time marginal members can be brought into the centre where the dialogue takes place. Finally, as we shall discuss in more depth in the next chapter, the knowledge leader insists that we must push the envelope, take charge of the information-rich environment we are in the midst of creating, embrace an exploratory ethic and create a world which vastly improves upon our experience. In formulating exploratory ethics, denizens of the network world see in radical innovation the possibility of the greatest good for the greatest number. The future is ours. We must, however, intelligently embrace greater doses of risk.

Let us turn to those who champion exploratory ethics – the knowledge leaders in the network worldview.

NOTES

1. See Charles Handy (1994), *The Age of Paradox*, Cambridge, MA: Harvard Business School Press.
2. Oliver E. Williamson (1975), *Markets and Hierarchies*, New York: Free Press, works out the original transaction cost analysis of how markets differ from hierarchies and clans as organizing governance principles. William Ouchi (1980), "Markets, bureaucrats and clans," *Administrative Service Quality*, **25**(1), pp. 129–41, explores the implication of a clan applied to an organization's culture. Andrew Chan (1997), "The corporate culture of a clan organization," *Management Decision*, **35**(1/2), provides case study treatment of DHL International as a clan organization with participative leaders at the centre.
3. Abraham Sagie and Meni Koslowky (2000), *Participation and Empowerment in Organization: Modelling Effectiveness and Applications*, Thousand Oaks, CA: Sage, emphasize the "how to" of empowerment. Gretchen M. Spreitzer and Robert E. Quinn (2001), *A Company of Leaders: Five Disciplines for Unleashing Power in Your Workforce*, San Francisco: Jossey-Bass, select empowerment as the first discipline for leaders developing teams and community.
4. Organizational learning has become a central motif in the cooperation pays story. See Peter M. Senge (1990), *The Fifth Discipline: The Art and Practice of the Learning Organization*, New York: Doubleday, for one of the originators of this idea. More modern applications, like that of Bob Garratt (2000), *The Learning Organization: Developing Democracy at Work*, London: HarperCollins, and Chris Argyris (1999), *On Organizational Learning*, Oxford: Blackwell, push the participative leader's talk towards learning how to engage in democratically structured dialogue which is highly tolerant of diversity in inputs.
5. Robert K. Greenleaf (1991), *Servant Leadership: A Journey into the Nature of Legitimate Power and Greatness*, New York: Paulist Press, captures the dynamics of the participative leader as steward or servant of the community. Alexander Pepper (2003), "Leading professionals: A science, a philosophy and a way of working," *Journal of Change Management*,

3(4), pp. 349–60, explores the position of the servant leader in peer-based communities.

6. Daniel Coleman, Richard Boyatzis and Annie McKee (2002), *Primal Leadership: Realizing the Power of Emotional Intelligence*, Cambridge, MA: Harvard Business School Press, tie this form of social intelligence to the effective participative leader. Malcolm Higgs and Paul Aitken (2003), "An explanation of the relationship between emotional intelligence and leadership potential," *Journal of Management Psychology*, **18**(8), pp. 814–24, investigate the role of emotional intelligence in boosting members' views of the participative leader.

7. The cooperation pays story is frequently referred to as high-involvement or people-centred management by those who take a human resource specialist's perspective on leadership. See, for example, Edward E. Lawler (1986), *High Involvement Management: Participative Strategies for Impairing Organizational Performance*, San Francisco, CA: Jossey-Bass, or for a focus on people-centred management see Jeffrey Pfeffer (1998), *The Human Equation: Building Profits by Putting People First*, Cambridge, MA: Harvard Business School Press.

8. Toxic handles diffuse those whose behaviour threatens the civility of the participative community. Peter J. Frost (2003), *Toxic Emotion at Work: Low Compassionate Managers Handle Pain and Conflict*, Cambridge, MA: Harvard Business School Press, portrays the empathic nature of the participative leader. Marcia Lynn Whicker (1996), *Toxic Leaders*, Westport, CT: *Quorum Books*, focuses on the toxic leader – the maladjusted, the enforcer, the street fighter and the bully – as potentially disruptive of what could otherwise be healthy participative communities.

9. Workplace diversity is treated as a central tenet in stimulating organizational learning and adaptation in healthy communities. See Frederick A. Miller and Judith H. Katz (2002), *The Inclusion Breakthrough: Unleashing the Real Power of Diversity*, San Francisco: Berrett-Koehler for an international perspective. Peruse Philip Robert Harris (2004), *Managing Cultural Differences: Global Leadership Strategies for the 21st Century*, Amsterdam: Butterworth-Heinemann. Patricia Arredondo (1996), *Successful Diversity Initiatives*, Thousand Oaks, CA: Sage, explains how indispensable trust is in building successful diversity programmes.

10. Sarah J. Noonan (2003), *The Elements of Leadership: What You should Know*, Lanham, MD: Scarecrow Press, highlights the need for leaders to discover their authenticity. Marie C. Wilson (2004), *Closing the Leadership Gap*, New York: Viking, addresses the ways in which participative leaders develop authenticity and the self-assurance that comes with it. Douglas R. May, Timothy Hodges, Adrian Chan and Bruce Auolio (2003), "Developing the moral component of authentic leadership," *Organizational Dynamics*, **32** (3), pp. 247–60, discuss the ethics component of authentic leadership from a communitarian worldview.

11. Michelle Reina and Dennis Reina (1999), *Trust and Betrayal in the Workplace: Building Effective Relationships in Your Organization*, San Francisco, CA: Berrett-Koehler, probe the dynamics of trust that give rise to social capital in the communitarian worldview. Robert M. Galford and Anne Seibold Drapeau (2002), *The Trusted Leader: Bringing Out the Best in Your People and Company*, New York: Free Press, focus on how effective participative leaders build trust.

12. Arie de Geus (1997), *The Living Company*, Cambridge, MA: Harvard Business School Press, conveys the sense in which a healthy culture confers a form of adaptive intelligence. Gilbert Fairholm (1994), *Leadership and the Culture of Trust*, Westport, CT: Praeger, draws attention to the adaptive intelligence ensuing from developing trust in a community.

13. The idea that "we are all one family" built into the trusting community plays havoc with the economic need to downsize which impacts all organizations at some time in their economic cycle. William Wolman and Anne Colamosca (1997), *Judas Economy: The Triumph of Capital and the Betrayal of Work*, Harlow: Addison-Wesley, capture the tension in communitarians violating the psychological contract in the workplace. For a discussion of how to deal with survivors of downsizing, see Marvin R. Gottlieb and Lori Conkling (1995), *Managing the Workplace Services: Organizational Downsizing and the Commitment Gap*, Westport, CT: Quorum.

14. For insight into the temporary nature of "hot" groups and communities of practice, see

Etienne Wenger, Richard McDermott and William Snyder (2002), *Cultivating Communities of Practice: A Guide to Managing Knowledge*, Cambridge, MA: Harvard Business School Press and Jean Lipman-Blumen and Harold J. Leavitt (1999), *Hot Groups: Seeing Them, Feeding Them and Using Them to Ignite Your Organization*, Oxford: Oxford University Press.

15.   See William D. Kipling (2001), *Ostracism: The Power of Silence*, New York: Guilford Press, for a thorough investigation of the psycho-social dimensions of silencing others. Robin P. Clair (1998), *Organizing Silence: A World of Possibilities*, Albany, NY: Albany State University, probes the wider implications of uses of silence to suppress, marginalize and create resistance.

16.   While communitarians do not have a monopoly upon contemporary discussions of social responsibility, their views do dominate this field. See, for example, Sandra A. Waddock (2002), *Leading Corporate Citizens: Vision, Values, Value-added*, Boston, MA: McGraw-Hill/Irwin, and Michael Hopkins (2003), *The Planetary Bargain: Corporate Social Responsibility Matters*, London: Earthscan Publications.

17.   The idea of a collective organizational culture is central to the communitarian worldview. Edgar Schein (1999), *The Corporate Culture Survival Guide: Sense and Nonsense About Culture Change*, San Francisco: Jossey-Bass, explores what corporate culture is built upon. Joanne Martin (2002), *Organizational Culture: Mapping the Terrain*, Thousand Oaks, CA: Sage Publications, provides an excellent synthesis of this literature.

18.   The emphasis in the organizational culture is upon employing commitment and shared values to overcome conflict and negotiate agreements. See Roger Fisher and William Ury (1991), *Getting to Yes: Negotiating an Agreement Without Giving In*, Boston, MA: Houghton Mifflin, for a classic presentation of this position. The mediator or conflict resolution component of the participative leader is explained by Michelle LeBaron (2002), *Bridging Troubled Waters: Conflict Resolution From the Heart*, San Francisco: Jossey-Bass.

19.   For the classic treatment of the virtual community see Howard Rheingold (1994), *The Virtual Community: Homesteading on the Electronic Frontier*, New York: Harper Perennial. Patricia K. Felkins (2002), *Community at Work: Creating and Celebrating Community in Organizational Life*, Cresskill, NJ: Hampton Press, provides a solid commentary on how technology and the virtual community modify the face-to-face nature of naturally occurring communities.

20.   The portrayal of the participative leader as change agent is pervasive in treatments of the communitarian worldview. Ken Clarke (2002), *End of Management and the Rise of Organizational Democracy*, San Francisco, CA: Jossey-Bass, portrays the participative leader as mobilizing change by shaping a culture of shared values, trust and integrity. Stanley Deetz, Sarah J. Tracy and Jennifer Lyn Simpson (2000), *Leading Organization Through Transitions: Communication and Cultural Change*, Thousand Oaks: Sage, portray the participative leader as guiding interpretations and framing options for the community.

21.   For the role of social capital in the communitarian worldview, see Dan Cohen and Laurence Prusak (2001), *In Good Company: How Social Capital Makes Organizations Work*, Cambridge, MA: Harvard Business School Press, and Mark C. Bolino, William H. Tunley and James M. Bloodgood (2002), "Citizenship behaviour and the creation of social capital in organizations," *Academy of Management Review*, **27**(4), pp. 505–23.

22.   See Thomas Donaldson and Thomas W. Dunfee (1999), *Ties That Bind: A Social Contact Approach to Business Ethics*, Cambridge, MA: Harvard Business School Press, for a clear statement of social contact ethics applied to instrumental leaders. For a critical treatment, attend to Mark Douglas (2000), "Integrative social contracts theory: Hype over hypernorms", *Journal of Business Ethics*, **26**(2), pp. 101–11.

23.   For a very interesting application of utilitarianism to business ethics, see John Raymond Boatright (2000), *Ethics and the Conduct of Business*, 3rd edn, Upper Saddle River, NJ: Prentice Hall. David P. Baron (2003), *Business and Its Environment*, 4th edn, Upper Saddle River, NJ: Prentice Hall, provides an excellent synthesis of the literature. The reader is encouraged to attend to Chapters 19 to 22 in this work.

5. Knowledge leaders: a portal to a new world story

> "We should do something when people say it's crazy. If people say something is good it means someone is already doing it."
>
> Fujio Mitarai[1]

What sort of position suggests go on crazy, stop on good? The answer, Fujio Mitarai and others hungry for innovation insist, is the knowledge leader's logic. It is shared by all those stimulated by the allure and excitement of the network worldview. Its focus is upon radical and meaningful innovation. The portal to a new world story is the tale of inventiveness, exploration and creativity. In this story, the best minds of every generation come together in loosely structured coalitions to customize, develop new prototypes and establish first-mover advantage via radical innovations.[2] Knowledge – its creation, transfer, sharing and embedding in markets – rises to the fore in the telling and retelling of this tale. The story is heard best when populations are confident that the future carries promise or that the past and our experience of the present can credibly be improved. The knowledge leader's story is less audible when a call for a return to the past (a fascination with nostalgia) and a search for the tried, tested and true grips the population. The optimistic call of the paradigm changer accompanies both new and old tales of significant breakthroughs – the invention of steel, the discovery of penicillin, the quest for and realization of human flight and the mapping of the genome.

Knowledge leaders recognize that, during periods in which change is framed as desirable, new and useful, knowledge called intellectual capital confers power.[3] The knowledge leader is a visionary or edge walker who presents him or herself as having access to new, useful and powerful knowledge. The knowledge leader is an embodiment of the aspirations and yearnings of creative participants in the network worldview. The credibility of the knowledge leader's claim to intellectual capital stems from the reputation conferred upon him or her by dedicated participants in the network and the hype, then investment, which accompanies certain projects. The network is a loosely structured coalition of participants high up on the learning curve in an area in which potential breakthroughs are plausible enough to attract sponsors, investors and/or patrons.[4] The network grows where capital can be raised to solve emerging problems or reformulate dated solutions. The network is seen by true believers as drawing the best and the brightest into pressing problem-solving situations. Once there, the loosely structured coalition of highly motivated participants seeks leaders who can stimulate creativity, enable collaboration, navigate in the midst of uncertainty and broker deals that foster further experimentation.

Three different players invest in and become integral components in the knowledge-based network. Each in their own way seeks to benefit from the potential to be realized in successfully generating a breakthrough. The successful knowledge leader knits the three participants together and keeps the network intact long enough to capitalize upon its potential. The first participants are the creatives or knowledge workers.[5] They invest their time, energy and knowledge in increasing the capacity of the network to generate new, original and useful ideas. Creatives are individuals and/or organizations that join the network to hedge the risk entailed in pursuing the breakthrough alone. Despite this strategy, creatives are loosely tied to the network. Projects are temporary. Many creatives possess contracts that lapse and are renewed depending upon whether their knowledge remains useful to the network. Creatives are continuously updating their skills. They battle knowledge obsolescence. Within each project in a network, creatives seek to gain a solid reputation from other creatives. This enhances the probability that, as projects are terminated or morph into networks taking hold of a new or different experiment, the creatives retain their involvement. The career trajectory of the creative in the network departs radically from that of the professional in either the communitarian or regulatory worldview.

The second players whom knowledge leaders bring into the network worldview tend to invest capital in the network. These individuals and/or organizations believe in the viability of the next new thing. They see the advent of early adopters of the innovation and are, as a consequence, willing to invest capital in the network. Theirs is a relatively speculative investment. The network possesses potential. To make this potential appealing to investors, the knowledge leader can point towards previous breakthroughs, the reputation of those involved in the network and/or existing pools of capital already accumulated. The knowledge leader must motivate investors without pointing to either an end product or a proven technique. In drawing investors into the network, the knowledge leader must reach out to those from other stories and reassure them not only that the projects have potential but that the projects underway are progressing. To reach investors under these constraints, the knowledge leader must be a skilled communicator. To communicate to buccaneers, the knowledge leader stresses the potential of the network to make profits. The network possesses a series of tactics which confer competitive advantages over its competitors. To attract communitarian investors, knowledge leaders frame the breakthrough sought by the network as reinforcing the inclusiveness, dialogue potential and learning capacity when applied to communities. The knowledge leader pitches the network breakthrough as aiding those in the regulatory worldview in stabilizing systems, reducing errors and generating greater reliability.

The third players that the knowledge leader must bring in and then keep involved in the network are intermediaries and allies. The creatives, after all, are knowledge sellers. They generate the new knowledge which the network attempts to disseminate and for which it seeks a good price. The investors, especially in the early stages of the network, support and buy the potential knowledge. Intermediaries bring buyers and sellers together. They provide the means for the network to make its presence known to others. Intermediaries are motivated by a desire to establish within their preferred story that they are on the leading edge. They are attuned to the next new thing. Intermediaries seeking to establish their access to powerful knowledge originate not only in the network worldview but in each of the others as well. Networks succeed, in part, when knowledge leaders find intermediaries who can become allies with those in the network. Intermediaries hype and amplify the prospects of the potential network. Intermediaries are credible to those who may feel uneasy dealing directly with a creative. Knowledge leaders who fail to create strong information signals via intermediaries may, in fact, generate breakthroughs but find that these are neither seen nor heard outside the creative arc of the network worldview.

Buzz is vital in the portal to a new world story.[6] To create the buzz in the entrepreneurial worldview and establish intermediaries, knowledge leaders lean on IPO specialists, financial advisors and investment houses, and they seek the endorsement of big-time buccaneer capitalists. Knowledge leaders and their creatives place alluring bottom-line advertisements, plant stories and seek media coverage as they attend to those avidly seeking to make a fortune. This is not as hard as it seems. Buccaneers are drawn to speculation. They hear about the big gamble with high payouts. Risk attracts rather than frightens them. However, the more the knowledge leader courts buccaneers as intermediaries, the more he or she must be wary. They need to protect the intellectual capital within the network from being pirated. To establish intermediaries and allies in the communitarian worldview, the knowledge leader attempts to get opinion leaders and influentials with the clan interested in improving or adding value to the community with the potential breakthroughs from the network. The knowledge leader must go slowly here. The process is best pursued by word of mouth and personal contact. The knowledge leader and creatives in the network must win the trust of communitarians. Care, however, must be taken when courting communitarian opinion leaders. The knowledge leader must keep the network competitive and open to revision even, at times, to the point when, in the eyes of communitarians, principles may be compromised and trust lost.

The most important intermediary and potential ally in the typical network is the large bureaucratic organization or rule-based system in the regulatory worldview. These hierarchical systems and the bureaucratic leaders within them are both attracted to and repelled by the skills of the knowledge leader. To establish the hierarchical system as an intermediary and ally, the knowledge leader must attenuate the attraction and play down or muzzle the fear. What those in the hierarchical system fear in the network worldview is the knowledge leader's willingness and ability to embrace uncertainty in the quest for novelty, creativity and innovation. Hierarchical systems reward subordinates for reducing uncertainty, adhering to precedent and minimizing errors. Nevertheless, those at the top of hierarchical systems are very interested in planned change and creativity when it can be implemented in a rational, prudent manner. The built to last story supports being prepared and keeping abreast of innovation. Thus, to keep abreast of what is new, slowly ramp up for innovation and to claim to be prepared for the future, large hierarchical systems often buy up small innovative networks or enter into subcontract agreements with them. One must, however, take care. When creative networks are under the direct control of a bureaucratic organizational culture, they often discover to their peril that their ability to innovate withers.

The portal to a new world story told in its six-point story template – origins, plot, audience, protagonist, genre and lesson – celebrates ours as a species confident in its ability to remake and improve the world. Knowledge is power.[7] It is the lever which self-consciously enables us to push away from the past and design the future. The future is a global experiment, a built environment increasingly improved and radically altered by inventions, vision and creativity. To true believers in this story, knowledge leaders are prophets or harbingers of a new and entirely desirable age. They flourish in times of an immense hunger for change, creativity and economic take-off. Knowledge leaders are stewards – not of the local and natural community, but of the newly designed, genetically engineered, temperature-controlled and behaviourally modified world. They are the explorers who do away with the rules, erase boundaries and, in time, transform hierarchies into networks. They are revolutionaries with an eye to profit but, unlike the buccaneer, they can defer profit taking and plunk down good money on research and development, exploration and the search for paradigm-altering ideas, technologies and prototypes. To true believers, the optimism in this story is palpable. Others whose hearts and minds are drawn to other stories, do not hear this optimism. They worry about the knowledge leader's cavalier attitude towards the possible harms of experimentation gone awry, the wanton destruction of local communities, the sacrifice and abuse of eco-systems, and the concentration of intellectual capital in fewer and fewer hands.

ORIGINS: KNOWLEDGE LEADER

The knowledge leader's story recasts the story of original sin. Adam and Eve, in the bosom of paradise, succumb to temptation, consume the fruit from the tree of knowledge and, in the midst of their enlightenment, forfeit their innocence and are as a consequence banished from the Garden of Eden. In the portal to a new world story, knowledge and the knowledge leader are reframed. The knowledge leader is not the serpent tempting humanity away from paradise but the prophetic self-made visionary to whom humanity must trust its fate and aspire to if it is to create a new paradise. In this recasting of the ancient tale, knowledge is the royal road to a better future. It is the human embodiment of progress.[8] The new paradise is not achieved by passively deferring to authority, relying upon the just-in-time gyrations of the invisible hand, or even in placing faith in nature and the naturally occurring community.

This version of a new and future paradise is dynamic and changeable. An improvement occurs when an idea is moved from its tacit stage to its embeddedness in the built environment. It is expected, in time, that a new series of ideas improving upon the old will emerge and be applied to a reconfigured world. The world is made, then remade *ad infinitum*. Each new version may not immediately be an improvement upon its predecessor, but in a short time, with the kinks taken out, the transition speaks to an improvement in the lot of our species as a whole. The knowledge leader stimulates this ongoing affirmation and celebration of change. The knowledge leader's story privileges the future. He or she heralds the leader as radically reformulating it (see Figure 5.1). In this sense, the knowledge leader functions as a pathfinder, not only scouting new options but bringing them into practice. As a pathfinder and change agent, the knowledge leader is sensitive to new ideas, a creative out-of-the-box thinker who is capable of building a loose coalition of participants to push these ideas into the fore-front.[9] As a leader bringing new ideas into practice, the knowledge champion must be able to navigate in the midst of the provisional. He or she must broker deals, thereby enhancing further exploration. The knowledge leader selectively attends to the past, critically evaluates the present, and skilfully weaves these two together in an attempt to generate credible and appealing claims to a better future.

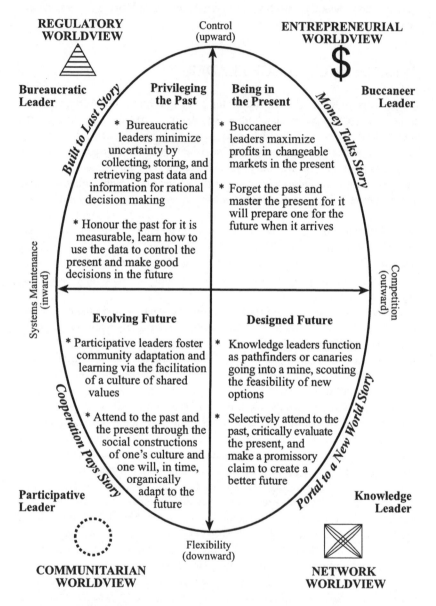

Figure 5.1   The kaleidoscope of time: four leadership stories

The lure of a perfectible future is looked upon with mistrust by those drawn to the entrepreneurial worldview. Leaders in the money talks story seek to maximize profits in continually altering markets. Theirs is a worldview which emphasizes being in control in the present (see Figure 5.1). This is where profits are made or lost. The future is provisional. Despite our desire to do so, it cannot be controlled. No one but the deluded believes that they possess sufficient control to create the future. Buccaneers see knowledge leaders as either deluded or, more often, as profit-seeking entrepreneurs hell-bent on cornering the market on intellectual capital and retiring young and wealthy. In fact, the buccaneers see effective knowledge leaders as entrepreneurs dressed up as knowledge leaders. The knowledge leader's propensity to critically evaluate or push off from the present (the buccaneer's temporal turf) is framed by buccaneers as knowledge leaders attempting to tout and hawk their wares. The buccaneers with their show me "now" attitude, take a sceptical view of that which cannot be sampled at the time of purchase and still promises tremendous benefits over that which can. Whenever the network worldview heats up and big money flows into it, buccaneers are never far behind. The adage of the buccaneer is simple – just do it! Master the present. When you have profits as a result of this mastery, stay with the profits. Never leap into the future when the present is sufficiently profitable.

The scepticism of the buccaneer towards the knowledge leader is not shared by the participative leader. Like the knowledge leader, the participative leader embraces change but strongly prefers innovation in an evolutionary rather than a revolutionary manner (see Figure 5.1). While the two celebrate collaboration, they suture it to different ends. This divergence results in an ongoing and persistent uneasiness between the two. The participative leader views the designed or radically reconfigured future as disrupting the very foundations of a healthy community built on trust, inclusiveness and dialogue-based learning. Participative leaders frame the radical innovations of knowledge leaders as emanating from elitist projects which employ temporary mercenary communities to generate ideas primarily for commercial interests. Ideas generated this way are hyped. They are neither integrated back into the community for discussion, nor tied to a concerted effort to discern whether the portended innovation is compatible with the shared values of community members. Communitarians fear a future in which new technologies dislocate and marginalize community members while at the same time they prepare for a new Mecca of globalization.[10] In this global future, participative leaders lament the loss or disruption of the local community.

Bureaucratic leaders have the greatest difficulty with the knowledge leader's celebration of the designed future; they honour that which has stood the test of time. The regulatory worldview, in its quest for certainty, privileges the past (see Figure 5.1). It is the known. It is the basis for the measurable, the reasonable and the factual. The past, insist those imbued with the regulatory worldview, is the best predictor of the future. Bureaucratic leaders are confident that those who lead us towards a new world via a careful scrutiny of the past are not only likely to avoid repeating errors, they are likely to reduce unnecessary risks. The bureaucratic leader worries about the knowledge leader's leap of faith with regards to the beneficence of a future founded on new-fangled gadgets, trends and often whimsical notions. The prudent bureaucratic leader prefers to rely upon the tried, tested and true and from that base, slowly and systematically plan new options. In the regulatory worldview the bureaucratic leader would move into the future preserving the best of the past. The bureaucratic leader seeks to implement rules, codes and protocols to lower what he or she perceives as the unintended harms of experimentation within the network worldview which, when left to its own devices, could go awry.

The origins of the portal to a new world story in the pervasive dream of a built environment not only celebrate human inventiveness and its practical application, but also reveal a distinct attitude towards nature. Nature is not to be emulated. It is to be improved upon. Those who think of themselves as scientists, divide into two camps. In the first camp are those who envision themselves as scientists within the regulatory worldview. These men and women seek to discover the hidden rules of the natural order and nature and make these known to *Homo sapiens*. Nature is a great system. Scientists discover its rules. These rules, when discovered, enable us to reduce error and generate greater systems reliance and dependability. Those in the second camp, scientists in the network worldview, see nature as the origin of many of our problems – death, storms, drought, illness – and seek to develop a synthetic or built environment that greatly improves upon the natural order. Parts and pieces of this new order are the basis for the new commerce. Intellectual capital explodes in waves of growing anticipation. Each successful version of an improved portal, whether a breakthrough in 1872 or 2005, leads to a proliferation of new possibilities, new worlds. In this multi-world universe redolent with options, the plot of the leader in the knowledge story is that of an explorer or inventor – in more contemporary terms, that of a cybertale or speculative adventure in science fiction. In this tale, the knowledge leader embodies the basic theme – that of transformation. The knowledge leader is depicted as a prophet or visionary. Those attuned to stories other than the knowledge leader's warn of the possible misadventures of those willing to blindly entrust their fate to the visionary.

PLOT: KNOWLEDGE LEADER

In the telling of the tale of the explorer, within the cybertale, the safe past is pushed aside and pulled forward into the designed future. The basic theme is that of transformation.[11] The knowledge leader is framed as the transformational visionary. In this capacity, he or she serves four interrelated functions within the portal to a new world story. He or she acts as a catalyst to creatives and knowledge workers in the network. To the public at large, the knowledge leader is a genius whose very presence in the network reassures and reduces the public's resistance to radical innovation or deep change. To those investing in the process, the knowledge leader is a skilled deal maker or broker possessing the capability of navigating in the midst of uncertainty and still delivering the goods. Finally, intermediaries and allies to the network frame the knowledge leader as a magnet who attracts the best minds of his or her generation and creates a network with sufficient depth and creative resources to retain its generativity over time.

The plot of the knowledge leader's story is a tale of overcoming human limitations and creating a future which disburdens. Vision in the portal to a new world entails not seeing what others do, but seeing creatively. The visionary knowledge leader is one third prophet, one third technician or scientist and one third practical business person. Despite this amalgam of skills, the plot of the portal to a new world story focuses upon the knowledge leader as a prophet. The term prophet, despite its resonance with biblical times, speaks of being on the cusp of new things, seeing the future before others. It places distance between itself and the other "profit". The term suggests that the prophet is in touch with a powerful force or forces (see Figure 5.2). It is precisely this that provides prophets with the gift of second, further, or creative sight. Moreover, the use of the term prophet to capture the visionary nature of the knowledge leader prepares the ground for the recognition that, despite their claim to extra sight, these individuals are frequently scoffed at by those who resonate with other stories.

What is important to recognize is that the plot of each story places vision and the visionary as one of the skills possessed by its preferred leader. In the money talks story, the buccaneer is understood as a visionary. The visionary in the entrepreneurial world is not the prophet, but the agile tactician who with pluck and courage leads followers to victory under adverse conditions. The tactician is a fierce competitor whose gift of sight permits them to see the field clearly and either leap upon opportunities or, with dexterity, avoid costly threats. Visionaries are proven and established winners. They capitalize upon the next new thing. They do not create it. They are adept at pirating. They are swift and opportunistic. They keep an eye open for the win. They are relentless. Since they are so likely to win, others use them as

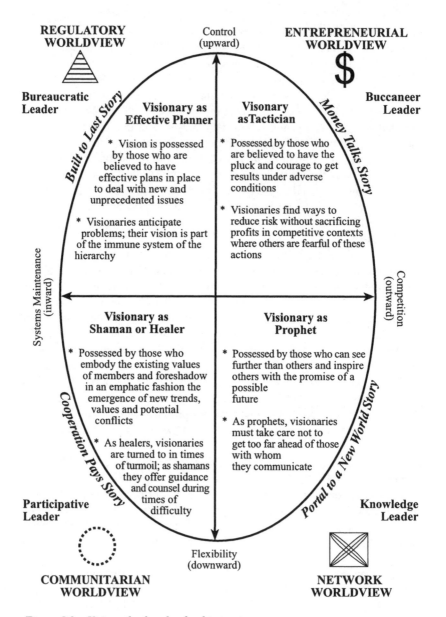

Figure 5.2   Vision: the four leadership stories

a cuing device or an indicator of what one ought to do or be in order to win. Followers seek buccaneer visionary leaders because it is they who will find the pot of gold before others.

The plot of the built to last story focuses upon the visionary as the effective planner (see Figure 5.2). Vision is possessed by those who are believed to have effective plans in place to deal with new and unprecedented issues. Visionaries anticipate problems and nip them in the bud. In the regulatory worldview, the visionary leader is prepared. He or she is proactive rather than reactive. The bureaucratic leader as a visionary leader is not a fire fighter. The visionary sits atop a hierarchical system with sufficient reliable information. He or she is prepared for all eventualities. Plans are in place to deal with emergent possibilities.[12] The information deployed to operate the system and deal with exigencies is not rooted in the so-called second sight or creative skills of prophets, but in facts amassed via discipline, hard work and attention to detail. Visionary bureaucratic leaders are helped by a cadre of specialists. They send relevant information up to their superordinate or leader. The visionary built to last leader knows what to do with this information. Visionary leaders are vigilant. As effective planners, visionaries earn the right to proudly proclaim that during their watch at the corporate helm, nothing untoward happens. The visionary in this story oversees that which is built to last. Vision in the built to last story leads to order and stability.

The plot in the cooperation pays story treats the visionary leader as a shaman or healer. Visionaries not only embody the values of the community, but are turned to in times of turmoil and stress.[13] As the shaman, the participative leader offers guidance and counsel, and tends to the perplexed. Unlike the knowledge leader's use of vision, the participative leader's use of vision is driven inward. They comfort and provide a model. Visionaries are wise. They know both the community and themselves. They possess integrity. Like the honoured elders of a clan, they resonate with communal values which have been handed down, modified and taken to heart. Visionaries in the communitarian worldview are open. They give voice to the concerns of those who are having a hard time being heard. They epitomize the community position and diplomatically represent it to outsiders. The tasks of the visionary in the cooperation pays story are to provide the community with the resilience to cope with adversity, sidestep divisive conflict, deal with social and personal anxiety and constantly remain open to dialogue and learning.

Foreshadowing our discussion in the next chapter, it is important to note that a contextualized treatment of leadership enhances our ability to make sense of the adage, "leaders must have vision". Vision, as we will discover, not only has different meanings in different stories, it requires other skills depending on the context. These skills are embedded in specific contexts.

Mastering the skills requires an understanding of contextualism. The audience, hearing each of the four faces of capitalism, all nod sagely when hearing that a leader must have vision. However, each formulates the visionary in a very different and at times contradictory manner. In the money talks story, visionaries are swift and clever tacticians who by pluck, courage and bravado take on risk and win. To be a visionary is to possess the confidence and decisiveness of the winner. In the cooperation pays story, the visionary leaders know themselves. They provide for those in distress, tend to the perplexed, nurture and care. The visionary as shaman or healer builds trusting communities, not by setting themselves apart from followers, but in the development of a trusting community. The visionary in the regulatory worldview is the effective planner, anticipating problems and acting as a loyal agent to the system by reducing uncertainty. The visionary leader as prophet in the portal to a new world increases uncertainty and creates ambiguity in the pursuit of creativity, originality and innovation.

The network worldview's audience is riveted by the belief that creative leaders are the real winners. It is, they insist, those who think outside the box and stimulate this in others who generate the template for new process that yield future profits. Advocates of the network worldview brush aside the buccaneer's concerns that most innovations are not only costly, they are never brought to market. Those attuned to the portal to a new world story believe that the out-of-the-box thinker is the most effective problem solver.[14] Not only does he or she anticipate problems unobserved by others, but uses cutting-edge techniques to render an appropriate solution. Champions of the knowledge leader are unsympathetic to the bureaucratic leader's perception that creative solutions violate precedent – they cause more problems than the initial dilemma which they purport to solve. The audience resonating to the knowledge leader's framing of creativity go so far as to insist that it is the out-of-the box thinking leader who best stimulates meaningful dialogue and enhances the resilience of the community. This audience brushes aside communitarian concerns with the temporary, mercenary and global concerns of creative knowledge leaders. They see it as indicative of the parochial concern of the communitarian leader. Let us now turn to the characteristics of the creative knowledge leader who entices audiences to the portal to a new world story.

AUDIENCE: KNOWLEDGE LEADER

Audiences drawn to the knowledge leader's story are optimistic about the future. They become anxious with those who, in their view, pine for the good old days, marvel at the quality of life in the present, or eagerly anticipate ample returns upon recent investments. The knowledge leader's story reduces their anxiety. It credibly promises true believers in the network worldview a new, better future or the possibility of extricating themselves from their present problems. The credibility of the knowledge leader's ability to design a new future or transform our experience of an irksome present rests in the audience's perception of the generativity of the network led by the knowledge leader. Those drawn to the knowledge leader's story seek the excitement and adventure of being engaged in exploring the edges of the unknown. They pride themselves on being early adopters of the next new thing.[15] True believers in the knowledge leader's story are firmly committed to all forms of exploratory rationality, and within it, the generative capacity of creative intelligence (see Figure 2.2). They see the rationality of other stories – procedural rationality in the regulatory worldview, psycho-social rationality in the communitarian worldview and market rationality in the entrepreneurial worldview – as misdirected.

Market rationality, with its emphasis upon tactical get rich quick intelligence, fails the test of the true believers in the knowledge leader's story because of both its short time frame and its total reliance upon satisfying the consumer or client. The true believer in the portal to a new world does not believe in quick fixes or the adulation of mimicry, even when accomplished swiftly and efficiently. To be intelligent, insist the denizens of the network worldview, one must push the envelope. The act of intelligence entails more than figuring out others' needs and then supplying these at a competitive price. The challenge is to design a future in which needs are both met in new ways and at times created. Exploratory rationality moves leaders towards the frontier.[16] Leaders who lead with creative intelligence introduce the very template copied and gradually disseminated by buccaneers. Upon closer inspection, the knowledge leader shares with the buccaneer leader a tremendous appreciation regarding the outward pull towards competition. Where exploratory and market rationality differ substantially is over flexibility. Creative intelligence embraces flexibility as the means of improving and remaining open to emerging phenomena. Market rationality is rooted in power. Wins form the basis of tactical intelligence. The proof of one's prowess, the very essence of one's intelligence, is established when others follow and do one's bidding.

Psycho-social rationality, with its emphasis upon the emotionally intelligent participative leader, is seen by knowledge leaders as necessary but insufficient for exploratory rationality. Emotional intelligence fosters dialogue and enables collaboration (both indispensable for creative intelligence), but it fails to focus upon specific ends or results. Psycho-social rationality, the trust-based logic of the communitarian worldview, reinforces cooperation but is made uneasy by the mobilization of competition. Exploratory rationality ties flexibility to competition. The very generativity of collaboration must be realized in contests with others for the rights of discovery and intellectual property. Creative intelligence in the network worldview is not merely learning – it is applied. It is knowledge made explicit and embedded in new goods or services. It is employed and rents are extracted by those whose claim to intellectual property rights are recognized. The investment in exploratory rationality must not only be intrinsically appealing to creative and knowledge workers in the process, but also meet the extrinsic needs of those investing in the innovative process and serving as network allies and intermediaries.

Procedural rationality with its roots in obedience to the rules and the honouring of tradition, reinforces the analytic proclivities of the bureaucratic leader. But while clear policies stabilize systems, they do not, insist knowledge leaders, permit one to either imagine or prepare for a future which is not firmly anchored in the past. Change in the built to last story is planned. It entails fine-tuning the hierarchical system. Despite the fact that exploratory rationality flies in the face of procedural rationality, the two form a symbiotic but unstable relationship. They do not share a talking point in the four faces of capitalism. Procedural rationality pulls up toward control and in toward systems maintenance; exploratory rationality pulls down toward flexibility and out toward competition. Each needs the other, but shares little with it. As a consequence, the bureaucratic leader who seeks to shake up the system may attempt to inculcate greater amounts of exploratory rationality. Knowledge leaders seeking capital or adding structure to the loosely coupled coalition in the typical network may attempt to introduce procedural rationality. Instability ensues. Exploratory rationality erodes certainty and procedural rationality plays havoc with creativity and constrains creatives.

The perception of creativity as a form of generativity which lends credibility to an optimistic rendering of the designed future requires that the leader synthesize rich files of interdisciplinary and cutting-edge information , think outside the box and inspire others to join in. This story does not envision creativity (see Figure 5.3) as an individual enterprise, but as a task undertaken in the midst of a buzzing, blooming welter of inputs from different sources. The coalition is a temporary community, often project-based, of individuals high up on the learning curve within a knowledge pool coming together to pose the "what if" questions. Creatives question authority. To lead in this context is to possess the skills of a improviser. The creative is not script bound. He or she sees the big picture, employs divergent thinking to stimulate options and refines the project as new, vital information emerges. Nevertheless, the knowledge leader works within deadlines, economic constraints and a very competitive field where networks flourish and other seek to compete with them.

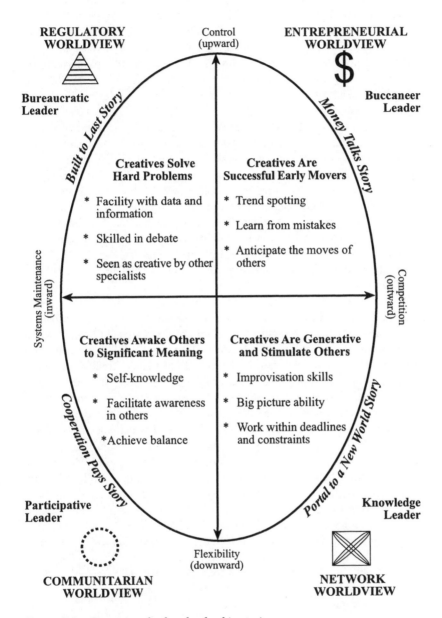

Figure 5.3   Creativity: the four leadership stories

Communitarians depict the participative leader as creative when he or she awakens others of the clan to significant meaning (see Figure 5.3). In this instance, creativity involves the leader's ability to plumb or gauge the deeper layers of group life. He or she highlights its meaning and relevance for a healthy adaptation to community life. In the cooperation pays story, the community is paramount. To realize the full benefits of membership, individuals must fit in yet retain their uniqueness. Achieving balance is central to creativity in the cooperation pays story. This requires knowledge of the self and the other.[17] Participative leaders employ self-knowledge to further their limits, to feel comfortable in their skin and to enable others involved in the community ventures. Creativity entails forfeiting a self-interested agenda for a cooperative one. The creative task is driven inward and downward. One discovers the genuine self in the creative work one engages in with others. Collaboration is not sutured to the task but to the ideals of developing a fully comprehensive and realized self in the midst of community. In the communitarian worldview, creatives are serene. They possess the spiritual calm of the enlightened. The creative leader in the cooperation pays story embodies this self-knowledge, serenity and enlightenment.

Those in the regulatory worldview frame the creative bureaucratic leader as the individual within the system who can be relied upon to solve hard or intractable problems (see Figure 5.3). Hard problems are sent upward within the procedural rationality of hierarchical systems; soft problems drop downward. They are delegated. In the built to last story, creativity involves working within the system to solve problems and, over time, introducing policies which create greater stability and prospects for systems longevity. In this story, creativity is neither the pursuit of originality nor the quest for significant meaning and enlightenment. The creative bureaucratic leader is skilful at preserving, enhancing and maintaining the system. The creative bureaucrat is a master of specialists, all of whom report upward. He or she is the person at the helm of the system, a cybertechnician in control of data and information, skilled in debate and seen by specialists as open to new ideas. In this story, remaining open to new ideas entails a willingness to rely on more than the routine advice one is given. Leaders add value to reports by synthesizing them followed by a clear, succinct justification and commitment to a line of action. Creative bureaucratic leaders are convincing. They have the evidence at their fingertips. Creative bureaucratic leaders employ procedures within the system to encourage planned changes.

In the entrepreneurial worldview creatives are successful early movers. Creativity involves a swift, decisive and successful break from the pack in competitive contests. Creativity is action-oriented. Those who have the idea but fail to act upon it are not creative leaders in the money talks story. Those who act upon sound ideas but fail to get the prize are also not creative. The creative buccaneer spots trends early, capitalizes upon them and gets out before the bubble bursts. This is not the story of the knowledge leader seeking to bring together the best minds and capital to explore options; it is the tale of the consummate warrior and his or her band of followers tracking down prey. These are not specialists. They go where the barriers to entry are low. They anticipate the moves of others. They mimic success stories. They learn quickly from their mistakes and rarely throw good money after bad. The creative buccaneers learn as they go. They remain aware that they are only as good as their last move. Even after a loss, they are eager to get back into the game. A good part of the creativity of the buccaneers is their infectious passion to succeed. The protagonist in the knowledge leader's story also has a passion to succeed. It is, however, rooted in an image of the future which is difficult to convey. Those who lead from the edge cannot reward their followers with quick returns – theirs is the promise to participate in the network of excitement and, in time, the possibility of fame.

PROTAGONIST: KNOWLEDGE LEADER

The hero in the portal to a new world story is the creative visionary with the capacity to meaningfully introduce and successfully disseminate radical innovations. He or she is framed by true believers in this story as a paradigm challenger and changer. Knowledge leaders thrive on the edge of dynamic knowledge pools. A dynamic knowledge pool attracts capital, educated knowledge workers, allies and intermediaries interested in giving form to the next new thing. In the past, dynamic knowledge pools surrounded the invention of the printing press, antibiotics, the automobile. In more contemporary parlance, dynamic pools adhere to bio-technology and genetics, electronic commerce and digital technologies. Those who claim to fully see or anticipate present dynamic knowledge fields are more likely than not to come from a buccaneer's predisposition. Buccaneers pirate the intellectual capital of others. They justify their actions as bringing innovations to those unable to pay the high prices of innovations. Innovations are costly because those who create them must recoup their costs of exploration and development. Knowledge leaders see themselves on the leading edge (see Figure 5.4), informed and enlightened and well connected within the amoebic-like contours of emerging networks.

The protagonist in this story is a champion or change agent who employs exploratory rationality to stimulate those in the network. The language used here is promissory, robust and ambiguous. The knowledge leader works with others who have both different knowledge bases and are accustomed to a

Bureaucratic Leader's View of Knowledge Leader	Buccaneer Leader's View of Knowledge Leader
Character * reckless * big talker, smooth talker * pro-innovation *Evaluation* * promises the sky * rarely delivers on time or as promised * low levels of accountability * useful when the innovation can help stabilize the system and keep abreast of changes	*Character* * a dreamer * blowing in the wind * talks out of the side of his or her mouth *Evaluation* * all smoke and mirrors * no clear tactics or game plan * talks about idea sharing, but does not execute * useful when he or she offers a good deal
Participative Leader's View of Knowledge Leader	**Knowledge Leader's Self-Portrait**
Character * all head, no heart * puts ideas before people * compromises principles *Evaluation* * views on globalization threaten local communities * mercenary uses/abuses of collaboration * lacks humanist vision * useful when the innovation can improve the quality of life in communities	*Character* * on the leading edge * informed and enlightened * well-connected *Evaluation* * a change agent who stimulates others * realistically captures trends and sees the big picture * can work with others from all points of view * useful in all circumstances calling for creativity, out of the box thinking and innovation

Figure 5.4   Knowledge leader: portraits

great deal of working autonomy. The knowledge leader challenges creatives and knowledge workers to avoid complacency and to see the big picture as one that, with poking, constantly presents new options. The knowledge leader invites participants to consider new questions. Exploratory logic is not rooted in the tactical fly-by-the-seat-of-your-pants position adopted by buccaneers, but by the insistence that creative intelligence bolstered by ongoing collaboration in highly competitive projects is applicable in all circumstances where new ways of doing things and organizing them are vital. Knowledge leaders do not limit exploratory rationality to complex or open-ended problems but, rather, see it as providing a competitive advantage to all leaders in all stories. To the knowledge leader, knowledge is power. Power is not a way to put others in their place; power in the hands of the knowledge leader is a call to innovate, explore and invent.

The self-portrait of the knowledge leader is not shared by other leaders. The buccaneer leader frames the knowledge leader as a self-indulgent, hypocritical dreamer who, in selling ideas in their developmental stage, is not much better than a snake oil salesperson. Knowledge leaders recoil at the accusation by buccaneers that they are hype masters. This wounds. The network advocates see buccaneers as individuals who invented the category. Buccaneers do not disagree. Rather they insist that their familiarity with hype enables them to call it when they see it. The hypocritical side of the buccaneers' critique is levelled at their belief that the knowledge leaders' call for "trust" on behalf of would-be investors, intermediaries and users of the apparent innovation is without merit. Buccaneers point out, as did many who refused to invest in the dot.com implosion, that knowledge leaders frequently go into business without a coherent action plan.[18] They present themselves as geniuses but actually seek, when and wherever possible, to transfer risk onto their clients. Knowledge leaders, buccaneers insist, are not "as advertised". Rather than share ideas, they seek to use intellectual property laws to fence in the frontier. The knowledge leader pushes the idea of property ownership into high gear and intends, despite the rhetoric of paradigm changes, to get as much control as possible.

The participative leader, rarely an ally of the buccaneer, joins in expressing his or her shock and outrage when pointing out that the knowledge leader fails to walk their talk (see Figure 5.4). In the eyes of communitarians, advocates of the network worldview employ the communitarian rhetoric but do not fully put it into practice. In practice, they are all head and no heart. They put ideas before people. They talk about sharing ideas, operating with diversity and rewarding dialogue but, in the crunch, the knowledge leader abandons those whose ideas are obsolete and cuts out whole groups when it is perceived that they no longer carry their creative weight. When push comes to shove, the knowledge leader weighs the merits of a new idea at its market value rather than its contribution to a sustainable community.[19] Still worse, knowledge leaders seem to espouse progress but, upon closer inspection, they reinforce universalism rather than particularism and thus play havoc with local indigenous communities. Communitarians are uncomfortable with globalization as proof of progress. The communitarian worries about the degree to which many knowledge leaders attempt to pass off the network worldview as an applied form of communitarianism. It is not. It is useful to communitarians only when the innovation sought is seen as both improving the quality of the community and does not involve selling out or badly compromising communitarian values and principles.

The prudent "if you can't measure it, you can't manage it" leader in the regulatory worldview frames the knowledge leader as a reckless, big talker with a pro-innovation bias (see Figure 5.4). Bureaucrats are uneasy with the knowledge leader's willingness to jettison the rules. They are uncomfortable with leaders who claim to know better than the system. They are aghast at the knowledge leader's assumption that innovation is good and beneficial. Most bureaucrats keep statistics on innovation. They are keenly aware, not only that most fail, but that only those that pass the bureaucratic test of time are integrated easily into the system. The regulatory worldview prefers fine-tuning the system, working within the rules and carefully attending to the implementation of new technologies and ideas. Those who worry about wide swings in the management fashion pendulum or the explosiveness of trendy new tools and heuristics for aspiring leaders, play on the tensions between the grounded consistency of the stay-at-home bureaucratic leader with his or her penchant for accountability, transactions and measurement and the mercurial knowledge leader and his or her propensities for exploration, transformation and creativity. The disparaging of the new as mere fashion plays to the bureaucratic leaders' strength.[20] Bureaucratic leaders do not attend to new-ness or creativity as an intriguing story. Ideas that are framed as innovative by bureaucrats are easily implemented. They bolster the reliability and longevity of the system and can be transferred from one department or part of the organization to others. That which is valuable withstands the test of time.

It is the unabashed belief that the knowledge leader is pushing the envelope and moving our species forward into a new world which makes him or her the quintessential hero in the network worldview. The network worldview marries the pull outwards toward competition with the pull downwards toward flexibility. Flexibility speaks to the collaborative potential and generativity of *ad hoc*, temporary coalitions. Competition addresses the vital and pressing fact that others in their networks seek to claim priority of discovery and harvest the returns to be garnered from successful break-throughs. The past is a poor predictor of the future. The genre of this story is that of a cybertale or science fiction treatment of the world. The future is no mere extrapolation of the present. The future is draped with new technologies and a treasure trove of opportunities. The new world is born in the minds of creatives working in networks and led by those who stimulate the search for innovation. Innovation is concretized in the emergence of new technology. The cybertale portrays the application of these technologies in blatantly optimistic terms.

GENRE: KNOWLEDGE LEADER

The cybertale is a utopian portrayal of the future. Science, human cerebrality and technology are synthesized. What ensues is the promise of a bold new future. In the portal to a new world story, creative intelligence harnessed by knowledge leaders opens new options for our species as a whole. The drama originally rooted in the entrepreneurial view shifts from the individual to the species. Rather than the self-made individual bootstrapping him or herself out of obscurity by bold and decisive moves, the knowledge leader combines the best minds on the planet with state-of-the-art technology and scientific/ artistic acumen to create breakthroughs. It is this struggle for breakthroughs by the best minds that elevates our species. The cybertale ruptures the highly scripted play of those in the regulatory worldview by labelling their self-acknowledged prudence as a fearful predisposition. It inhibits necessary exploration. Those who adhere to the genre of the highly scripted play are framed as resistant to change, frozen and inert by champions of the network worldview. Despite this rupture or perhaps due to it, the advocates of the network worldview expect a proportion of bureaucratic leaders to become investors or intermediaries contributing to network development.

The cybertale has its most perplexing and ideologically fraught relationship with the open-line talk show, the populist genre of the communitarian worldview. While both strongly resonate with the benefits of sharing, trust and the inclusion of diverse impulses into decision-making, each takes these in very different directions – ones that are growing increasingly acrimonious within contemporary geo-political and cross-generational positions. The cybertale boldly hitches its star to technology, corporatism, globalization, and the celebration of the built, planned, or engineered environment. The open-line talk show rallies its listeners to a small, local and "simple is beautiful" theme. This principled moral position embraces technology only when it is viewed by users as humanizing. It views the natural eco-system or biosphere as a sacred heritage requiring conservation and care. Ironically, when the crowds gather to protest at the World Trade Organization (WTO) for example, one witnesses a tension-filled conjunction of the cybertale and the open-line talk show – a tension that, as it gives birth to a protest movement, has shed blood on urban streets.[21]

The clash between and among genres can be explained most easily in turning our attention to how each genre frames technology (see Figure 5.5). In the cybertale technology is not only a route to new possibilities, it is evidence of creative intelligence. It is the master stroke of a species that cannot outrun the cheetah, endure drought as well as the camel or explore the ocean as well as the whale. Nevertheless, due to technology, our species outshines these others. Just as the steam shovel extends the human hand in its ability to move material, so too exploration in genetics permits us to modify life forms, including our own and those we digest. The digital revolution in our midst accelerates the creation, transfer and storage of information on a planetary level. Technology is embedded creative intelligence. It embodies the efforts of humans to harness the best practices of the best minds in our species and flexibly employ this creative intelligence to manage the planet and direct our destiny. The cybertale is clear – we are makers of our destiny. There will be some glitches and accidents with technology, but the costs of stifling our creative intelligence and failing to capitalize upon our competitive advantage as a species are far too great.

In the highly scripted play – the genre which girds the regulatory worldview – technology is framed as a means to reduce uncertainty, enhance reliability, and reduce errors on behalf of hierarchical systems. It is an embodiment and concretization of procedural rationality. Technology reduces uncertainty by curtailing human idiosyncrasies, routinizing, standardizing and calibrating. It lends itself to the objective, dispassionate collection of data. Hierarchical systems adopt technology when it can be integrated without too much disruption and there is evidence that the technology can be repaired, maintained and replaced in a cost-efficient manner. In the regulatory worldview, technology is the handmaiden of planning. It enhances control. It does not revolutionize systems; instead, it maintains them. Technology is not intended to impact the ends towards which the system is directed by those at its helm. It is viewed as a means of more assuredly achieving these ends. Technology is most secure or difficult to dislodge in the highly scripted play when it enhances the power or authority of those at the top of the system. Technology empowers those at the helm of large systems. It is best employed when it reduces error and helps to get things just right. What it means to get things right is determined by those at the helm of the hierarchy.

In the genre of the entrepreneurial worldview – the continuing drama or struggle – technology is a means of enhancing goal attainment in the midst of competition. It is a means to an end in a story in which there is only one desirable end – winning. Technology is adopted when one believes it provides a competitive advantage. Technology which is easily imitated provides less of an attraction. In the continuing drama or struggle technology is

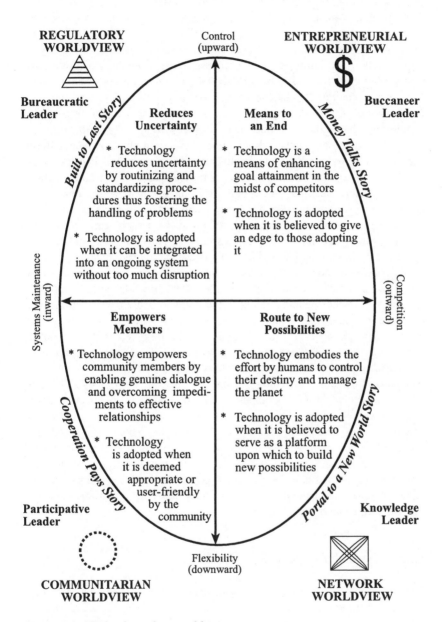

REGULATORY WORLDVIEW — Control (upward) — ENTREPRENEURIAL WORLDVIEW

Bureaucratic Leader

Built to Last Story

Reduces Uncertainty

* Technology reduces uncertainty by routinizing and standardizing procedures thus fostering the handling of problems

* Technology is adopted when it can be integrated into an ongoing system without too much disruption

Means to an End

* Technology is a means of enhancing goal attainment in the midst of competitors

* Technology is adopted when it is believed to give an edge to those adopting it

Buccaneer Leader

Money Talks Story

Systems Maintenance (inward)

Competition (outward)

Empowers Members

* Technology empowers community members by enabling genuine dialogue and overcoming impediments to effective relationships

* Technology is adopted when it is deemed appropriate or user-friendly by the community

Route to New Possibilities

* Technology embodies the effort by humans to control their destiny and manage the planet

* Technology is adopted when it is believed to serve as a platform upon which to build new possibilities

Cooperation Pays Story

Portal to a New World Story

Participative Leader — Flexibility (downward) — Knowledge Leader

COMMUNITARIAN WORLDVIEW

NETWORK WORLDVIEW

Figure 5.5   Technology: four worldviews

presented as both a prize and a problem. As a prize, it succeeds in providing entrepreneurs with a competitive advantage. In this manner it can swiftly change losers into winners or, if successfully instigated by winners, propel them upwards to risk their now even more substantial wealth by playing for higher stakes. As a problem, entrepreneurs frame technology as notoriously costly and fickle. It is costly because the creation of technology requires large amounts of capital. Purchasing technology is costly and maintaining it is cumbersome. Even more problematic is the possession of a particular technology that reduces a buccaneer's ability to quickly shift from one business venture to another. Buccaneers insist that the continuing drama cannot be won by purchasing technology on the open market. Those selling it would be employing it to make money if it delivered even one half of what it promised. Moreover, once a technology is on the market, the competitive advantage it confers upon a purchaser is limited if all have equal access. Buccaneers are attracted to the role of pirate as a rapid early mover and imitator. Lastly, technology depreciates rapidly. Those who buy in late in the cycle get the best price, but find little if any competitive advantage.

The open-line talk show, as we have seen, rubs shoulders uncomfortably with the cybertale. Technology in the open-line talk show empowers members. It evokes genuine dialogue and helps to overcome impediments to effective relationships. Technology is accepted when it is seen as user friendly by members in the community. In this depiction, technology humanizes. It is not, as in the highly scripted play, a means of tying the human into the system or the person into the position in order to enhance a mechanized system. Technology is not, as those in the money talks story would have it, a means to compete more efficiently. In the communitarian worldview, technology is embraced only when and if it fosters cooperation, enhances dialogue and reinforces the trust upon which solid, enduring, relationships are built. As we have seen, the conditional embrace of technology by communitarians puts it at odds with the portal to a new world story. Those drawn to the open-line talk show portray technology as a gamble or a game of snakes and ladders. If one lands on a snake, the downward trajectory into the future can be devastating.

LESSON: KNOWLEDGE LEADER

Leaders in the portal to a new world story are convinced that generative knowledge is power. It will shape our future. It pushes the boundaries and refocuses our collective attention. It celebrates learning by experimentation. As well, it speaks to a global market and a new world order redolent with heretofore unexperienced potential. To realize this potential knowledge leaders must employ some of the basic skills of the other leaders, yet customize them to fit the network world. Indeed once we begin to think in terms of what skills or knowledge leaders possess we shift, albeit subtly, from telling the leadership stories to making sense of leadership practice. Practice hybridizes stories. It addresses the actions and skills guided by knowledge that differentiates between our four archetypal leaders. Practising leaders, like the knowledge leader, must put together a skill portfolio. This enables him or her to provide others with a clear signal as to their leadership capabilities.

The knowledge leader, as we shall discuss far more thoroughly in Chapter 6, must clearly signal his or her ability to meet the needs of participants. On the other hand, knowledge leaders who continually attract followers, subordinates and/or members, fail to align their story signals with their practice. They confuse others. Thus the knowledge leader who creates a story emphasizing creativity, innovation and generativity yet in practice penalizes others for making errors, creates confusion. The knowledge leader's story is being followed by bureaucratic leaders' practices. Or, to take another example of the misalignment between story and practice, imagine a dedicated knowledge leader who signals in his or her leadership story the ongoing need to push on in experimentation. He or she then sells the potential new breakthrough to the first possible purchaser and leaves the field. In this instance a knowledge leader's signal is supported by buccaneer practice. Participants conscious of their autonomy, creativity and freedom to push the envelope in search of new breakthroughs are drawn to the knowledge leader's signals within his or her story. They then conclude upon reflection of the leader's practice that the knowledge leader is less interested in pushing the envelope than in maximizing profits.

Knowledge leaders are particularly susceptible to story and practice misalignment. Theirs is a story rife with uncertain outcomes. It speaks to the future. It uses the language and aims at transformative practices. It is global in its reach and it aims for universal practice. The improvisational quality of leadership in the network worldview is open to drift.[22] These are not rigid rules. Norms keep changing. Markets open up, get heated, then swiftly turn ice cold. In story–practice misalignment, practice alters as leaders face new challenges. Challenges arise with great frequency in the network worldview. Stories change as leaders facing new challenges seek a means of effectively signalling to followers, participants, members or subordinates. Stories draw audiences who can hear them. The leadership story reduces anxiety. It seems credible. The story laced with procedural rationality summons the deferential subordinate. Market rationality rife with rewards for tactical intelligence and honours for winners draws followers. The mentoring skills of the emotionally intelligent leader beckon those who seek a meaningful existence. Exploratory rationality, the call of creative intelligence, lures participants.

To encapsulate this notion of misalignment between story and practice in the knowledge leader, imagine the following example. A knowledge leader, drawing upon creatives in the area, initiates a successful network of applying a miniature remote sensing device injected into the bloodstream to monitor stroke development in patients who seem to manifest early warning signs. The knowledge leader, let us call her Glenda, puts together considerable expertise and begins to generate intellectual capital. However, despite three great years, Glenda finds it difficult to generate sufficient income to draw a good salary. As a result, she takes a job in a well-established medical apparatus firm known for its stable hierarchy and longevity. In the three years at the edge of the medical remote sensing network, Glenda's story – the portal to a new world story – was consistent with the skill base or practice. In transitioning out of the network worldview and into a far more regulatory worldview, what does Glenda do?

It is clear that in the four faces of capitalism, leadership stories are not so easily transferred. This holds true not only for the knowledge leader. The participative leader whose firm is aggressively acquired by a buccaneer raider, the bureaucratic leader whose department is privatized and the buccaneer whose company is nationalized or unionized, all in varying degrees find their leadership stories in transition. In fact, in writing this book and relying upon discussion and input from 24 practising leaders (six in each of the four faces of capitalism), the one thing they agreed upon is that leaders who are worth their salt customize their stories as they grow and learn. To this end, the next two chapters investigate how, when and why leaders change their stories. Equally vital is what practising leaders do to use their existing skills to align and realign leadership stories with leadership skills or practices.

In Chapter 6 I look at how, within each leadership story, practising leaders develop skills which are adapted to the four functional pulls – upwards towards control, downwards towards flexibility, inwards toward system maintenance, and outwards toward competition. Leaders who develop reach as the basis for story transition develop their "within-story reach". They are local leaders. They effectively learn to develop within-story skill transitions. They interpret other leaders' stories through the prism of the practices within their worldview. For example the knowledge leader who seeks to increase "people" skills within the network worldview will look to the emotional intelligence of the mentor in the communitarian worldview. However, the knowledge leader anchored in innovators' skills will adapt the members' skills to suit the temporary, project-based and competitive nature of the network worldview. The knowledge leader who chooses to stay within the network worldview takes on the skills of the collaborator when seeking to develop and enrich his or her people skills.

The within-story skill transition discussed and mapped out in Chapter 6 provides a systematic means of developing skills, building upon existing skills for the leaders interested in staying within their story. In the final chapter, I turn to the cosmopolitan leader. Cosmopolitan leaders are capable of reinventing themselves. They are reflective practitioners within the four faces of capitalism. In practice this means that they engage in ACTs (anchor cross-story transitions). In ACTs, cosmopolitan leaders not only cross story lines but, over time, alter anchor skills. Cosmopolitan leaders extend their reach, but often at the expense of confusing their followers, subordinate members or participants. As leaders change stories they alter their skills or practices. They must learn to leave behind those who cannot hear their new leadership story. Leadership comes with a price. The contextual model of leadership makes it clear that there are no easy answers to those seeking to act as leaders. It entails hard work and the ability to customize your leadership story and align this with both skill and practice. Those who believe that leadership is simply doing what effective leaders do are on the right track. However, since leaders come in so many shapes, sizes and forms, and each is effective in a particular context, how does a leader put the stories together with the skills and practice?

Let us address this question. We will now enrich our perspective by moving from the four leaders' stories to the skill portfolios of local and then cosmopolitan leaders in the four faces of capitalism. In shifting our attention, we move from a focus upon the leaders and their worldviews or cognitive sense-making to the skills leaders employ to put a worldview or combination of worldviews into practice.

NOTES

1. The quotation from Fujio Mitarai, the CEO of Canon, can be found in Shira White and G. Patton Wright (2002), *New Ideas About New Ideas: Insights on Creativity From the World's Leading Innovators*, Cambridge, MA: Perseus. See page 211 for the quote. This book does an excellent job of stimulating insights on knowledge leaders based upon interviews with, for example, John Seely Brown (Xerox), Dale Chihuly (glass artist), Frank Gehry (architect), John Loose (Corning). Interestingly, among the interviews are recent ethics/law violators Jeff Skilling (Enron) and Sam Waksel (ImClone).
2. For varying insights into radical or disruptive innovation, see Alan Barker (2002), *The Alchemy of Innovation: Perspectives From the Leading Edge*, London: Spiro, and Christopher M. McDermott and Gina C. O'Connor (2002), "Managing radical innovation: An overview of emergent strategy issues," *Journal of Product Innovation Management*, **19**(6), pp. 424–38, Andrew Hargadon (2003), *How Breakthroughs Happen: The Surprising Truth About How Companies Innovate*, Cambridge, MA: Harvard University Press, stresses the use of existence of recombinant knowledge in breakthrough creation.
3. For the roots of power in intellectual capital, see Thomas A. Stewart (2001), *The Wealth of Knowledge: Intellectual Capital at the Twenty-First Century Organization*, New York: Currency, and Alan Burton-Jones (1999), *Knowledge Capitalism: Business, Work and*

Learning in the New Economy, Oxford: Oxford University Press. To capture the relationship between networks or clusters and intellectual capital see Stephen Tallman, Mark Jenkins, Nick Henry and Steven Pinch (2004), "Knowledge clusters and competitive advantage," *Academy of Management Review*, **29**(2), pp. 258–71.

4. Henry Mintzberg (1983), *Structure in Fives: Designing Effective Organizations*, Englewood Cliffs, NJ: Prentice Hall, calls these loosely structured organizations "adhocracies". Michael Porter (1990), *The Competitive Advantage of Nations*, London: Macmillan, draws attention to groups of loosely linked organizations as a new face in the network worldview. Todd H. Chiles and Alan D. Meyer (2003), "Managing the emergence of clusters: An increasing returns approach to strategic change," *Emergence*, **3**(3), pp. 58–9, give an excellent background to the reason for the emergence of adhocracies, clusters and networks in the knowledge-based economy.

5. To get a sense of the distinction between the professionals and the knowledge worker, see Frances Horibe (1999), *Managing Knowledge Workers: New Skills and Attitudes to Unlock the Intellectual Capital in Your Organization*, New York: John Wiley. Mats Alvesson (2004), *Knowledge Work and Knowledge Intensive Firms*, Oxford: Oxford University Press, captures the distinction between practice and rhetoric in the knowledge leader's depiction of creatives. Finally, Craig L. Pearce (2004), "The future of leadership: Combining vertical and shared leadership to transform knowledge work," *Academy of Management Executive*, **18**(1), pp. 47–57, explores the changing skill portfolio as leaders move to working with knowledge workers.

6. "Buzz" is indispensable in diffusing innovation. For a technical discussion of the diffusion of innovation that has stood the test of time, see Everett M. Rogers (1995), *Diffusion of Innovations*, 4th edn, New York: Free Press. Emanuel Rosen (2000), *The Anatomy of Buzz: How to Create Word-of-Mouth Marketing*, New York: Doubleday, attends to the need to hype products and services with which the client or consumer has little previous experience. Dominic Power and Mats Lundmark (2004), "Working through knowledge pools: Labour market dynamics, the transference of knowledge and ideas, and industrial clusters," *Urban Studies*, **41**(5/6), pp. 1025–44, explain how buzz works in disseminating innovative ideas in a prominent cluster in Stockholm.

7. Stewart Clegg (2003), "Managing organization futures in a changing world of power/knowledge," *Oxford Handbook of Organization Theory*, Oxford: Oxford University Press, explains the changing notion of knowledge to power in the network worldview. For a more optimistic treatment of knowledge as power in the network worldview, see Verna Allee (2003), *The Future of Knowledge: Increasing Prosperity Through Value Networks*, Amsterdam: Butterworth-Heinemann.

8. For an insightful treatment of technology in the political economy of the network worldview, see Joel Mokyr (2002), *Gifts of Athena: Historical Origins of the Knowledge Economy*, Princeton, NJ: Princeton University Press For a less linear view of knowledge as the embodiment of progress, read Siva Vaidhyanthan (2004), *The Anarchist in the Library: How the Clash Between Freedom and Control is Hacking the Real World and Crashing the System*, New York: Basic Books.

9. Arnoud de Meyer, Soumitra Dutta and Sandeep Srivastava (2002), *The Bright Stuff: How Innovative People and Technology Make the Old Economy New*, London: Financial Times/Prentice Hall, explore via case studies how creative leaders are capable of regenerating firms like Charles Schwab, Barnes and Nobel, and General Motors. To explore the leader in the network worldview as a creative knowledge activist, see Georg von Krogh, Kazuo Ichijo and Ikujiro Nonaka (2000), *Enabling Knowledge Creation: How to Unlock the Mystery of Tacit Knowledge and Release the Power of Innovation*, Oxford: Oxford University Press.

10. To sample the ballooning anti-globalization literature written from a communitarian point of view see Noreena Hertz (2001), *The Silent Takeover: Global Capitalism and the Death of Democracy*, London: Heinemann; Brink Lindsey (2002), *Against the Dead Hand: The Uncertain Struggle for Global Capitalism*, New York: John Wiley; and David Held and Anthony McGrew (2002), *Globalization/Anti-Globalization*, Cambridge: Polity Press.

11. Transformation as used in the network worldview signals the knowledge leader's interest in

and pursuit of deep change. See Dean Anderson and Linda Ackerman-Andersen (2001), *Beyond Change Management: Advanced Strategies for Today's Transformational Leaders*, San Francisco: Jossey-Bass/Pfeiffer, for a psychological treatment of the transformational leader. Kim S. Cameron (2003), "Organizational transformation through architecture and design: A project with Frank Gehry," *Journal of Management Inquiry*, **12**(1), pp. 88–93, captures the creative design aspect of Gehry's design and transformation of a management school.

12. The bureaucratic leader's capacity to anticipate problems and design systems for stability under control is described by John Roberts (2004), *The Modern Firm: Organizational Design for Performance and Growth*, Oxford: Oxford University Press. Hugh Courtney (2001), *20/20 Foresight: Crafting Strategy in an Uncertain World*, Cambridge, MA: Harvard Business School Press, outlines the four levels of residual uncertainty in strategic planning and provides bureaucratic leaders with an uncertainty toolkit.

13. Debra M. Amidon (2003), *The Innovation Superhighway: Harvesting Intellectual Capital for Collaborative Advantage*, Boston, MA: Butterworth-Heinemann, captures the knowledge leader's sense of vision; James M. Kouzes and Barry Z. Posner (2002), *The Leadership Challenge*, 3rd edn, San Francisco: Jossey-Bass, explore the participative leader's vision.

14. To get a sense of the knowledge manager as the most effective problem solver, see Pervaiz, K. Ahmed, K.K. Lim and Ann Y.E. Loh (2002), *Learning Through Knowledge Management*, Oxford: Butterworth-Heinemann and James W. Cortada (2001), *21st Century Business: Managing and Working in the New Digital Economy*, Upper Saddle River, NJ: Financial Times/Prentice Hall.

15. For the role of early adopters and others in the communication of change in ideas, see William R. Spence (1994), *Innovation: The Communication of Change in Ideas, Practices and Products*, London: Chapman and Hall. Eric Brousseau (2003), "E-commerce in France: Did early adoption prevent its development?" *Information Society*, **19**(1), pp. 45–57, explores the paradox of how the early adoption of a form of the Internet in France slowed down its adoption of the form used elsewhere.

16. In their "New theory of the firm," Alex Bennet and David Bennet (2004), *Organizational Survival in the New World: The Intelligence Complex Adaptive System*, Amsterdam: Butterworth-Heinemann, explore why and how knowledge leaders push into the frontier and set up deep schisms with bureaucratic leaders. J. Stewart Black, Allen J. Morrison and Hal B. Gregersen (1999), *Global Explorers: The Next Generation of Leaders*, London: Routledge, employ the frontier metaphor to make sense of exploratory rationality in the knowledge leader.

17. The importance of self-knowledge is emphasized in Robert E. Quinn (1996), *Deep Change: Discovering the Leader Within*, San Francisco: Jossey-Bass. James C. Collins (2001), *Good to Great: Why Some Companies Make the Leap and Others Don't*, New York: Harper Business, characterizes the level five leader as one steeped in self-knowledge and aware of the other.

18. Paul Krugman (2003), *The Great Unraveling: Losing Our Way in the New Century*, New York: W.W. Norton, explores the antecedents to the digital ponzi scheme. Daniel Quinn Mills (2002), *Buy, Lie and Sell High: How Investors Lost Out on Enron and the Internet Bubble*, London: Prentice Hall/Financial Times, probes the popping of the Internet bubble. See Janet Rovenpor (2003), "Explaining the e-commerce shakeout," *E-Service Journal*, **3**(1), pp. 53–76, for case studies of the failure of Internet-based business in 2000 and 2001.

19. For an excellent conceptual treatment of the knowledge life cycle, see Joseph M. Firestone and Mark W. McElroy (2003), *Key Issues in New Knowledge Management*, Boston, MA: Butterworth-Heinemann, and Julian Birkenshaw and Tony Sheehan (2002), "Managing the knowledge life cycle," *Sloan Management Review*, **44**(2), pp. 75–83.

20. For critical treatment of the management fashion cycle, see Brad Jackson (2001), *Management Gurus and Management Fashions*, London: Routledge. Patrick Thomas (1999), *Fashions in Management Research: An Empirical Analysis*, Aldershot: Ashgate, provides a good background to Brad Jackson's treatment of the shifting popularity of varying management gurus. Danny Miller, Jon Hartwick and Isabelle Le Breton-Miller

(2004), "How to detect a manpower fad – and distinguish it from a classic," *Business Horizon*, **47**(4), pp. 7–16, explore what goes into making what initially seems like an innovation in thinking about management and leadership into a mere fad.

21. For a sense of the protest, tension and social movement impetus against globalization, see John Clark (2003), *Worlds Apart: Civil Society and the Battle for Ethical Globalization*, Bloomfield, CT: Kumarian Press; Paul Kingsworth (2003), *One No, Many Yeses: A Journey to the Heart of Global Resistance*, London: Free Press; and Jonathan Neale (2002), *You are G8, We are 6 Billion: The Truth Behind the Genoa Protests*, London: Vision Paperbacks.

22. For recent work plumbing the depths of the jazz metaphor for the improvisational skills of the knowledge leader, see Karl E. Weick (1008), "Improvisation as a mindset for organizational analysis," *Organization Science*, **9**(5), pp. 543–55; Kathryn Pavlovich (2003), "All that jazz," *Long Range Planning*, **36**(5), pp. 441–58; and Ken Kamoche, Miguel Pina E. Cunha and Joao Vieira da Cunha (2003), "Towards a theory of organizational improvisation: Looking beyond the jazz metaphor," *Journal of Management Studies*, **40**(8), pp. 2023–51.

6. Leadership skills in context

> "Different contexts require different styles, but you are asking about my general management style. There are times when I have to make the call to be autocratic, but the norm that I am working to is team based and participative."
>
> Bill McLaughlin[1]

The skilled leader is a contextualist. He or she can both read the changing stories as they hybridize and transition to skills or competencies relevant to shifts in their own leadership story. As Frito Lay Europe began moving from its primary mooring in the entrepreneurial worldview to a greater awareness of the cooperation pays story, Bill McLaughlin, the former President and CEO, intuitively sought to come to terms with the demands for new competencies. When the money talks story unabashedly reigned supreme at Frito Lay Europe, Bill McLaughlin felt comfortable calling the shots. He saw himself as the boss, primary partner, fire fighter, star performer and deal maker. However, in McLaughlin's own words, "as the work became more complex and decisions faster, I realized that I was not smart enough to make all of the decisions". McLaughlin, however, is plenty smart. He is doing precisely what smart leaders do. McLaughlin is aware of a new set of pulls and pressures, in contextualist terms, the imposition of a new story upon the old money talks story. McLaughlin is signalling that the buccaneer leader's skill set, while certainly not disappearing at Frito Lay, is altering. Greater complexity and interdependence in the operation are calling for new leadership competencies to be added to the old.[2] In Frito Lay's case, the new competencies are drawn from the communitarian's and, to a lesser degree, the knowledge leader's skill set.

A contextual approach to leadership views leadership skills as dynamic. A recurrent theme in the literature on contemporary leadership is simply, but powerfully, that a leader is many things to many people. As a consequence, skilled leaders possess a diversity of competencies which they mobilize at the right time and use in proportions suitable for a particular context. While this insight flirts with a contextualist's approach to leadership, it falls short. It does so because it fails to systematically identify the array of skills required. It neglects tying leadership skills to specific contexts. In particular, this approach disregards how leaders who have developed their skills to cope with problems and issues transition to or learn new skills as contexts alter. Thus, in reading many well-written books on leadership, we learn that leaders must have vision or be able to execute. The typical leadership book is rather selective. Its author prizes certain leadership skills as vital, and disparages or pushes off other skills as quite beside the point. What we fail to learn when we adhere to these well-intended approaches to leadership is what it means, in our example, to provide vision or to execute successfully and effectively in different contexts.

With the basic four faces of capitalism model as our foundation, we learn that vision, or for that matter execution, not only means different things but, as we move from the model to practice in this chapter, that it involves quite distinct skills. To briefly illustrate this, attend to vision and execution in the buccaneer and bureaucratic leaders' stories. The leader with vision in the built to last story monitors and prudently depicts a credible, measured future rooted in closely examined forecast data. The leader with vision in the money talks story is a confident, self-made individualist who in a boss-like manner presides over a future while others are mesmerized by the imminence of quick wins to be accrued following the leader. Similarly in the money talks story, execution is embodied by the leader who enacts a series of swift and bold tactics aimed at beating others. In the built to last story, execution is a decision taken by leaders after attending to the facts, adhering to procedures and eventually committing the system to a line of action. What is important in a contextualist approach to leadership is that as we move from model to practice, we must recognize that the skills required to lead vary with the context and the leader's story.

To lead within a worldview is often to fail to recognize that one's skills will be appreciated only if the conditions for the predominance of this worldview stay intact. Leaders who execute like buccaneer leaders are duly rewarded for their pluck and propensity toward risk. However, they will soon have their wings clipped if their unit is bought or taken over by a large bureaucracy. It is clear that "just do it" is not the rallying cry of the prudent bureaucratic leader. Or imagine an edge-walking knowledge leader accustomed to boldly challenging those on his or her team and then their services are sold to a communitarian non-governmental organization interested in technology transfer to the third world. It is likely that, in the domain of the participative leader's quest for consensus and buy-in, the bold challenging style of the knowledge leader will require tempering. Each of us as leaders or potential leaders lives in a dynamic world of practice.[3] Practice requires that we muddy our models. We must begin to discuss how and why, for example, participative leaders who find themselves increasingly in an entrepreneurial or network worldview begin to doubt the utility of the skills that were hugely rewarded earlier in their career. In the contextual approach to leadership, hybridization is the process wherein leaders recognize that no worldview is self-contained. In practice, archetypes wither. They do not, however, lose their usefulness. A contextualist approach to leadership insists that well-intended prescriptions such as "a leader ought to have a vision" require context specification with regard to skills. A contextual approach to leadership demonstrates how leaders can use their understanding of the four faces of capitalism and their worldview within this model to temper and fuse their skills to accommodate the ongoing and dynamic pulls and pressures of others' stories. In practice, worldviews are not static.

The aim of this chapter is to employ the contextualist approach to explore how leaders develop reach in their skills to protect, buffer and adapt their worldview to that of others. To accomplish this, I will first depict, using the four faces of capitalism model, the underlying skills in each of the leadership stories, then discuss the forces that bolster and weaken these skills. Skill portfolios are aggregates of the skills required by a leader to communicate his or her leadership to potential followers, subordinates, members or participants. In developing their skill portfolios and adapting these to the pulls exerted upon them by other worldviews, the leader adapts. He or she develops a reach which nurtures and protects their preferred worldview. In the final chapter, I explore cosmopolitan leaders. These develop ACTs or anchor cross-story transitions. They are leaders whose reflective practice enables them to broaden their reach and reinvent themselves.

THE SKILL PORTFOLIO: HOLISTIC DEPICTION

In practical terms, a contextualist approach to leadership recognizes that all competent leaders are talented but that in each worldview an effective leader possesses very different skills. This helps explain why, for example, the knowledge leader with his or her willingness to embrace uncertainty in the pursuit of innovation is not typically cherished in a context which rewards the prudent bureaucratic leader for monitoring the system and reducing uncertainty. The buccaneer leader in his or her rush to get results will be depicted as an autocrat by communitarians and a bull in a china shop by bureaucrats. In this discussion I remain sympathetic to leaders who stay in their worldview but seek an appreciation of the spectrum of leadership skills required to enhance their ability to deal with pulls and pressures from other worldviews. In this discussion I address how leaders develop and sustain reach within their preferred story. Effective leaders "within" a story have skills which enhance their anchor skill. Reach enables leaders to deal with those who are not true believers in the leader's story.

Skills are the talents we both possess and acquire that form our response to the demands which arise in or dominate our preferred worldview. In practice, very few of us live our lives solely within a worldview. We have a footprint in all four worldviews. Nevertheless, we anchor our portfolio in one using the others as subsidiary or fall-back skills. This is not a function of our biological or genetic capacity, but a dictum built into the psycho-social dynamics of leadership. The more likely we are to be seen and accepted by others as leaders, the more clearly we signal our skills to these others. Generally speaking, those with 25 percent of their skill portfolio in each of the four faces of capitalism are perfectly poised to endure as players in a form of instrumental behaviour, however, they are unlikely to lead. The leader signals a preferred set of skills to others. Leaders are made when their skill set is seen as desirable by others and they can, in time, deliver on these skills.

This creates an irony. Leaders overstate or exaggerate their story so that this clear signal of competency within a worldview can be picked up by those who seek a leader. Participative leaders who send out buccaneer signals will have an easier time drawing followers than they will members. As we shall see, this is more likely when the buccaneer leader anchors in the boss's skills. Bureaucratic leaders who consistently put out communitarian signals or attempt to anchor in mentoring skills in lieu of monitoring, will not draw subordinates eager to do the bidding of the system. They will draw members enthusiastically motivated to question expertise and interpret the rules using their discretion. This cross-signalling creates tension. Leaders who continue to do so will imperil their role as a leader. Imported leaders must learn to tie their practice or skills to their story or over time they must effectively alter their stories.

Interestingly, to lead requires the clear signalling of a dominant leadership story, a worldview preference and the ability to back this up with a contextually relevant skill set. This is not to say that one cannot become an effective leader with a footprint in each of the four faces of capitalism. In my own case, I assess mine to be invested 15 percent in the regulatory world-view, 45 percent in the communitarian, 25 percent in network and 15 in the entrepreneurial worldview. The contextual approach to leadership suggests, as we shall see, that I invest my time and energy in developing my preferred story – the participative leader's – by anchoring in the mentor's skill and developing, in the following order, diplomat's skills (network), facilitator's skills (regulatory) and advocate's skills (entrepreneurial). These are skills that all fit the cooperation pays story (see Figure 6.1). They accommodate the footprint of an individual who resonates with and seeks skills in the cooperation pays story. These skills signal to others that I am a leader interested in dialogue, inclusiveness, community and developing a culture of trust. Those seeking membership and a meaningful existence will be drawn

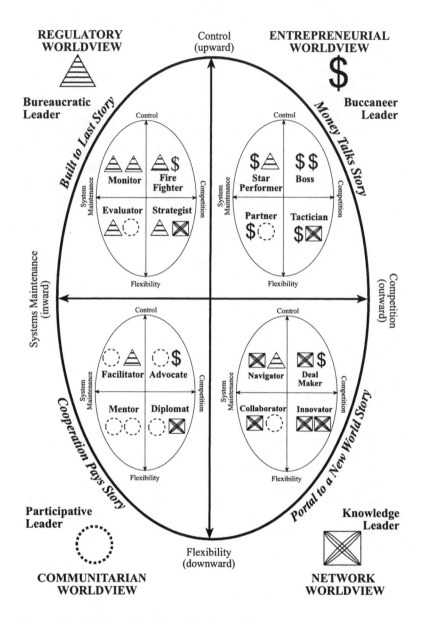

Figure 6.1   Skill sets of leaders: holistic model

to my message. My signals are competitive with other leaders. Each is ideally tied to your preferred worldview. Once these jive with your own skills, not only will you be able to meet these demands and feel good about yourself and your relationship to your leadership role but, as well, you will feel that you are having an impact as a leader.

The holistic model of the skill sets for each leadership story is outlined in Figure 6.1. Note in this Figure that the pull upward towards control by the few, downward towards flexibility, outward towards competition and inward towards preservation of the status quo is now reflected at two distinct but interrelated levels of analysis. First, these pulls hold for the relationship between and among each of the four leadership stories within the four faces of capitalism and, now, within each of the leaders' stories. The small ovals within the quadrants modify and apply the pulls within a leader's story. This is the domain of the local leader. In this domain, flexibility, for example within the money talks story, does not exist at the same intensity or convey the degree of flexibility within the model as a whole or, in the Figure, in the big oval. Flexibility in the money talks story signals flexibility within a worldview that prizes control and competition. Thus the buccaneer leader who takes on an active partner must, even within the entrepreneurial worldview, begin to develop the skills of listening, collaboration and attending to the views of his or her partner. Similarly, the buccaneer who begins to think outside the box tactically seeking an edge in critically scrutinizing his or her present means of making a profit, moves, albeit in a buccaneer's fashion, towards the flexibility one finds far more developed in the network worldview.

In the holistic model we view 16 skills (see Figure 6.1). In practice, no leader can simultaneously possess fully blown skills in all four faces of capitalism. The leader's anchor skills along the diagonals in the holistic model are opposed. They are difficult to possess at the same time within one's skill portfolio. We shall see this when we look at gradient two transitions in the next chapter. Anchor skills epitomize the leader's story. Not only do true believers recognize this skill, but outsiders associate it with leaders who, on the whole, they neither esteem nor seek out. Each leadership story possesses an anchor skill. In the contextual model of leadership, anchor skills are doubly reinforced. Thus the monitor's skill (the anchor skill in the regulatory worldview) is conveyed by the symbol of the double hierarchy or triangle in Figure 6.1. Anchor skills respond to the same pulls at both levels of analysis. The monitor's skill pulls upward and inward towards control and systems maintenance both within the story and in the larger oval in the holistic model (see Figure 6.1). Anchor skills bind the story and serve as the basis or jumping-off point for the development of a leader's transitional skills.

Boss's skills (\$\$) pull towards control and competition both between and among leadership stories (the big oval) and within the money talks story (the small oval). Boss's skills anchor the entrepreneurial worldview.[4] These skills, as we shall see when we probe the skill portfolio of buccaneers (small oval) provide both those within the money talks story and those viewing it from afar with the basic image of the buccaneer leader. Those seeking followers are strongly advised to develop, signal and make credible their skills as a confident boss and take-charge leader. Monitoring skills denoted by the double hierarchy symbol (ΔΔ) pull upward towards control and inward towards system maintenance at both levels of analysis.[5] Bureaucratic leaders who seek willing subordinates and compliant superordinates are advised to develop their skills at monitoring and providing clear data and information in a rationally evident manner.[6] The monitor manages, measures and distributes information. Mentoring skills (○○) anchor the cooperation pays story, pulling downward towards flexibility and inward towards the maintenance of shared values at both levels of analysis. The mentor serves as exemplar of the values of those who aspire to and find meaning in their contributions or membership in the community. Innovating skills denoted by the double network symbol (⊠⊠) pull outward towards competition and downward towards flexibility, both between and among leaderships stories (the big oval) and within the portal to a new world story (the small oval).[7] Those seeking participants to enter into the risky world of the network are strongly advised to develop, signal and make credible their skills as creative, leading-edge practitioners who can generate intellectual capital.

Anchor skills, not surprisingly, anchor one within a story. They provide the strong, pure signal necessary to draw followers (buccaneer leader), subordinates (bureaucratic leader), members (participative leader), and participants (knowledge leader). As leaders further develop their anchor skill within a leadership story, it becomes more difficult for them to be attuned to other pulls and pressures emanating from other stories. Transitional skills enable those with a preferred worldview to remain within that leadership story and simultaneously begin to accommodate the influences and pulls of other stories. The dynamics of transitional skills are such that each one is not equally easy for a leader with well developed anchor skills to acquire. In the holistic model, transitional skills on the diagonal from the anchor skill are more difficult to develop than those contiguous to it. This is not nearly as important a problem in developing local reach as it will become when we look at leaders who develop skills outside their preferred leadership story. For example, this means is that the participative leaders anchored in mentoring skills (○○) will have more trouble acquiring the transitional advocate skills (○\$) than either facilitator (○Δ) or diplomat skills (○⊠). Transitional skills on the diagonal share no talking point with the anchor skill. Thus the anchor skill in the cooperation pays story shares not one of the pulls (flexibility, competition, system maintenance, or control) with the transitional advocate skills. Without this talking point, the participative leader will have a harder time, but certainly not impossible, in taking his or her turn as a thoroughly convincing advocate.

The skill set for leaders (see Figure 6.1) in the entrepreneurial worldview is the anchor or boss skills and the transitional skills of the star performer (Δ), tactician ($\boxtimes$) and, somewhat harder to acquire as it rests on the diagonal, the partner ($\bigcirc$). Not all bosses are star performers. The star's skills speak to the production capabilities of the buccaneer. They are a specific means of contributing to the buccaneer's goal of making a profit. High producers win. They make big dollars, euros or pounds sterling. This is especially true in end-results or commission-based payment systems. The star's pull within the buccaneer leader's story is toward the regulatory worldview. Buccaneers who produce within a game, and are duly rewarded for it, remain reluctant to change games. They become wedded to the measures and procedures which provide them with solid winnings. Tactical skills realign the buccaneer's game such that he or she attends to alternate investment opportunities. In the buccaneer leader's pull towards the network worldview the motive is to both trounce one's competition and win. The buccaneer with well-honed tactical skills looks ahead to the future. He or she attempts, within the entrepreneurial worldview, to think outside the box. Partnering skills are the hardest for the thoroughgoing buccaneer to develop and maintain since it means giving up control and reducing competition. The pull towards the cooperation pays story is acknowledged when the buccaneer needs resources badly and is willing, as a consequence, to enter into a co-leadership relationship. The thoroughgoing buccaneer will prefer a silent or compliant partner. The presence of a partner requires consultation, compromise and, within the tolerance of the thoroughgoing buccaneer, trust.

The skill set for leaders in the regulatory worldview (see Figure 6.1) is anchored in the monitor's skills ($\Delta\Delta$) and the transitional skills of the fire fighter ($\Delta\$$), evaluator ($\Delta\bigcirc$) and along the diagonal, the strategist ($\Delta\boxtimes$). Typically, monitoring skills entail carefully measuring and attending to the maintenance of a system so that it can be kept under control. Fire fighting skills are mobilized when the system must either run roughshod over or disregard the rules and procedures because of the vehemence or disruptive potential associated with a particular problem. The pull here is towards the entrepreneurial worldview. Fire fighting skills, like brief but useful bursts of adrenalin, enable a system to cope with large doses of uncertainty. The goal of the fire fighter, unlike the full-fledged boss in the entrepreneurial worldview, is to return the system to standard operating procedures. Evaluator's skills pull the analytically minded, objective bureaucrat toward interpreting the rules, measurements and routines so they will be intelligible to systems users. These skills are rooted in dialogue, developing relationships and establishing a culture of trust. The need to have performance evaluations and other measures accepted in the hierarchical system pulls the bureaucrat towards the cooperation pays story. Strategist skills address innovation. These are hard for the bureaucratic leader to develop. They are on the diagonal. Strategist skills do not lend themselves to uncertainty reduction. The bureaucratic leader interprets innovation as planned change. Within the regulatory worldview, this network pull stresses the future, the need to think outside the routines of the system, and the need to create alliances.

The skill set for participative leaders (see Figure 6.1) in the communitarian worldview is anchored in mentoring skills (○○) and the transitional skills of facilitators (○△), diplomats (○⊠) and, along the diagonal, advocates (○$). In their mentoring skills, participative leaders provide an anchor by embodying – in their walk and talk – the shared values of an open, trusting, dialogue-based community. The facilitator's skills stabilize the community. Facilitators reduce and channel conflict into constructive forms. They informally coordinate people and events and permit structures to become relaxed without losing a sense of reliability and/or trustworthiness. A diplomat's skills focus upon the community's interaction with those beyond its borders. Participative leaders must not only demonstrate the values of the community to members, they must symbolically project these so that those outside the community can enter into alliances or discover an interactive distance which works. Left on their own, communities over time can become insular and xenophobic. The diplomat's skills empower interdependent relationships and exchanges between and among varying communities. Advocates' skills are difficult for the mentor to develop. The advocate, as a representative of the entrepreneurial worldview in the participative leader's story, champions an idea or subculture within a larger community. Advocates politicize communities. They are activists. They believe that, when the community as a whole implements their ideas, it will be far better off. The advocate's idea of a "win" is to better the community, even if it requires running roughshod over others' views.

The skill set for knowledge leaders (see Figure 6.1) in the network worldview is anchored in the innovator's skills (⊠⊠) and in the transitional skills of the collaborator (⊠○), the deal maker (⊠$) and, along the diagonal, the navigator (⊠△). In developing skills as an innovator, the knowledge leader provides an anchor by initiating and sustaining the generative or creative processes which draw participants to the project-based cluster. The collaborator's skills, whether experienced face-to-face or virtually, enhance the sharing of ideas in the midst of competition and encourage participants to make tacit ideas explicit in the name of the project. Collaborators with their people skills build a sense of *esprit* in the midst of the blooming buzzing confusion that accompanies loosely structured networks. The deal maker's skills bring the bottom line profit motive and hustle required to raise money and attain resources for projects within highly competitive contexts. To succeed in bringing breakthroughs to market, networks need business acumen. The public needs to see or experience a product. It must be marketed, promoted and a demand created. The deal maker brings the entrepreneurial spirit to the network laboratory. The navigator's skills create order in the midst of the loosely structured, often temporary network – an order that works only if it does not impede or inhibit the creative process. Even in the midst of the creative process, stability is required. The navigator's skills are hard for innovators to develop.

In the holistic model, each of the four faces of capitalism – entrepreneurial, regulatory, communitarian and network worldviews – all signal a leader with a very different skill set. It is not necessary for two leaders in the same skill set to possess the same footprint or ratio of transitional skills to anchor skills within that worldview. Leaders who stay within the story recognize the archetype of the leader within their story, and then piece together a unique and personal skill set. In the next section I will turn to four skill sets: the buccaneer leader's skill set within the money talks story; the bureaucratic leader's in the built to last story; the participative leader's in the cooperation pays story; and the knowledge leader's in the portal to a new world story. Expanding upon these within story skills (small oval, Figure 6.1) serves two functions. It helps leaders who are confidently anchored within a leadership story to adapt their skills to pulls from other stories and, second, it serves as a platform for understanding how and why leaders reinvent themselves.

BUCCANEER LEADER'S SKILLS: MONEY TALKS

Those who seek to develop a footprint well established in the anchor skills of the boss and the transitional skills of the star performer, tactician and partner, will do well to recognize the conditions which reinforce the money talks story. Buccaneer leaders are selected in contexts in which the problem faced is relatively simple, in which resource scarcity is believed to prevail, substitutes are readily available to replace those who fail to survive in market contests and, lastly, where decisive end-results oriented action are sought and rewarded. The entrepreneurial worldview shades into other stories as the complexity of problems and the need for specialists rise. This is also true as conditions of munificence replace scarcity, long-term buy-in or planning replaces short-term actions, and regulation and safety replace risk-taking when the public loses faith in the creative destruction of markets. In the former conditions, the boss's skills rise to the fore. The anchor dominates the buccaneer leader's skill footprint. As the latter conditions emerge, transitional skills rise in usefulness within the buccaneer leader's skill set. These transitional skills adapt the money talks story to other pulls.

The boss's skills epitomize the struggle motif in the money talks story. Bosses walk the winners' walk (see Figure 6.2). Bosses act as if they were proprietors. They exude confidence. The boss is the consummate person in control. He or she gives clear orders and expects followers to do their bidding. The exchange relationship between followers and leaders is rooted in capital. This relationship takes priority over friendship and personal bonds. The statement, "this is nothing personal, it is just business" permeates the no nonsense relationship between bosses and followers. In the boss role one's private life is separated from one's public life. The boss unabashedly provides directions to followers. The purpose of the boss–follower relationship is to get results. The stronger the relationship, the greater the profits. The greater the profits, the more followers are drawn to the boss. The lion's share of the profits goes to the boss. The boss can disband the group of followers and seek others should he or she choose to create a new means of extracting rents with entirely new personnel. The boss is an agent for him or herself first and is therefore unabashedly self-interested. The embodiment of rugged individualism and survival comes to the forefront most clearly in the boss's skill portfolio. Bosses who fail to get results soon find themselves followers. This skill speaks to scarcity, market contests and getting to the bottom line as quickly as possible. The boss lives in and is aware of the "spread". This is the difference between how much it costs him or her to keep an employee or follower and their return to the firm. The higher the spread, the more valuable the follower.

Bosses' skills begin to accommodate the regulatory worldview as their skills shade from the director of action to the leader as the competent doer of action, or star performer.[8] The more the boss is immersed in doing rather than overseeing the task, the more likely the boss shades into the star performer. The star is deferred to by followers as a top performer in a competitive task. When the boss is an overseer, the star is a valuable employee with a substantial spread. When the boss is the doer, the boss becomes a star. The star performer gains control as followers defer to his or her expertise at the task. They acknowledge the superior monetary rewards to be achieved by working for or submitting to the star. The star's skills stress execution, setting priorities and working with others (see Figure 6.2). The pull towards the regulatory world is clear. The star knows what routines and practices work best. While not eager to share ideas, thereby aiding followers in possibly dethroning him or her, the star is concerned with developing best practices

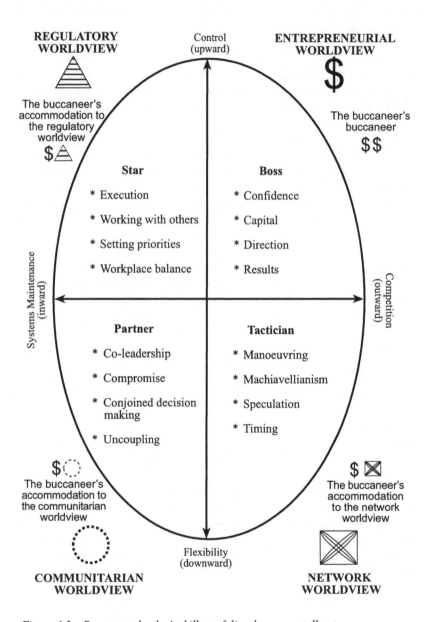

Figure 6.2   Buccaneer leader's skill portfolio: the money talks story

and establishing routines that can bolster productivity.

While the boss can easily jettison a mechanism for rent extraction in pursuit of a more profitable one at less risk, the star has vested interests in staying in the game in which his or her skills are so amply rewarded. This pull toward systems maintenance within the buccaneer's story does not negate the star's relentless and driven desire to increase profits by improving productivity. Ageing is problematic for the star. As he or she ages, there is a tremendous pressure to keep producing as younger followers begin to come into their own. The burnout rate for stars is high. Theirs is a skill set in which, as one ages, the call to workplace balance becomes increasingly problematic. Interestingly, as we shall see in the next chapter, ageing stars often make the transition of the buccaneer's skill set into the fire fighter's in the built to last story. When the pay for this transition is lucrative and met with the option of a handsome pension, the ageing star may be motivated.

In enlarging his or her tactical skills, the buccaneer leader with a dominant footprint in the bosses' skills turns to think outside the box, looks at options, and begins to manoeuvre (see Figure 6.2).[9] Tactical skills are the buccaneer's accommodation to the network worldview. Rather than stay within the rent extraction game embedded in a given set of competitors and a known industrial configuration or setting, the tactician seeks greater wins. He or she is willing to increase risk, speculate and embrace bold change. Timing is central in this skill set. The buccaneer with tactician's skills is interested in moving early into a lucrative field, often by joining with others. Yet in true buccaneer fashion, the collaboration sought is quite Machiavellian and it requires excellent timing. The tactician seeks to maximize inputs from the network by joining the network early and using this entry status as a means of getting more from the network than he or she returns to it. Exchanges early on have initial members receiving information from later arrivals; later exchanges usually see the tactician exiting the network before reciprocation is necessary. The buccaneer with tactician's skills can make the transition to the deal maker in the network worldview. The tactician focuses on repositioning the buccaneer's game, the deal maker raises capital and tends to the business side of the network.

Partnering skills emerge when bosses in search of capital or contacts take an equal.[10] Co-leadership is a great compromise for a control-oriented boss or even a boss who has developed his or her star skills. Buccaneer leaders do not view compromise as winning. The buccaneer typically has great difficulty developing partnering skills. There is another in the game with whom one must consult and enter into dialogue (see Figure 6.2). This slows down one's ability to "just do it". Partnering skills are the buccaneer's reluctant accommodation to the communitarian regime. This pull increases, not only when the leader seeks capital or connection to bolster profits, but when the buccaneer begins to recognize the complexity of problems at hand and now requires diverse inputs. Most buccaneers merely flirt with partnering skills. These are, after all, rugged individuals whose view of the good world is one free of encumbrances. Reciprocity exchanges, while acknowledged, are seen as binding convention. Buccaneers typically recognize that they are in over their heads in terms of problem complexity when profits sag. They then sell or exit. Indeed, as soon as resources are plentiful, buccaneers typically seek the opportunity to uncouple from or dump partners and either move up or return to their anchor in the "I'm boss here" view. When buccaneers do take to partnering skills, they frequently start trying to modify the boss's skill in search of respect, purpose and meaning. The boss who late in life turns to philanthropy, establishes foundations and turns to community service, is, as we shall discuss in the next chapter, a prime (albeit rare) candidate for a gradient two anchor cross-story transition (ACTs). While the buccaneer with a strong sense of community giving is rare, it is not at all impossible.

For those interested in employing insights from the contextual approach to leadership to developing buccaneer leaders' skills, it is vital to remember that one never leaves the money talks story. This is the story where all skills yield clear monetary rewards to the skill wielder. The game is clear. It is action oriented. Only end results count. The boss is the consummate symbol of the winner. The star embodies the grace and ability of super performers – those who set the pace and establish the mould for others to follow. The partner speaks to the wise conciliatory buccaneer who can lead while heeding the counsel of others and attending to views other than his or her own. The tactician is the restless buccaneer always seeking to reposition the game and move to the frontier where the winnings are even greater and the competition has yet to assemble. The chant in all the skills is a resounding "win, baby, win". These are aggressive skills courted by ambitious men and women who will do what they have to do to win and move on. In this story it is leaders who win and, when time and/or money are scarce, who better to turn to than the skilled, self-made buccaneer.

BUREAUCRATIC LEADER'S SKILLS: BUILT TO LAST

Bureaucratic leaders, unlike buccaneer leaders, are not self-made. They are either credentialled or can provide proof of their ability to satisfy the criteria embedded in pre-established job descriptions. The anchor skills of the monitor and the transitional skills of the evaluator, fire fighter and, on the diagonal, strategist, all address concerted efforts to maintain stable hierarchical systems. The skills which flourish in the built to last story come into their own as competition is driven inward, requiring that individuals compete for positions within levels of a hierarchy. Resources are plentiful and individuals in systems are confronted by complex and recurring problems with which they or their predecessors have had a history of efforts at managing. In the bureaucratic leader's skill set, prudence, patience and reliability trump speed, explanation or dialogue-based learning. The bureau-cratic leader adheres to precedent, is an agent for others in the system and must, as a consequence, be able to justify his or her decisions to those for whom he or she serves as an agent. The regulatory worldview shades into other stories when the rules of the system must be altered swiftly, human emotion and values must be brought into the system to achieve buy-in, and out of the box theory is required to aid problem-solving and reconfigure set routines within the hierarchial system.

The monitor's skills (see Figure 6.3) epitomize the uncertainty reduction motive at the heart of the built to last story. The monitor establishes, reinforces and oversees the routines and policies that go into the ongoing standard operating procedures of the hierarchical systems. Monitors assure that the standard operating procedures at the core of the system are not only protected but are sufficiently resilient to withstand the test of time. Monitors ensure that the information that is used to make prudent, rational decisions governing the system is reliable. Unlike the money talks story, action is pushed down; decision making and careful attention to data and information are elevated. The monitor attends to the vast amount of information retained by the system and lends relevance to it by setting priorities and policies, and placing certain issues on the system's agenda while removing others. The monitor determines what is measured in the built to last story. What is measured is taken seriously and it is understood as the means of maintaining order, achieving stability and enhancing the durability of the system.

The evaluator's skills take the anchor skills of the monitor in the built to last story towards the cooperation pays story.[11] Evaluators interpret measurements. They put the rules into practice and evaluate the data generated by those who work in the system. While monitors' skills are cerebral in nature (weighing options and embedding policies and procedures into public documents) evaluators bring them into practice. Evaluators put abstract rules and policies into practice so that those who occupy positions within the system can understand how their efforts are coordinated. The built to last story is one which neither empowers nor enables subordinates to employ discretion in the interpretation of the rules and measurements used within the system. Evaluators strive to get those who put policies and procedures into practice to internalize these in the manner intended by monitors. Evaluators align policies and procedures with practice so that, over time, error and deviation are reduced. In effect, those who make their numbers are, in time, promoted; those who consistently fail to do so are evaluated negatively and

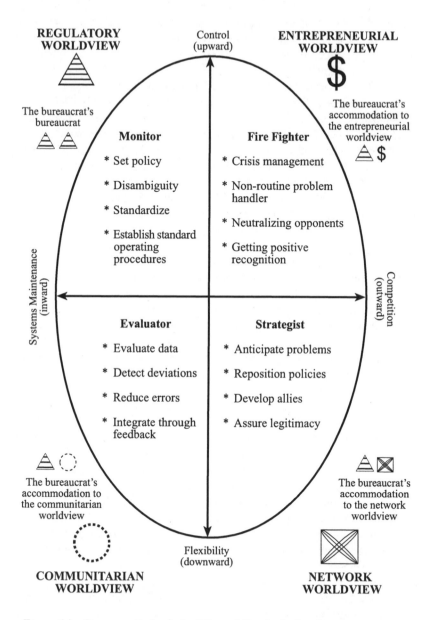

Figure 6.3   Bureaucratic leader's skill portfolio: the built to last story

left to languish at the same level within the hierarchical system until they see the light of day. Evaluators stay within the built to last story and do not cross over into facilitators' skills in the cooperation pays story because they are preoccupied with reducing error noise and surprise in the system and not with empowering members.

The skills of the fire fighter (see Figure 6.3) pull the built to last story toward the entrepreneurial worldview.[12] These skills speak the language of the results-oriented crisis manager or turnaround artist working within a system concerned with returning as soon as possible to stability and reliability. The fire fighter's skills heat up when the system must either flaunt or disregard its own rules in order to swiftly and expeditiously cope with either pressing and pervasive threats or alluring but demanding opportunities. Fire fighters' strengths rest in deliberate action. They take the reins when careful decision-making procedures are insufficient to assure the perpetuation of the system. If one imagines a complex, hierarchical system which cannot be directly monitored and requires a panel board or a series of lights to indicate and measure the state of problems and issues for the system to deal with, then, when a routine problem lights up, the monitor turns to the evaluator. The evaluator's task is to get the lights turned off or the problem measures reduced. When, however, the panel board lights up with "emergency", the monitor turns to the fire fighter. Fire fighters specialize in non-routine matters. Rather than thinking outside the box (see strategist's skills below), they cut swiftly and directly to the heart of the matter. They neutralize opponents, chop out dead wood, cut through red tape, reduce budgets and downsize. They are, metaphorically speaking, licensed to work outside the standard operating procedures of the system and to do all that they can to return the system to stability. They are in, and work for, the system. They do not seek to capitalize upon the emergency and, as the star performer would in the money talks story, make it the centre of a lucrative rent extraction game.

Within the built to last story, the strategist (see Figure 6.3) seeks to reposition the system or reconfigure its policies in order to cope with future exigencies.[13] The strategist's skills push the envelope within a worldview that privileges the past. This is a hard skill for the bureaucratic leader to cultivate. The strategist employs data from and of the past to build models, scenarios and contingencies which are intended to prepare the system for new options and alternatives. Within the tradition-based built to last story, the strategist points to the need to redesign, re-engineer or reconfigure structures in a system that rewards certainty and stability and honours tradition. In my experience, within the skill set of bureaucratic leaders, strategists push the envelope within the rules and data preferences of the system. In this sense, the strategist mobilizes data to build models, plan scenarios and mobilize contingent policies. The aim is to prepare the system for new options and viable alternatives. While the pull towards the network worldview is evident – ask the "what if" question, think outside the box, develop allies – the talk is typically of systems redesign, re-engineering or repositioning. Strategists' talk of change is heard when it is framed as moving the system towards greater long-term stability; it is heard as shrill and foreign when pitched as revolutionary, innovative and leading edge. This, as we shall discuss in the next chapter, is the domain of the navigator, the knowledge leader's accommodation to the regulatory worldview.

The skill portfolio of the bureaucratic leader in the built to last story turns the egoism of the self-interested leader so prevalent in the money talks story into a matter of duty and a demonstration of loyalty to the system. The monitor anchors the hierarchical system. Monitors must follow the rules for changing rules. He or she is entrusted with overseeing and updating the policies, procedures and routines that rest at the core of the system. The leader's aim is to protect the core routines, policies and procedures and therein reduce uncertainty. The system requires ongoing tuning by the evaluator. The evaluator aligns the standard operating procedures (formal rules) with those in practice (rules in use). Evaluators' skills bring the human equation into the cool lattice of objective reasoning preferred by the analytically minded monitor. When the system receives an unexpected jolt or whack on the side of the head, the fire fighters' skills are mobilized. Fire fighters are crisis managers who, in the midst of emergency, often run roughshod, albeit for a short time, over the system's rules and procedures. The job is to return the system to order as quickly as possible. The strategist's skills come to the fore when the system and those at the top seek to prepare it for long-term, planned change. In the bureaucratic skill set, the aim is to reduce error, uncertainty and noise. Leaders are disciplined. They show an allegiance to the system. The ideal leader is a rational decision maker who works within the constraints of the system and, over time, helps to routinize or tame complex persistent problems. In the tradition of the classics, the bureaucratic leader succeeds when he or she is perceived to have contributed to a system that withstands the test of time.

PARTICIPATIVE LEADER'S SKILLS: COOPERATION PAYS

Those seeking to develop a footprint well established in the anchor skill of the mentor, the transitional skills of the facilitator, the diplomat and, along the diagonal, advocate, would do well to attend to the conditions which reinforce their story. The cooperation pays story flourishes when competition is reduced and control gives way to flexibility. These occurrences are likely with an increased perception of the importance of change and complexity. The cooperation pays story downgrades top-down autocratic leadership in preference to leaders who empower members, seek diverse inputs, and build a culture of trust. In the communitarian worldview, there are often several acceptable solutions to a problem or issue. The test of leadership is how inclusive, participative and dialogue-based processes are employed to arrive at these results. Action, the preoccupation of leaders in the money talks story, gives way to compassion. Compassion in leadership practice binds members into a cohesive yet open, trusting community.[14] These adaptive communities rise to the challenge of change by developing a high involvement culture which fosters dialogue and nurtures learning. In the midst of the open learning culture, objectivity and analytic models, so prevalent in the built to last story, give way to the quest for authenticity, meaning and ethical and/or spiritual development.

The idealism in the cooperation pays story is pragmatically anchored in the skills of the participative leader as mentor (see Figure 6.4). The mentor embodies or gives human form to the values of the community and therein serves as a guide, counsellor and socializing agent for those seeking membership. The mentor exemplifies the values of the culture to veteran members and, as a conduit or fusion point, brings the best of the values of new members into contact with those of long-standing members. The culture at the heart of the mentoring process is dynamic or flexible yet stabilizes in a particular set of shared values. Over the generations, mentors meld the new with the old. Mentors are change agents who subtly help a community adapt over time by providing it with a culture that empowers learners. Mentors require a large dollop of self-knowledge in order to acknowledge their limits as leaders. This enables others to carry on. Mentors share leadership. They excel in getting others to realize their leadership potential. In preparing the next generation, the mentor explicitly grapples with the ephemeral nature of leadership and how very good leaders prepare others to take on the calling of the leader.

The facilitator's skills grow within the cooperation pays story when the community becomes more complex, formal and rule bound.[15] In a community which is growing rapidly, some members are strangers to one another. They must be introduced. The facilitator is a trust-builder. The task of the facilitator is to put people at ease and establish that the community is a safe place in which a person can speak from the heart without fear of recrimination. Facilitators' skills, unlike mentors', are largely invisible. The facilitator succeeds when others feel that it is they who have done the hard work of creating an orderly, healthy community. Order is achieved, unlike that in the built to last story, with a minimum of formal structure and rules. This

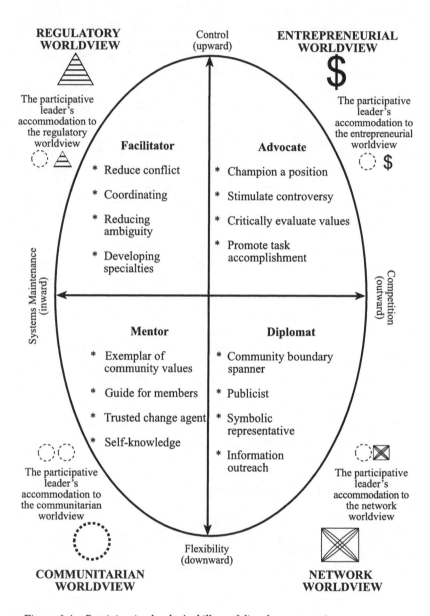

Figure 6.4   Participative leader's skill portfolio: the cooperation pays story

informal order, aided and abetted by a capable facilitator, generates civility, and appreciation of civility leads to the development of committed teams. To build order, the facilitator reduces conflict. Teams flourish when facilitators leaning upon appreciative inquiry and mediation encourage feedback, group support and nurturing of others. To foster involvement, team members are empowered, provided with autonomy and given the discretion to set their own challenges. To capitalize upon the synergies of enthusiastic teams, the facilitator presents the community as a shared destiny in which, as the whole develops and becomes enriched, so too do all the parts. Facilitators coordinate tasks informally, trying to help the community educate its specialists but not encourage them to claim expertise and then talk down to others.

Diplomatic skills arise when communities seek to interact with other communities who do not share their values (see Figure 6.4).[16] Diversity within a community and multiculturalism or pluralism among communities express the participative leader's keen recognition that no healthy community is an island. The diplomat conveys a sense of the community and its values to outsiders. The diplomat must think outside the box and be sensitive to other cultures' stereotypes and blind spots. The diplomat is a cultural boundary spanner or symbolic representative of one community to others. He or she brings images of other cultures to the focal culture and, likewise, images of the focal culture to others. Like all boundary spanners, there are dangers here. He or she may be seen as too involved with outsiders to be fully accepted at home, and far too foreign to be accepted as anyone but a visitor by outsiders. In this shifting space between and among cultures, the diplomat's skills flourish. The diplomat is a publicist for the focal community; he or she seeks information to determine whether other communities have the potential to become allies, enemies or neutrals, and under what conditions each is possible. The diplomat is not an innovator but a bridge builder, developing an alliance that reaches from deep inside a community to those outside it in order to serve both the focal community and the ideals of diversity and multiculturalism.

Advocacy skills are difficult for most participative leaders to fully develop (see Figure 6.4).[17] These skills exist on the diagonal with the anchor skill of mentoring. Advocacy skills flourish as communities become political and certain subcultures give rise to leaders who take a position at odds with others in the community. Advocacy skills challenge the compassion and harmony producing skills of the mentor. Neither the facilitator's nor the diplomat's skills are eager to ally with the advocate's. As advocates thrive within a community, controversy rises. The facilitator's efforts to reduce conflict and attain stability are challenged. The diplomat's ability to symbolically represent the values of a community does not become easier as activists seek to push their ideas to the forefront. Advocates are action-oriented champions who take strong positions in the community. They sincerely believe that the position which they hold, if enacted, will greatly benefit the community as a whole. They are community-minded activists who seek to win. The advocate's skills are the participative leader's accommodation to the entrepreneurial worldview. The advocate, unlike the mentor, does not try particularly hard to hear all sides of a discussion or dialogue. Rather, they use persuasive skills to get their position recognized. In their view, positions compete and it is the job of competent leaders to make sure that winning positions are implemented. Advocates have far less tolerance for the "let a thousand flowers bloom" position of the mentor. Those outside the community are often confused when they perceive open debate passing for dialogue within the cooperation pays story. Insiders, however, are tolerant of advocates as long as they do not actually silence others' positions and agree to submit theirs, even though boldly or forcefully presented, to the scrutiny of the community as a whole.

It is a credo of the cooperation pays story that we learn to collectively adapt as we embrace the other. In proximity we shed our fears and anxiety and discover a safe place from which to grow. The participative leaders walk a disciplined line. On the one hand they foster and nurture a safe place; on the other they must remain vigilant against complacency, conformity and groupthink. Keen-eyed mentors recognize that the shared values of the community must be put into practice. Dialogue is not just talk – it is committed talk. The facilitator's skills ensure that conflict in the community is constructive and that consensus is not a form of compliance. The diplomat's skills are attenuated when the community escalates relations with other communities. The diplomat symbolically and concisely embodies the values of the community to outsiders. The advocate's skills come to the fore in the midst of controversy. Community members who openly disagree with others have faith that the community can and will select wisely among or between contesting positions. It is this faith in the wisdom of the everyday member of the community that is the great leveller in the cooperation pays story. The leader in this story is neither above nor pushes the community toward new vistas; leaders must possess and be perceived as possessing the integrity of the trusted other.

KNOWLEDGE LEADER'S SKILLS: PORTAL TO A NEW WORLD

Knowledge leaders push networks or temporary clusters of communities toward new vistas. Networks are loose coalitions of best minds brought together for relatively short time periods to create breakthroughs. Knowledge leaders are visionaries and prophets. The anchor skills of the innovator and the transitional skills of the collaborator, the deal maker and along the diagonal the navigator, all address concerted efforts to push boundaries, heighten creativity and generate new products, ideas and/or techniques. The skills which flourish in the portal to a new world story come into their own when there is sufficient optimism about the future. This optimism is expressed when people are willing to invest time, money and energy in outcomes and/or processes which have yet to be clearly mapped. As well, there needs to be a credible means to protect intellectual property and a pool of knowledge workers or creatives interested in working on speculative projects. In the portal to a new world story, improvisation, creativity and the ability to diffuse innovations trump instant profits, stability and meaningful membership in a community. The knowledge leader employs exploratory rationality to convey the possibility of a new, synthetic or designed future in which human burdens will diminish. The anchor skill in the network worldview innovating shades into other stories when emotional intelligence is required to facilitate sharing. In the midst of competitive, temporary coalitions, greater structure is required to coordinate events and schedule in an *ad hoc* or *laissez-faire* culture and capital is required to kick-start, maintain and/or disseminate the results of network productivity.

The innovator's skills[18] anchor and epitomize the leading edge or mind-stretching originality of those who seek to lead in the portal to a new world story (see Figure 6.5). The innovator acts like a magnet drawing participants to the edge of knowledge within a problem field. He or she convinces creatives and knowledge workers that, with their contribution to the project, a breakthrough is imminent. These are uncharted waters. Those drawn to the network soon realize that the innovator's solution is actually not imminent at all, but requires ongoing development. There is little to copy in this process. The innovator must improvise. The creative process is cross-disciplinary; it values originality, exploration, invention and serendipity. The innovator creates a momentum in which best minds are drawn together in search of intellectual capital. As the project develops and alters its focus, knowledge becomes obsolete and participants formerly in the limelight find their contracts lapsing. The goal is clear. The innovator is in search of intellectual capital. To assure participants that this intellectual capital will not be pirated by others, the innovator must not only push towards discovery or invention, but do so in a manner in which competitors will be unable to easily imitate the results and waltz off with the prize.

Collaborators' skills shade into the innovators' when either the knowledge workers or creatives become disgruntled with the lack of progress in the network or feel that there are inequities or injustices in it.[19] The collaborator is the team builder in the network worldview. This is much more difficult than team building in the communitarian worldview. In project-based

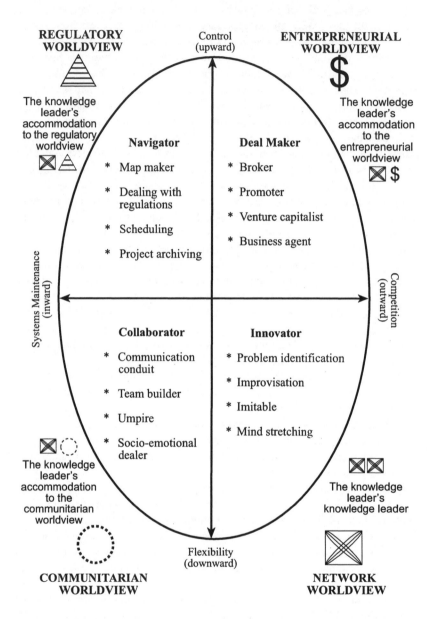

Figure 6.5   Knowledge leader's skill portfolio: the portal to a new world story

networks, the pursuit of creativity requires idea sharing, but this must proceed in the midst of temporary or short-term contracts, frequent shortages in capital, ongoing competition, and often pervasive yet credible rumours of downsizing. The collaborator's skills are those of the socio-emotional leader – hearing out problems, attending to wounded egos and reinforcing the benefits to be accrued from heightened commitment to the team. Collaborators act like umpires or referees, helping to deal with disputes between and among participants in a network. While conflict is not frowned upon as it is in the communitarian worldview, it requires direction. Conflict and tension which stimulate independence of thought and fortify the willingness to challenge others' ideas are encouraged; conflict which results in the silencing of other creatives is to be thwarted. The complexity of teams within projects and within networks, all loosely held together by lapsing contracts and/or multiple network involvements, stimulates the very uncertainty which gives rise to creativity. However, this combination of complexity and lack of structure makes it exceedingly difficult to get information from one part of the network to another. The collaborator uses the informal culture around the water cooler and the grapevine within the network to make sure that ideas originating in one part of the network and useful elsewhere get disseminated.

Deal makers' skills rise in importance within the skill set of the knowledge leader as the network seeks resources to sustain itself and disseminate its innovations in the marketplace.[20] Deal makers' skills (see Figure 6.5) represent the knowledge leader's accommodation to the entrepreneurial worldview. Deal makers promote the network. They work as venture capitalists in the early stages. They raise interest and draw attention to the potential being put together by knowledge leaders. Deal makers create the stir surrounding a potential innovation. They act as business agents representing the network to investors and intermediaries and then they secure resources – personnel, financial capital, goodwill and sponsors. While the innovators push creativity and seek to stretch the minds of participants, the deal makers push the project into the market. The deal maker is interested in the bottom-line results of innovation. The deal maker is not interested in whether or not the innovation is perfect in the engineering sense, but whether it is likely to capture the market and yield hefty returns. Deal makers bring sales prowess and market savvy to the network. Not only do they help sell the network to investors, but they help sell the end results of the innovative process to potential buyers.

The navigator's skills within the skill portfolio of the knowledge leader focus upon a concerted attempt to employ a more formal means to accomplish order and knowledge transfer within the amoeba-like conditions of the typical creative network.[21] These skills are difficult for the innovator to develop. The navigator's skills pull on the diagonal toward the regulatory worldview (see Figure 6.5). Navigators' skills call for a curtailing of creativity in the pursuit of order. These skills grow as do both the degree of interdependence between and among projects and the need to make sure that the person with the right knowledge gets to the appropriate project at the correct time. Navigators are creative map makers. They deftly sketch and resketch the altering configurations of teams within projects and within networks. These provisional maps are short-lived but serve a function similar to that of the organizational chart in the much more stable regulatory worldview. The navigator has none of the definitive measures or quantitative and repetitive inputs of the monitor but, relying upon his or her creative skills, the navigator uses surrogate measures – estimates, assessments and educated guesses – to piece together a sense of order when, in fact, so much is in flux. This sense of order enhances the knowledge leader's ability to schedule, draw up and enforce contracts, attend to budgetary matters, archive relevant project material and deal with both intermediaries and investors. Without this approximation of order, few outside the network worldview would be willing to get involved in the network.

The skill set of the knowledge leader is at home in the initiation, development and consummation of exploratory processes. This is a visionary quest for originality and generativity. The network is a loose constellation of participants drawn by diverse motives to the dream of the innovator. The anchor skills of the knowledge leader require the ability to establish credibility as a magnet drawing the best minds at the edge of a knowledge field and, at the same time, possess the skill of improvising in the midst of a process that is rife with unpredictable occurrences. The development and sustaining of the creative process in the network draws upon the skills of the collaborator. The collaborator's skills direct competition and conflict towards creative engagements, empower teams and enhance idea sharing among participants. The navigator's skills create a provisional order in the buzzing, blooming confusion of a multiplicity of simultaneously occurring projects within a typical network. The navigator's skills enhance the leader's ability to plan, schedule and budget in the midst of ongoing change. The deal maker's skills bring the bottom-line problems of rent extraction, financing and returning a profit to the fore. The skill set of the knowledge leader remains within the portal to a new world story. Success entails mobilizing and then owing intellectual capital.

Whether we focus our attention upon the knowledge, bureaucrat, participative or buccaneer leader, developing local leadership skills requires that the leader understands how to learn. In the four faces of capitalism learning is situated.[22] Leaders learn skills that provide solutions to the problems they face. Learning is more probable and takes place more easily when two types of compatibility occur. First, learning is more probable when the new skill or practice sought is built upon the leader's existing skill set, and second, that the new skills sought are compatible with the leader's story. Let us close this chapter with a discussion of how the contextual model of leadership provides leaders with a systematic means of developing reach and acquiring new skills.

LEARNING NEW SKILLS

In this chapter I have been concerned with how, and to a lesser degree why, leaders who remain in the same story acquire new skills. On the whole, I have been very disappointed in the way this topic is typically handled in the literature on leadership. Without a contextual approach, the within-story skill acquisition of various leaders has been treated very differently in each worldview. Worse, the anchor cross-story transitions (ACTs) or instances of leadership reinventions are portrayed as the outcome of a magic skill possessed by leaders. They can, like a chameleon on a Persian rug, alter their colours to successfully meet the demands of a changing environment. In this discussion I will first examine how the contextual model of leadership creates a unified view of how, and to a lesser degree, why leaders learn new skills within a leadership story. In conclusion, I address how the four faces of capitalism provide students and researchers in leadership studies with a systematic means of explaining and/or assisting leaders in reinventing themselves.

Without a contextual approach, the acquisition of new skills by leaders is usually explained within the basic premises of a particular worldview. Thus participative leaders or scholars whose work is lodged in the communitarian worldview explain how the leader learns new skills by placing this leader in the community. As the community develops new values or alters its existing norms, the leader who is an embodiment of the values and practices of the community must adapt. The participative leader is conceptualized as a dynamic force. He or she both influences the community as a function of his or her role as leader and is influenced by the community. The participative leader in this explanation is descriptively attuned to the participative leader's mentoring skills and these alone. Participative leaders who develop advocacy skills are portrayed as violating the conditions under which leadership learning should occur. While the skills of the facilitator and diplomat are admitted into the skill portfolio of the participative leader they are not developed as jumping-off points to enable the participative leader to cross leadership story lines and reinvent them.

Similar to the participative leader, a knowledge leader is portrayed as learning new skills by enlarging his or her capacity to innovate. The bureaucratic leader increases his or her ability to monitor and the buccaneer strives to effectively direct or alleviate his or her boss's skills. Without the contextualist model, worldviews do not systematically influence one another. Each is treated as a self-sufficient story. I experience this in my discussions and teaching with executives in an MBA leadership education programme. The mid-life students in this programme ask me why the entrepreneurial worldview, and within it the buccaneer leader, is highlighted in their course in finance. In their organizational behaviour or human resource management course, the participative leader is praised and put on a pedestal. Likewise, the bureaucratic leader as decision maker in their strategic management course and the network worldview in their courses on knowledge management. Their point, as I have learned to appreciate it, is not one which rails at the fact that different skills are useful in putting together a skill portfolio, but rather that each claims to be most important.

In the contextual model, the plasticity of leaders is not treated as infinite. The model begins with the leader understanding the four worldviews, tied to the four functional requisites (upwards/downwards/inside/outside) that allow us to make sense of instrumental behaviour. Then the leaders with some experience in leadership must work on understanding their preferred leadership story and their footprint, at any one point in time in the four faces of capitalism. Practice begins when leaders move from the theory of worldview comprehension – a series of rational sense-making assumptions that can be taught in the classroom – to the acquisition of skills. In the contextual model one learns skills in practice. Moreover, new skills are not acquired randomly. They build upon skills which share the same pulls in the four faces of capitalism. We build upon the scaffolding of already acquired skills to deal with problems and issues that are in use. We learn poorly when we attempt to acquire skills that do not build upon our existing abilities or which deeply violate our sense of what is to be valued in our leadership story. What is important is what can be learned and applied by a practising leader in the context as they understand it.

In the next chapter I lean heavily upon the work I have done with 24 executives and leaders in different countries and from very different occupations – architect, city planner, financial analyst, master chef, ship's captain, and so on – who were selected because six of each strongly identified with one of the four faces of capitalism. With this group I worked to find out how practising leaders, using the four faces of capitalism, felt that they customized their stories, acquired new skills and over time transitioned from one worldview to others. The act of leadership reinvention explains how practising cosmopolitan leaders, all of whom had over 20 years in their leadership roles, create ACTs (anchor cross-story transitions). In the four faces of capitalism ACTs address paths of skill development wherein leaders self-consciously move from one anchor skill, for example the boss in the buccaneer leader's story, to the innovator in the knowledge leader's. Let us turn to skill acquisition in the act of leaders reinventing themselves. In the four faces of capitalism this is not treated as a magical skill possessed solely by master leaders with special talents, but as a systematic quest for leadership reach. It requires hard work, attention to detail, and patience.

NOTES

1. Bill McLaughlin is former President and CEO of Frito Lay Europe. The quote opening this chapter is found in an interview with John R. Childress (2000), *A Time for Leadership: Global Perspectives From an Accelerated European Market Place*, Los Angeles: Leadership Press.
2. Michael Zwell (2000), *Creating a Culture of Competence*, New York: Wiley, discusses the analytical shift required to move from story-based models to skill discussion of practical leaders. Robert E. Quinn, Sue R. Faerman, Michael P. Thompson and Michael R. McGrath (2003), *Becoming a Master Manager: A Competency Framework*, New York: Wiley, provide a model of leadership competence that informs and provides structure to the four faces of capitalism. Robert E. Kaplan and Robert B. Kaiser (2003), "Developing versatile leadership," *Sloan Management Review*, **44**(4), pp. 19–27, develop the "leadership versatility index" which probes both the competency of leaders and how they can develop reach, balance and accommodation of other leaders' stories. For a more scholarly treatment of the versatility index, see R.E. Kaplan and R.B. Kaiser (2003), "Rethinking a classic distinction in leadership: Implications for the assessment and development of executives," *Consulting Psychology Journal: Research and Practice*, **55**(1), pp. 15–25.
3. Terrence L. Gargiulo (2002), *Making Stories: A Practical Guide for Organizational Leaders and Human Resource Specialists*, Westport, CT: Quorum, explores how to move from stories about leadership to developing skills. In a less theoretical fashion, Dennis Carey and Marie-Caroline Von Weichs (2003), *How to Run a Company: Lessons from Top Leaders of the CEO Academy*, New York: Crown Business, get leading edge CEOs to discuss how they move from theory to practice in their leadership development and solution of specific problems.
4. For illuminating discussions of the boss's anchor skill in the money talks story, see David M. Dealy and Andrew R. Thomas (2004), *Defining the Really Great Boss*, Westport, CT: Praeger. Abraham L. Gitlow (1992), *Being the Boss: The Importance of Leadership and Power*, Homewood, IL: Business One Irwin, captures the role of power and the context in which it is most useful to aspiring leaders. Deborrah Himsel (2004), *Leadership Sopranos Style: How to Become a More Effective Boss*, Chicago, IL: Dearborn Trades Publishing, employs Tony Soprano, the fictional Mafia boss in the US television show "The Sopranos" to illustrate the effective traits of the boss as leader.
5. Patricia C. Pitcher (1997), *Artists, Craftsmen and Technocrats: The Dreams, Realities, and Illusions of Leadership*, 2nd edn, Toronto: Stoddart, captures monitoring skills in her robust depiction of the leader as a technocrat. Malcolm A. Birkin (2000), *Building the Integrated Company*, Aldershot, Hampshire: Gower, looks at how leaders develop coordinated systems, particularly in the context of complex international business and systems. Danny Samson and David Challis (1999), *Patterns of Excellence: The New Principles of Corporate Success*, London: Financial Times Management, focus on the need for those in hierarchical systems to develop the skills of loyal agents – measurement, decision making, planning, prioritizing and the like.
6. Brad W. Johnson and Charles R. Ridley (2004), *The Elements of Mentoring*, New York:

Palgrave Macmillan, explore what excellent leaders do to mentor. The community-building and dialogue aspects of the leader as mentor are depicted by Patricia J. Fritts (1998), *The New Managerial Mentor: Becoming a Leader to Build Communities of Purpose*, Palo Alto, CA: Davies-Black.

7. Tim Jones (2002), *Innovating at the Edge: How Organizations Evolve and Embed Innovation Capability*, Oxford: Butterworth-Heinemann, looks at innovations at Dyson, Smint, eBay, Google, Bluetooth and others to make sense of the skills innovators use in practice. John E. Tropman (1999), *The Management of Ideas in the Creating Organization*, Westport, CT: Quorum, explores what he terms the five Cs of idea-leadership and idea-management.

8. Sunny Stout Rostrun (2002), *Accelerating Performance: Powerful Techniques to Develop People*, London: Kogan Page, provides an intellectually rigorous account of how to think like a star performer in developing a skill portfolio for productive leaders. Larry Bossidy and Ram Charon (2002), *Execution: The Discipline of Getting Things Done*, New York: Crown Business, speak to the leader as producer in their notion of execution. I believe Charles Cox and Gary L. Cooper (1988), *High Flyers: An Anatomy of Managerial Success*, Oxford: Basil Blackwell, successfully portray the complex inner life of the leader as producer.

9. The "outside the box thinking" that is grounded in a tactical notion of sense-and-respond is described effectively by Stephan H. Haeckel (1999), *Adaptive Enterprise: Creating a Leading Sense-and-Respond Organization*, Cambridge, MA: Harvard Business School Press. William G. Forgang (2004), *Strategy-Specific Decision Making: A Guide for Executing Competitive Strategy*, Armonk, NY: M.E. Sharpe, focuses on the short-term specific decisions required of the buccaneer leader with tactical skills.

10. Yves L. Doz and Gary Hamel (1998), *Alliance Advantage: The Art of Creating Value Through Partnering*, Cambridge, MA: Harvard Business School Press, make the argument for partnering. Marvin Snider (2003), *Compatibility Breeds Success: How to Manage Your Relationship With Your Business Partner*, Westport, CT: Praeger, and Anne Deering (2003), *The Partnering Impact: Making Business Partnerships Work*, New York: John Wiley, both focus on how to successfully develop skills as a partner in competitive contexts.

11. Danny G. Langdon (2000), *Aligning Performance: Improving People, Systems and Organizations*, San Francisco: Jossey-Bass, gets at the skills of the evaluator in the regulatory worldview. David Wade and Ronald Recardo (2001), *Corporate Performance Management: How to Build a Better Organization Through Measurement-Driven Strategic Alignment*, Boston, MA: Butterworth-Heinemann, treat the process architecture skills of the evaluator as a mainstay in creating, implementing and measuring routines on complex systems.

12. J. Chris Skinner and Gary Mersham (2002), *Disaster Management: A Guide to Issues Management and Crisis Communication*, Oxford: Oxford University Press, address the skills of the fire fighter in the corporate setting. John Laye (2002), *Avoiding Disaster: How to Keep Your Business Going When Catastrophe Strikes*, New York: John Wiley, and Rene A. Henry (2000), *You'd Better Have a Hose If You Want to Put Out the Fire: The Complete Guide to Crisis and Risk Communications: Professional Tips, Tactics, Dos, Don'ts and Case Histories*, Windsor, CA: Gollywobbler Productions, deal with the how-to of fire fighting.

13. Richard A. D'Aveni, Robert Gunther and Joni Cole (2001), *Strategic Supremacy: How Industry Leaders Create Growth, Wealth and Power Through Spheres of Influence*, New York: Free Press, focus on the need for bureaucratic leaders to rethink their routines. Stephen G. Haines (2000), *The Systems Thinking Approach to Strategic Planning and Management*, Boca Raton, FL: St Lucie Press, treats the strategist as working within a hierarchical system with an agenda of planned change. Richard S. Handscombe and Philip A. Norman (1993), *Strategic Leadership: Managing the Missing Links*, London: McGraw-Hill, draw out the leadership skills that strategists require.

14. Nancy J. Eggert (1998), *Contemplative Leadership for Entrepreneurial Organizations: Paradigms, Metaphors and Wicked Problems*, Westport, CT: Quorum, discusses the role of

compassion in building a participative community which can compete with others. Judith A. White (1998), "Leadership through compassion and understanding: An interview with Aung San Suu Kyi," *Journal of Management Inquiry*, **7**(4), pp. 286–93, pushes Eggert's point into practice.

15. David Straus (2002), *How to Make Collaboration Work: Powerful Ways to Build Consensus, Solve Problems and Make Decisions*, San Francisco: Berrett-Koehler, discusses the skills of the effective facilitator. Annette Simmons (1999), *A Safe Place for Dangerous Truths: Using Dialogue to Overcome Fear and Distrust at Work*, New York: AMACOM, runs through the seven basic skills of the leader as a facilitator.

16. Manuel London (1999), *Principled Leadership and Business Diplomacy: Values-Based Strategies for Management Development*, Westport, CT: Quorum, discusses the dynamics of being a leader diplomat. At the macro-analytic level of multiculturalism, John Hooker (2004), *Working Across Cultures*, Stanford, CT: Stanford Business Books, makes the case for the cross-cultural diplomat as leader in contemporary ventures. Vincenzo Perrone, Akbar Zaheer and Bill McEvily (2003), "Free to be trusted? Organization constraints on trust in boundary spanners," *Organizational Sciences*, **14**(4), pp. 422–39, remind us of the double-edged sword which pulls boundary-spanning leaders in the communitarian worldview.

17. Colin Coulson-Thomas (2002), *Transforming the Company: Manage Change, Compete and Win*, 2nd edn, London: Kogan Page, addresses the need for leaders to develop a clear position and argue it strongly. Richard M. Perloff (1999), *The Dynamics of Persuasion: Communication and Attitudes in the 21st Century*, Mahwah, NJ: Lawrence Erlbaum, explores the shifting way in which we frame the advocate in the communitarian worldview. Barry Edward Eckhouse (1999), *Competitive Communication: A Rhetoric for Modern Business*, Oxford: Oxford University Press, looks at the skill of making messages which refute and directly compete with others.

18. Wayne Miles Bundy (2002), *Innovation, Creativity and Discovery in Modern Organizations*, Westport, CT: Quorum Books, discusses the practice of structuring exploration in network contexts. Clayton M. Christensen and Michael E. Raynor (2003), *The Innovator's Solution: Creating and Sustaining Successful Growth*, Cambridge, MA: Harvard Business School Press, probe how innovators embed their practices in the network and over time develop a means of extracting sustainable profits. For a stimulating look at alternative models of inducing creativity in and among knowledge workers, see Robert J. Sternberg, James C. Kaufman and Jean Pretz (2002), *The Creativity Conundrum: A Propulsion Model of Kinds of Creative Contribution*, New York: Psychology Press.

19. Within the network worldviews, Jeffrey Shumas and Janice Twombly (2001), *Collaborative Communities: Partnering for Profit in the Networked Economy*, Chicago: Dearborn Trade, capture the ongoing nature of creative collaboration. In an interesting book, Harvey Seifler and Peter Economy (2001), *Leadership Ensemble: Lessons in Collaborative Management from the World's Only Conductorless Orchestra*, New York: Times Books, look at how to generate creativity in the absence of clear and formal leadership.

20. Don Tapscott, David Ticoll and Alex Lowy (2000), *Digital Capital: Harnessing the Power of Business Webs*, Cambridge, MA: Harvard Business School Press, look at the deal maker as a generator of capital in the digital agora. Jeff Papows (1998), *Enterprise.com: Market Leadership in the Information Age*, Reading, MA: Perseus, attends to the role of the participant in the cluster as a deal maker. Fiona Czerniawski and Gavin Potter (1998), *Business in a Virtual World: Exploiting Information for Competitive Advantage*, Basingstoke, Hampshire: Macmillan Business, call attention to deal making in the area of competitive intelligence.

21. Malcolm Warner and Morgen Witzel (2004), *Managing in Virtual Organizations*, London: Thomson Learning, examine the skills of the virtual general manager as a creator of order in the midst of flux. The techniques of the knowledge leader as navigator – mapping, scheduling and engineering – are explored by Jay Leibowitz (2001), *Knowledge Management: Learning From Knowledge Engineering*, Boca Raton, FL: CRC Press. Tony Morgan (2002), *Business Rules and Information Systems: Aligning IT With Business Goals*,

Boston, MA: Addison-Wesley, applies data processing and business rules to navigating in information rich clusters.

22.   For the classic statement on situated learning and its application to leadership practice, see Jean Lave and Etienne Wenger (1991), *Situated Learning: Legitimate Peripheral Participation*, Cambridge: Cambridge University Press. Julian Orr (1995), "Ethnography and organizational learning: In pursuit of learning at work", in C. Zucchermaglio, S. Bagnara and S. Stucky (eds), *Organizational Learning and Technological Change*, Berlin: Springer, for an excellent conceptual treatment of situated learning. See Silvia Geharadi (2000), "Where learning is: Metaphors and situated learning in a planning group", *Human Relations*, **53**(8), pp. 1057–80, for a treatment of how learning requires an awareness of context and the limits of practice.

7. Leaders reinventing themselves: the ACTs of the reflective practitioner

"Leadership is both active and reflective. One has to alternate between participating and observing. Walt Whitman described it as 'being in and out of the game.' For example, Magic Johnson's greatness in leading his basketball team comes in part from his ability to play hard while keeping in mind the whole game situation, as if he stood in the stands."

Ronald A. Heifetz[1]

Reflective practitioners reinvent themselves in the flow of action. To become a masterful leader, the incumbent must be capable of immersing him or herself in the very actions that provide leadership and at the same time be able to reflect and make sense of the larger context in which these acts have meaning and consequences. In the contextual approach to leadership, being "both in and out of the game" requires that a leader is entrenched in the anchor skills, yet able to develop skills that provide him or her with a bridge to other stories. Reflective practitioners learn how to cross the bridge. They see the big picture. The big picture view entails the leaders' ability to work on their anchor skills while developing skills from other leaders' stories. The reflective practitioner as described by Heifetz and others is the hero in the story of the cosmopolitan leader. Cosmopolitan leaders have reach.[2] They develop reflective practices that challenge and push the internally consistent logic of any particular worldview. The reflective practitioner is not only aware of other leadership stories, but develops anchor cross-story transitions (ACTs) that serve as a bridge for leaders to reinvent themselves and make their stories unique.

ACTs is the acronym I use throughout this chapter to systematically portray how the contextual approach to leadership provides an insight into the process of becoming a more reflective practitioner. ACTs indicate how and when leaders who seek to develop their reach move out from their anchor skill within their preferred story, through select transitional skills within their story (small oval Figure 7.1) and develop skills in other leadership stories (large oval Figure 7.1). In the previous chapter, we focused on the small oval within the four faces of capitalism, I portrayed the local leader who is

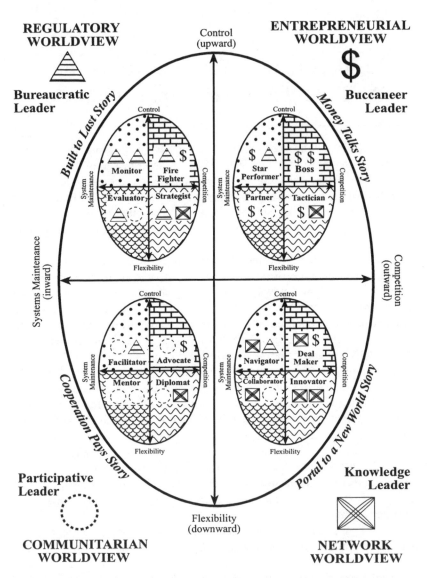

Figure 7.1　Anchor cross-story transitions (ACTs): four instrumental leaders

beginning to develop reach. The local leader stops short of developing a bridge (ACTs) to others' stories. The awareness of others' skills is not focused outwards but is harnessed to the leader's story. This is a benefit and a limitation. The local leader will be lauded for both nurturing a clear and consistent worldview and helping those within it resolve issues – profit, stability, meaningful existence, and innovation. Thus if one strongly values the cooperation pays story, one would do well to select a leader anchored in mentoring skills with some within-story transitional skills in one or more of the facilitator, diplomat, and advocate's skills. The local leader meets the demands of those who stay within the story. The limitation here, one that is common in the assessment of leaders in the realm of politics, is that the leader merely mirrors the needs of his or her followers (subordinates, members or participants).[3] He or she fails to reflect upon practices beyond those at hand, and does not achieve the reflective arc – a mighty ambitious one – which enables leaders to reinvent themselves and remake their stories.

ACTs or anchor cross-story transitions are for leaders interested in increasing their reach and enhancing their ability to work between and among worldviews. Leadership reinvention, the core of reflective practice, the very "being in and out of the game", is not magic. It requires hard work. But this, as was the case in developing a leader's local reach, is discernible in a pattern within the four faces of capitalism model. This pattern aids leaders in developing skills in a self-conscious and systematic manner. One starts within the model by recognizing one's anchor skills as a boss ($), monitor (Δ), mentor (○) or innovator (☒). Now, rather than focus upon skills within one's preferred worldview, one consciously opts to work on skills that match one's preferred worldview as found in others' leadership stories (see Figure 7.1). Skills in the contextual model of leadership cannot be built upon a base which has little fertile soil. The motto of ACTs is build on your strengths as a leader, but continue to push towards other worldviews. It is important to note that the further the distance, the greater the reach, the larger the potential for reflective practice.

The contextual approach to leadership ties skills to worldviews. Leaders must have proficiency within their anchor skill and at least one other transitional skill within their story before they can begin to think of developing ACTs. Without this proficiency reflective practice is simply a form of pattern recognition. The leaders notice that others do not take them seriously as a leader and then attempt to alter their behaviour to meet the demand. Victory in this method is pyrrhic.[4] The leader has no understanding of others' stories and where they lead. He or she is merely using surface clues to get by. Reflective practice emerges when the leader achieves distance by understanding or being able to reflectively practise the skills emerging in other stories and bringing these to bear upon his or her anchor skills. The reflective practitioner as a cosmopolitan leader goes out into the world to develop skills that make a story which suits a hybrid audience.[5] He or she leaves the archetype of the leader and begins to develop a unique leader's story. Leaders with reflective practice customize their leadership journey.

What is interesting in the contextual approach to leadership is that the unique leader's story is built upon a basic vocabulary of anchor cross-story transitions (ACTs) just as a unique author uses paragraphs, sections, chapters to move ideas from one context to another and achieve a sense of unity. The four faces of instrumental behaviour or capitalism in this model provide the basic vocabulary. These four worldviews are not haphazard. They neither constrain the individuality of a particular leader, nor compel the leader aspiring to reach to move in directions incompatible with his or her personal views. The model is pragmatic. It requires that the leaders meet the challenge of balancing their skill portfolio with their preferred worldview. They must work with their skills to meet, push and make sense of the needs of followers, subordinates, members and/or participants. Each of the four ACTs addresses the reach of a particular leader within the four faces of capitalism – the buccaneer leader in the money talks story, the bureaucratic leader in the built to last story, the participative leader in the cooperation pays story and the knowledge leader in the portal to a new world story.

Each of the ACTs is depicted by different pattern in Figure 7.1. Let us look at each individually. The buccaneer leader's ACTs in the brick pattern anchors in the boss's skills ($$) in entrepreneurial worldview. It follows the money symbol to the cross-story transitional skills of the fire fighter (Δ$) in the regulatory worldview, the deal maker (⊠$) in the network worldview and along the diagonal, to the communitarian worldview, the advocate's skills (○$). The bureaucratic leader's ACTs in the built to last story (see dotted pattern in Figure 7.1) anchors in the monitor's skills (ΔΔ). It transitions across stories to the facilitator's skills (○Δ) in the cooperation pays story, the star's skills ($Δ) in the money talks story and the hardest to achieve by the bureaucratic leader, the navigator's skills (⊠Δ) in the portal to a new world story.

The participative leader's ACTs (see scales pattern in Figure 7.1) anchors the mentor's skills (○○). It follows the circle with the broken circumference to the transition skills of the collaborator (⊠○) in the network worldview, the evaluator (Δ○) in the regulatory worldview and, along the diagonal, the notion of partnering ($○) in the entrepreneurial worldview. The knowledge leader's ACTs (see waves pattern in Figure 7.1) anchors in the innovator's skills (⊠⊠) in the portal to a new world story, and transitions cross-story to the tactician's skills ($⊠) in the buccaneer leader's skill portfolio, the diplomat's skills (○⊠) in the participative leader's skill portfolio, and along the diagonal to the strategist's skills (Δ⊠) in the bureaucratic leader's skill portfolio. Each of these four leaders' ACTs has its own rhyme and reason.

Drilling down into the ACTs depicted in Figure 7.1 requires attending to two important dynamics. First, leaders attempting to expand their reach can anchor their skills in only one worldview at a time. As they cross stories, reflective practitioners carefully shift worldviews as they move from one anchor skill to another.[6] This requires deliberate effort and hard work and is rewarded by the reflective practitioner's ability to fully reinvent him or herself. In this way, a buccaneer leader anchored in boss's skills ($$) can, as noted in Chapter 5, enlarge his or her within-story tactician's skills ($⊠). This is a response to the buccaneer leader's interpretation of the network worldview. Then to develop what will be called a gradient "1" buccaneer leader ACTs (see Figure 7.2) the leader can,[7] with attention to detail, transition from the boss's skills to the tactician's and out of the entrepreneurial worldview to the deal maker's (⊠$) skill in the knowledge leader's skill portfolio. Once comfortable and at home with the deal maker's skill, the buccaneer leader can diminish his or her boss's skills and upload, albeit slowly and with considerable precision, the innovator's anchor skills. Once at home with the innovator's skill, a shift that can take years, the buccaneer leader has reinvented him or herself as a knowledge leader. In Figure 7.1, we move from the bricks pattern of the boss's skills to the waves pattern of the innovator's. In the world of practice, as knowledge leaders we give off signals to creatives and knowledge workers in lieu of followers. Once the innovator's skill anchor is intact, the reinvented knowledge leader works within the network worldview developing his or her within-story skills of the collaborator (⊠○), deal maker (⊠$) and, along the diagonal, the hardest for an innovator to acquire, the navigator's skills (⊠Δ). The leader is now set to reinvent him or herself again within their career if they elect to do so.

The second dynamic adapts the diagonal notion in the within-story skill transition to three distinct gradients in the ACTs. Within the four faces of capitalism, leadership skills on the diagonal, whether within a leadership story (small oval) or in the ACTs (large oval), do not share a talking point. Thus the money talks story shares no talking point with the cooperation pays story and, similarly, the built to last story shares nothing with the portal to a new world story. The others share "control" (regulatory/entrepreneurial), "flexibility" (communitarian/network) as talking points. In the four ACTs, the three leadership skills – an anchor and two ACTs transitional skills – that share talking points will be referred to as gradient "1" ACTs; those along the diagonal will be labelled gradient "2" ACTs; and those that fully reinvent leaders – anchor to new anchor leadership skills – are gradient "3" ACTs. Gradient "1" ACTs are within the reach of most leaders seeking to expand their skills beyond their leadership story. Gradient "2" ACTs are possible. However, they rarely if ever result in full leadership reinvention. The anchor skills along the diagonal contradict or oppose one another. As some leadership scholars have pointed out, they are rife with competing values.[8] Leaders who attempt gradient "2" are more likely to remain anchored in their preferred anchor skills than to reinvent themselves. Those who systematically elect gradient "3" and patiently persevere can fully reinvent themselves several times within their lifetime.

First I will turn to each of the four ACTs, and within each one to the three cross-story gradients. The book concludes with a brief discussion of how the contextual approach to leadership provides leaders with a basic understanding of the manner in which reflective practice adds breadth and depth to their capabilities as leaders. The contextual model of leadership provides a means of making sense and critically adopting the prescription of many leadership gurus that leadership is, for example, all about executing, building, visioning, strategically aligning structure and policy, establishing intellectual capital, developing trust, acting with integrity and the like. In the contextual approach leaders fill in, for example, what it means in practice to build a vision in very different leadership contexts and how and why over time leaders learn to change and systematically reinvent their leadership stories as they become reflective practitioners.[9]

BUCCANEER LEADER'S ACTS

Consistent with the entrepreneurial worldview, buccaneers reinvent themselves in the pursuit of money and the desire to win.[10] They stay within the money talks story if this can best be accomplished and thereby satisfy the needs of successful buccaneer leaders. In this manner their reach is limited to the small oval within the four faces of capitalism. The leader in the money talks story who is thriving or expects to do so will anchor in the boss's skills ($$) and develops within-story reach by augmenting the anchor, when needed, with tactician's skills ($⊠), star's skills ($Δ) and along the troublesome diagonal, partner's skills ($○). Buccaneer leaders who enlarge their tactician's skills are attractive as deal makers (⊠$) to knowledge leaders in the network worldview. Those who upload on star skills are potential fire fighters (Δ$) or turnaround artists in beleaguered hierarchical systems and along the diagonal, those with partnering skills are sought after as advocates (○$) and philanthropists in communities that are either awash in controversy or seek assistance from well-heeled winners.

The shift from the brick pattern of the boss's skills through the local skills of the tactitican and star to the deal maker and fire fighter's skills marks the origins of the gradient "1" and "2" ACTs in Figure 7.2. It is either in pursuit or protection of wealth that successful buccaneers venture out of the boss's

Anchor Skill

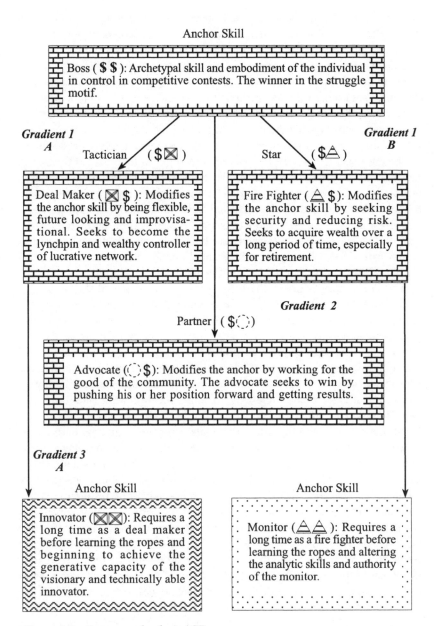

Boss (**$ $**): Archetypal skill and embodiment of the individual in control in competitive contests. The winner in the struggle motif.

Gradient 1
A

Tactician ($⊠)

Gradient 1
B

Star ($△)

Deal Maker (⊠ $): Modifies the anchor skill by being flexible, future looking and improvisational. Seeks to become the lynchpin and wealthy controller of lucrative network.

Fire Fighter (△ $): Modifies the anchor skill by seeking security and reducing risk. Seeks to acquire wealth over a long period of time, especially for retirement.

Gradient 2

Partner ($◌)

Advocate (◌ $): Modifies the anchor by working for the good of the community. The advocate seeks to win by pushing his or her position forward and getting results.

Gradient 3
A

Anchor Skill

Anchor Skill

Innovator (⊠⊠): Requires a long time as a deal maker before learning the ropes and beginning to achieve the generative capacity of the visionary and technically able innovator.

Monitor (△△): Requires a long time as a fire fighter before learning the ropes and altering the analytic skills and authority of the monitor.

Figure 7.2   Buccaneer leader's ACTs

anchor skills. The gradient "1" ACT, boss ($$) → tactician ($☒) → deal maker (☒$) was a well-trodden route to a lucrative career in the dot.com boom that marked the last years of the twentieth century. As high technology soared, buccaneer leaders eager to capitalize upon their skills uploaded on tactician's skills within the money talks story and either pushed their way as deal makers into the network worldview or were enticed by stock options and agents fees that could finance a small country. Tactical skills within the money talks story enable the boss to begin to think outside the box, consider future options and seriously look at alternative money making propositions. Brokering deals is still key in enabling networks. In the post 9/11 *zeitgeist*, networks have sprung up around applications of high technology to security, especially in the employment of retinal scanning, prevention of identity theft, bio-toxin detection and leading edge military and anti-terrorist applications.[11] The rush of capital into bio-technology remains firm and increasingly credible evidence that e-commerce and those who push it in new directions are far from dead. Where there is substantial money to be garnered in broker- ing deals, the buccaneer leader will not be far behind.

The cross story reach in the boss → tactician → deal maker's ACT is established as the boss with ample tactician's ability migrates from the entrepreneurial to the network worldview of the deal maker. Reflective practice commences when leaders alter their anchor skills to adapt them to new stories. The adaptation here requires that the boss accustomed to full and total control over followers must now deal far more flexibly with participants who are loosely interdependent and at times totally autonomous. Followers adhere to authority in their quest for wealth. Followers want what the leader has. They seek to either emulate or, interestingly, depose and replace him or her in their concerted efforts to accumulate control and money. Participants in the network worldview of the deal maker are loosely bound. Participants question authority, attempt to have it work on their behalf and want a strong say in how capital can be employed to enable breakthroughs and to make more capital over time. The deal maker must not only bring resources into the network, but do so in a manner which is perceived by participants as advancing the network. While self-interest is not lost in the shift from tactician to deal maker's skills, it is tempered by the reflective need for the leader to develop practices which establish and develop his or her reputation as a contributor to the network's needs. Those deal makers who are seen as overly self-interested are not asked to re-enter the network as it reformulates itself around new and emerging projects.

The gradient "1" boss → tactician → deal maker ACT pushes or pulls the entrepreneurial boss into the portal to a new world story anchored by the skills of the innovator. With time, effort, and a genuine willingness to immerse him or herself in the network worldview, the cosmopolitan leader can fully reinvent him or herself by attending to the gradient "3" ACT – the shift from the boss's anchor skill to the innovator's. This shift, boss ($$) → tactician's ($⊠) → deal maker (⊠$) → innovator (⊠⊠), from the bricks pattern of the buccaneer to the waves pattern of the knowledge leader takes time. The buccaneer leader who has developed deal maker's skills is drawn to the excitement and lucrative potential of innovation. He or she begins to get captured by its heady blend of creativity when it is applied in the pursuit of wealth and fame.[12] To access their creativity, buccaneers tie their confidence and willingness to commit to a line of action with the give and take of working with creatives. The buccaneer leader taking on a deal maker's skills acclimatizes to flexibility and increasingly relinquishes, albeit painstakingly, the need for control. They begin to extend their time line for getting results and can establish a visionary perspective especially when tied to their credible ability to execute. Once comfortable in the knowledge zone, the innovator begins to reduce his or her reliance upon deal maker's skills (⊠$) and with the innovator as an anchor skill (⊠⊠) begins to take on the transitional skills of the navigator (⊠Δ) and, along the diagonal, the collaborator (⊠○).

Gradient "2" in Figure 7.2 shows the impact of competing values on the ACTs of the buccaneer leader. The boss ($$) → partner ($○) → advocate (○$) ACT never leaves the brick pattern of the money talks story (see Figure 7.2). It is not followed by a gradient "3" transition. Bosses will find it very costly to reinvent themselves as mentors, the anchor skill of those in the cooperation talks story.[13] They share no talking point. The boss is heavily invested in "control" and "competition"; the mentor in "flexibility" and "system or cultural maintenance". The boss can, however, upload on his or her within-story partnering skills and, as a consequence, take the time for dialogue and to develop some trust in a co-leader. Once this is established, and this is far from a stable propensity of the control-oriented boss, the boss with partnering skills can cross over into the advocate's role in the communitarian worldview. Note that gradient "1" ACTs are easier for the incumbents than gradient "2" ACTs, while leaders can fully reinvent themselves with the former but not the latter. Gradient "2" ACTs require that the leader develop skills that conflict and contradict his or her worldview. This is possible in following one's transitional skills across the story line, but not in moving from one's preferred anchor skill to one which contradicts it.

The buccaneer is drawn to advocates' skills (○$) when there is either money or status to be accrued.[14] Many buccaneers find themselves drawn to public causes less out of altruism or a deep abiding quest for the common good than as a means of representing a position which will improve their lot and, in so doing, increase the welfare of the community. Buccaneers have no trouble whatsoever convincing themselves that what is good for them is very good for the community. Buccaneers with people skills developed through partnering are drawn to the advocate's skills when communities are either willing or pushed into tolerating controversy and accepting those who jockey for ascendant positions. As to status, the buccaneer leader is also drawn to the public recognition and respect given to buccaneers who, as advocates, give their time, money and energy to the community. Many a buccaneer leader, often later in life, turns to advocacy in creating foundations and backing causes in the community. The motives for this are, I believe, complex.[15] The buccaneer in advocate's clothing seeks to retain some control over the process and wherever possible have his or her people manage it and help to harvest the goodwill and reputational capital likely to accrue as a result of the public's recognition of their largesse. This is not the anonymous and selfless contribution of the mentor nor the attempt to listen attentively so as to discern the community's wishes.

While the gradient "2" ACT is not a matter of leader reinvention, it does require the buccaneer with partner's skills to develop reach and engage in reflective practice. As an advocate the buccaneer must alter the "follow me or be out of sight" position that those who seek control adopt when they begin to recognize that members in the community want their leaders to reflect members' values. This is difficult. To succeed, the buccaneer leader transitioning from the boss with partner's skills to the advocate must be able to recognize and speak to values other than the quest for profits and status. Buccaneers are competitive. They share neither their ideas nor their personal values with others in the community. Buccaneers are rugged individualists.[16] They look upon sharing as a conspiracy hatched by the weak (losers) to rob the strong (winners). Once they can "hear" of the benefits of paying their dues and becoming a member, even a rather demanding one, in a community, this enables them to take on the role of the advocate in the communitarian worldview. Oddly, for those more sociologically minded than myself, it is in honour of the advocate in the gradient "2" buccaneer's ACT that many monuments, buildings and public squares are named. Presently there is a fascination with corporate donors who contribute sums of money to name sports complexes and other community amenities after themselves.[17]

Buccaneer leaders reinventing themselves as monitors in the built to last story, a transition amalgamating buccaneer leader's gradient "1B" and "3B" ACTs, in Figure 7.2, is a relatively well-worn transition to students of the contextual model of leadership. In the regular course of affairs, two interrelated motivations for this boss (\$\$) → star (\$Δ) → fire fighter (Δ\$) and still later and much more difficult to accomplish ("3B"), fire fighter (Δ\$) → monitor (ΔΔ) transition, exist. First, as bosses succeed and enlarge their star performer skills, they often concentrate their efforts on a particular area with great success. This results in the star (\$Δ) reaching toward the built to last story to instil order in an organization given increasing complexity. The boss's skills ($$) thrive when all relevant information must be filtered through the leader. This becomes more difficult as the firm begins to require the input of lawyers, logistics specialists, accountants, marketers and human relations experts. In the relatively rapid transition from a small proprietorship or family business to an increasingly successful and more complex firm, the star is motivated over time to leap to the built to last story in order to engage in the functions of the fire fighter (Δ$). Second, there is no pension, no security and little assurance as one ages in the money talks story. The star, with age, will retain his or her earning proclivities as a high producer. New, young, hungry talent challenges the star.[18] The star with a reputation for getting results is often courted by those in the regulatory worldview. The star when harnessed to the fire fighter's task is excellent at crisis management and non-routine problem solving; he or she is eager, as well, to cash in on the pension, security and back-ended pay regime practised in hierarchical systems.

As the boss with enlarged star's skills transitions to the fire fighter in the built to last story, the fire fighter with a buccaneer past begins to see and appreciate the rewards of a hierarchical system. The control is something the boss turned fire fighter requires little reflective practice to appreciate. The built to last emphasis upon systems maintenance, however, requires reflective practice. The fire fighter is fully alive in the midst of crisis. However, as the system returns to standard operating procedures, the fire fighter must succumb to the rules, precedents and routines of the system. The fire fighter accommodates this constraint less out of a desire to be penned in than a recognition that in the regulatory worldview the rules can solve many problems if used well and, more realistically, that the remuneration for those at or near the top in the regulatory worldview (especially if looked at within the larger time frames with compounding interest) satisfies many a once-daring buccaneer.

The gradient "3B" ACT from fire fighter (Δ$) to the anchor skill of the monitor in the built to last story takes time and dedication to complete. Fire fighters reduce their fire fighting skills as they develop an understanding of where the real power and control rest within the hierarchical system. Being fierce and relentless competitors eager to expand their control and enlarge their earning potential, the fire fighter with a buccaneer's past is motivated to learn the ropes and acquire the master skill of the leader in the built to last story. The monitor, the anchor skill in the regulatory worldview, earns his or her position by combining credentials which attest to his or her skills combined with hard work; the boss in quest of the monitor's recognition is a self-made individual who stays close to those at the top of the hierarchy. He or she learns through close observation, ingratiation with those at the top, and execution of hard tasks with solid results. This "active" monitor suits many systems seeking people who can not only lead during periods of stability and careful planning, but who possess the stick-with-it-ness to shine when the going gets tough.

Buccaneer leaders' ACTs indicate that they are not entrapped in the money talks story, but can, anchoring in the boss's skill, adapt their story and capabilities so as to flourish and win the respect of others outside the money talks story. In the next section, I turn to how and why the leader in the built to last story moves out of this story and can, in the right circumstances, reinvent him or herself. The bureaucratic leader is, however, much more prudent. He or she moves out of the planned and well-tended system much more reluctantly than the buccaneer leader hell-bent upon acquiring status and making a fortune.

BUREAUCRATIC LEADER'S ACTS

Consistent with the regulatory worldview, bureaucratic leaders reinvent themselves and venture out of the built to last story in pursuit of order, stability and security. When the hierarchical system, which grounds the bureaucratic leader's domain, is orderly, stable and secure, the built to last leader remains satisfied. He or she is a leader at the top of a complex, rule-bound system entrusted with overseeing the system so as to assure its stakeholders of its continued reliability, longevity and stability.[19] The leader in the built to last story who attains these ends or expects to do so will anchor in the monitor's skills ($\Delta\Delta$). He or she will develop within-story reach by augmenting the anchor, when needed, with evaluator's skills ($\Delta\bigcirc$), fire fighter skills ($\Delta\$$) and along the diagonal, strategist's skills ($\Delta\boxtimes$). The monitor enlarges his or her evaluator's skills (see gradient "1A"; Figure 7.3) on perceiving the source of instability in the system as arising in a misalignment of the organization's culture – for example, people increasing errors by failing to adhere to the policies, measures and routines of the system. When crisis is seen as imminent within the system, the monitor increases his or her reliance upon fire fighting skills (see gradient "1B"). Along the diagonal, the monitor attempts to amplify his or her strategic skills (see gradient "2"; Figure 7.3) when it is thought that the system requires new thinking, change and redesign.

The bureaucratic leader's ACTs appear as a dotted pattern with reinvention possible within the scale pattern of the mentor and the brick pattern of the boss (see Figures 7.1 and 7.3). The bureaucratic leader is a by-the-book leader. He or she is loyal and dutiful to the system and its orderly development, prolongation and management. To be in the dotted area in Figure 7.3

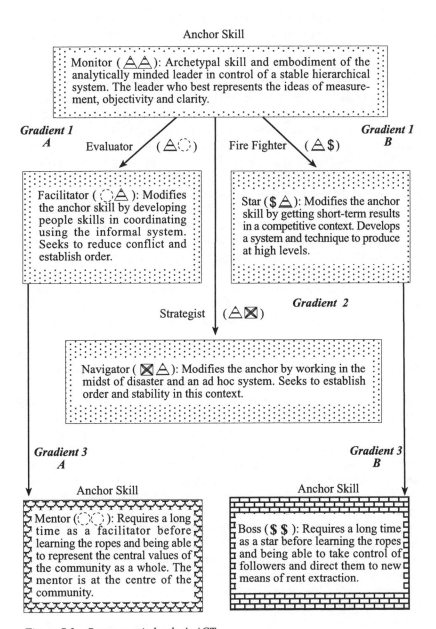

Figure 7.3 Bureaucratic leader's ACTs

is to recognize, with varying degrees of comfort, that skills which build and create order in systems are vital. The gradient "1A" ACT enables the monitor (ΔΔ) who enlarges his or her facilitator skills (Δ○) to cross over into the cooperation pays story by adopting the skills of the facilitator. This requires reflective practice because the facilitator's skills require the monitor to give up control and relinquish a strong preference for analytic distance and objectivity. The facilitator epitomizes "order with people" skills in the co-operation pays story. The facilitator reduces conflict, coordinates members' dialogues and employs the informal system to enhance trust and increase members' commitment to the team. The monitor gives up control when the subordinates in the system demand to be treated as members. The monitor with evaluator's skills begins to value the skill of the facilitator when delegating this to others no longer enhances system stability. To develop facilitator's skills, monitors will get involved in the interpretation of subordinates needs. The leader who satisfies subordinates needs helps them to feel as if they are members. It is expected that they will heighten their commitment and involvement with the system and its operation.

When the facilitator with a bureaucratic leader's background becomes comfortable with his or her people skills, he or she may see the usefulness of the cooperation pays story in creating, maintaining and sustaining order in systems that over time begin to resemble communities. The "3A" ACT, monitor (ΔΔ) → evaluator (Δ○) → facilitator (○Δ) → mentor (○○) pushes the bureaucratic leader into the heart of the quest for a meaningful existence. At first the facilitator with a bureaucratic leader's past takes up the coopera-tion story as a means of establishing order in systems. As they buy in when they see that it works, some percentage of monitors in this skill transition come to be full believers. They seek to flatten levels of hierarchy, empower members and develop multi-functional teams, and look for opportunities to stimulate dialogue and enhance learning in the organization. The develop-ment of mentor's skills requires that a bureaucratic leader see and believe that, in periods of rapid, unpredictable change and systems disturbance, it is wise to empower individuals and enable cross-functional teams that are capable of working through new issues rather than relying upon tightly for-mulated policies and performance evaluations.[20] The gradient "3A" ACT is accomplished by bureaucratic leaders who employ their leadership to trans-form a hierarchical system into a trust-based community. This ACT requires reflective practice. The bureaucratic leader who changes from the built to last story to the cooperation pays story must feel comfortable with communitarian values. He or she cannot feign openness, trust or the ability to listen. The mentor is at the centre and embodies the values of a viable, trusting community.

Along the diagonal in the four faces of capitalism, bureaucratic leaders anchored in the uncertainty reducing skills of the monitor cannot easily or systematically reinvent themselves with the creative skills of the anchor in the network worldview – the innovator. The two anchor skills clash. Thus the gradient "2" ACT, monitor ($\Delta\Delta$) → strategist ($\Delta\boxtimes$) → navigator ($\boxtimes\Delta$) increases the bureaucratic leader's reach, but does not readily enable leadership reinvention. The basic dynamic of this ACT goes like this. Monitors augment their within-story strategist's skills when they attempt to reconfigure, redesign or restructure a hierarchical system. Strategist's skills speak to planned change, out-of-the-box thinking and a future orientation within the built to last story. There are two interrelated reasons for monitors with highly developed strategies being lured over the line into the portal to a new world story. The first reason addresses the sporadic manner in which bureaucratic leaders with strategist's skills are heard in the hierarchical system. During periods of planned change in the system, they are taken seriously; during periods of stability, their views gather dust in largely unread reports. The data addressing how and when to deal with emerging issues and plan for change are viewed, like insurance, as documents to be taken seriously when the appropriate time arises. On the other hand strategists who go to work as navigators in the network worldview are constantly challenged and alert, and vie for input on important functions. Those with strategist's skills who have trouble getting their change message on the agenda, ironically are seen as the source of much-needed stability in the adhoc-ratically structured network.

The second reason for the bureaucratic leader crossing over into the network worldview addresses the manner in which many hierarchical systems attempt to purchase the potential to innovate rather than create innovation within their orderly system. To purchase innovation, bureaucratic leaders often acquire young, agile network firms and keep them at a distance.[21] Bureaucratic leaders susceptible to the ACT are aware that their top-down culture of rule-based deference to authority, if permitted to infiltrate the new acquisitions, will stifle innovation in its tracks. At first, those at the top of the hierarchical system attempt to leave the newly acquired agile firm to its own devices. However, reporting requirements guided by stakeholders' concern about the money spent on the new acquisition will lead to demands that the bureaucratic leader with strategist's skills be put in charge of the agile network firm. Bureaucrats trust bureaucrats – even those with strategists' skills. They do not feel comfortable with the mercurial knowledge leader at the helm. Those that cross the storyline become navigators; they subjugate their need for order to meet the creative needs of the network. Those who remain in the built to last story stifle creativity in the quest to integrate the potentially innovative projects into the greater needs of the hierarchical system.

The gradient "2" bureaucratic leader's ACT requires reflective practice. The monitor with strategist's skills navigating in the network worldview must be confident in his or her ability to achieve a semblance of order in the midst of an ever-changing, temporary system. This confidence cannot depend upon the top-down communication style of the bureaucratic leader, but on the ability of the navigator to develop an understanding of the key issues related to the knowledge pool in which the participants in the network are immersed. To create a sense of order, navigators cannot rely solely upon rules, policies and routines, but must bank on their ability to create provisional maps and contingent options to accommodate the alterable structure and processes within the amoeba-like network.[22] Leaders catching things on the fly and creating a sense of order is different from improvising. It moves one's skill set from control to flexibility. It lends order and coordination to the work of many improvisers working at breakneck speed in competition with others for the network capital to be garnered from radical innovation.

The gradient "1B" ACT, monitor ($\Delta\Delta$) → fire fighter ($\Delta\$$) → star ($\$\Delta$), when appended to the gradient "3B" bureaucratic leader's ACT, pulls or pushes the leader from the dotted pattern of the monitor's skills to the brick pattern of the boss's. Figure 7.3 outlines how and why a bureaucratic leader anchored in the skills of the monitor can reinvent him or herself as a boss in the money talks story. This trajectory is not simply the reverse of the boss → monitor leadership reinvention discussed in the buccaneer leader's ACTs. The monitor to boss ACTs are engaged in by leaders at the head of systems that are seeking more freedom and extrinsic reward; the boss to monitor ACTs are engaged in by buccaneers seeking greater security and stability. The monitor ($\Delta\Delta$) with highly developed fire fighter's skills ($\Delta\$$) comes to the fore when the system is in crisis and requires a turnaround leader. As a fire fighter, the bureaucratic leader in search of high financial returns can transition to a star ($\$\Delta$) within the entrepreneurial worldview. The monitor with fire fighting skills who is motivated to become a star in the money talks story modifies the monitor's anchor skill. He or she seeks short-term bottom-line results in a competitive system. The star is focused upon him or herself, not the system. The star employs his or her analytical skills to develop a system which enhances his or her ability to out-produce others and reap the lion's share of commissions or rents within an entrepreneurial game.

As stars develop a taste for winning, they alter their skill set. In lieu of highlighting their producer's abilities in one particular rent extraction game within the entrepreneurial worldview, they begin to hire other stars and over time feel comfortable anchoring in the boss's skills. As bosses they go where there is money to be made. Monitors who cross over the built to last story into the entrepreneurial worldview are in search of big wins – wins for the "self", not the system or community. They are seeking freedom of action.

They found this difficult to attain as monitors. They are willing to live by their wits in a "just do it" worldview. They are willing to take the fall when the market calls them a failure. Reflective practice here speaks to the psychological transition from prudence to risk-taking and from a recognition of duty to a quest for freedom.

Bureaucratic leaders' ACTs are increasing as the stability of hierarchical systems is tested. Whether we think of downsizing, outsourcing, re-engineering, organizational flattening, making systems more transparent, more socially responsible and the like, bureaucratic leaders are being pushed into trying out new skills.[23] Many of the contemporary tools mobilized to improve organizations are rooted in efforts to reduce the cost of running bureaucracies, to enable bureaucracies to adapt by empowering those within to build a culture of trust and to make hierarchical systems more innovative. Paradoxically, bureaucratic leaders, those who consistently seek stability and order, are provided with ample motivation to engage in ACTs that, once beyond the built to last story, question the basic authoritative premises upon which the regulatory worldview is constructed.

PARTICIPATIVE LEADER'S ACTS

Authority in the cooperation pays story rests in the all-inclusive team or community. Leadership is distributed and shared. It is not vested in the rules or in the position of the leader as in the regulatory worldview. Participative leaders are selected by the community because they are seen as embodying and exemplifying the values of the team. Leaders are caring, trustworthy colleagues. In line with the communitarian worldview, participative leaders venture out of the cooperation pays story and, in time, reinvent themselves in the search of a meaningful existence. In practice, a meaningful existence is created, insist communitarians, by building a community of trust in which dialogue and learning enhance the resilience and adaptive capacity of the collective. When this can be accomplished within the cooperation pays story, there is no motive for participative leaders to leave their preferred worldview. The leader in the cooperation pays story who has found a meaningful existence will anchor in the mentor's skills (○○) and develop within-story reach by augmenting the anchor, when needed, with the diplomat's skills (○⊠), facilitator's skills (○△) and, along the diagonal, advocate's skills (○$). Participative leaders who develop their diplomat's skills are attractive as collaborators to knowledge leaders; those who cultivate facilitator's skills are of value as bureaucratic leaders eager to get buy in from subordinates and along the diagonal those with advocate's skills are sought after as partners by buccaneers eager to get access to resources.

In Figure 7.4, I outline the process within the four faces of capitalism wherein participative leaders reinvent themselves as knowledge leaders (gradient "1A" appended to gradient "3A"), as bureaucratic leaders (gradient "1B" appended to gradient "3B") and, along the diagonal, the transition from a participative leader to a potential partner in the money talks story. In each of these ACTs, the participative leader moves out of the cooperation pays story and develops reach. The reach dilutes the strength of the cooperation pays story, but compensates by enabling the leader in the midst of an ACT to develop reflective practices. The gradient "1A" ACT, mentor (○○) → diplomat (○☒) → collaborator (☒○) appended to gradient "3A", collaborator → innovator (☒☒) enables the participative leader to think outside the box or community, make alliances with outsiders and, in time, impart new ideas from outside communities into the focal team or community. The gradient "1B" ACT, mentor (○○) → facilitator (○△) → evaluator (△○) appended to gradient "3B", evaluator → monitor (△△) enhances the participative leader's ability to create order, stability and structure within a flexible community. Finally the gradient "2" ACT, mentor (○○) → advocates (○$) → partner ($○) enables the participative leader to form resource-based, albeit temporary, partnerships with others in order to get results.

In the contextual approach to leadership, leaders do not randomly reinvent themselves. Participative leaders anchored in mentoring skills will augment these skills with diplomat skills when the focal community finds itself engaged in increasingly uncertain and problematic relations with other communities outside its boundaries.[24] Mentors with diplomatic ability represent the values of the community to those outside it. They serve as boundary spanners establishing relationships with outsiders needed by the focal community. Mentors with well-developed diplomat skills make excellent collaborators in the network worldview. They bring together people in teams with varying positions within a given pool of knowledge. They know how to act as knowledge conduits. Collaborators with a participative leader's past develop the reflective practice of working in temporary, project-based communities. They stress the sharing of ideas. They help bring projects to their completion. Collaborators care about the intellectual capital embedded in the grey matter of participants.[25] Their goal is to develop trust between and among participants in the network in order to turn tacit knowledge into useful intellectual capital. In the gradient "3A" ACT, collaborator (☒○) → innovator (☒☒), the collaborator over time attends to the knowledge itself and diminishes his or her concern with its transfer. The motivation for collaboration within participative leaders to reinvent themselves as innovators rests on their desire to be the creative source of ideas and to reap the rewards that accrue to those who possess this anchor

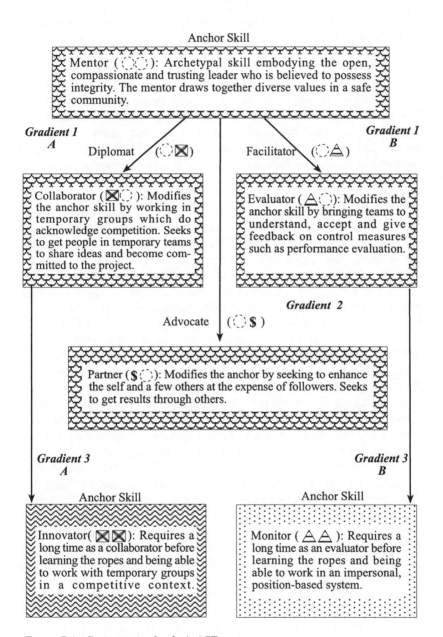

Figure 7.4 Participative leader's ACTs

skill. In the network worldview, the innovator claims priority of discovery, fame and, at times, the money that accompanies successful breakthroughs.[26] The reflective practice in the gradient "3A" ACT emphasizes the collaborator's willingness and ability to enlarge his or her perspective. In lieu of stressing the people and relationship component of the innovation equation, the collaborator learning the ropes of the innovator must immerse him or herself in technical content, funding opportunities, creation of the prototype, knowledge obsolescence and speed of other networks in pushing the envelope on this breakthrough. The collaborator is excellently placed in the network to acquire these skills. He or she goes between and among participants and has access to the knowledge base upon which the innovation is built.

In the participative leader's gradient "1B" ACT appended to the gradient "3B" (Figure 7.4), the participative leader over time reinvents him or herself as a bureaucratic leader. The shift is a function of the increasing demands for accountability and a clear plan of action demanded by those who will, for example, withdraw their support for a non-profit organization unless it establishes a clear and more formal chain of command.[27] In the field of business ethics, one finds the call to increase regulation, introduce codes of conduct and establish greater accountability as a direct outcome of the perception that groups are violating trust, engaging in self-serving behaviour and/or are involved in blatant conflicts of interest. Bureaucratization is the process whereby rules, standards and codes replace the employee's use of discretion. In the process of bureaucratization of communities, mentors enlarge their facilitator skills.[28] The emphasis is placed upon reducing conflict, coordinating events and achieving stability and order in the community. The facilitator is drawn to develop evaluator skills as members in a community are transformed into subordinates within a system.

It is the call to control via measurement that is the reflective practice of the mentor with facilitator skills crossing over the ACT line into the regulatory worldview. In my experience in the work world, I have discovered that when a bureaucratically structured firm acquires or merges with a company with a clan-like culture, pressure grows to turn the facilitator into an evaluator. The shift is from flexibility to control. As an evaluator, the leader is reinforced for tying human relations and trust to obtain buy-in on specific ways to standardize and measure human performance. The evaluator is not particularly motivated to aid members in maximizing their human potential as are facilitators. The evaluator's aim is to tie the person to the position in a manner which increases order and adds stability to systems. The reflective practice here emphasizes a willingness to utilize one's people skills in sustaining an effective system. The system takes priority over the person. Community is a means to reinforce order. Order is seen and understood as necessary to structure the community and make it more like a system.

As the system takes priority over the person, the evaluator is motivated within the process of the hierarchical system to compete in the internal labour market for more of the monitor's skills. The gradient "3B" ACT in which leaders with a communitarian past reinvent themselves as bureaucratic leaders involves the reflective practice of taking control of key measures and setting an agenda. This serves to focus the attention of subordinates within the system. The monitor oversees the rules, sets policies and highlights precedents within the creation of a routine or standard operating procedures. This provides the order and stability in the complex system. While rising up the hierarchy, the evaluator takes on more monitor's skills within the built to last story. He or she is entrusted with seeing the big picture, working in an impersonal, position-based system and providing procedurally rational accounts of events. The monitor must synthesize the information sent upwards by specialists and experts. This information must be integrated and tied to the ongoing sustainable operation of the system.

Along the diagonal, the participative leader's gradient "2" ACT, mentor ($\circ\circ$) → advocate ($\circ\$$) → partner ($\$\circ$) moves from the cooperation pays to the money talks story. In the gradient "2" ACT, the participative leader typically fails to fully reinvent him or herself. The transition stays within the scale pattern in Figure 7.4. The mentor and boss skills, both anchors in their respective leadership stories, conflict. The mentor is the steward of the community – a servant leader; the boss is unabashedly a self-interested agent. What does occur in participative leader's ACT "2" gradient is that a mentor with well-developed advocate skills – a participative leader interested in winning by advancing a position – crosses the communitarian story line in pursuit of wealth and control. Advocates turned partners seek to utilize their connections in the community for their own personal advancement. Accustomed as they are to dialogue and compromise, the partner from the communitarian worldview is easy prey for the aggressive buccaneer leader. The buccaneer leader seeks resources. This often entails not merely financing, but also access to the niche market of a viable community. The partner, over time, will be seen as a "sell out" by true believers in the cooperation pays story.

The participative leader's gradient "2" ACT of the buccaneer with partnering skills often ends badly. The incumbent who crosses the story line from community to self-interested behaviour is depicted as a turncoat by communitarians. He or she is no longer trustworthy.[29] They now give voice to views which are no longer seen as either authentic or in the best interest of the community as a whole. They are viewed as opportunists. On the other hand, the leader with partnering skills (precisely because they are amenable to compromise and open to negotiation and dialogue) are used rather shabbily by those fully anchored in the boss's skills. Those with boss's skills embrace their partner when they have an urgent need for resources but easily push them to the side when the need is either fulfilled or no longer of great importance. Too compassionate and mindful of others to be a boss yet now having been seen to cross the line from advocate to partner, they are precariously caught between the two. They will have a hard time regaining acceptance from their communitarian colleagues and an even more arduous time attempting to anchor in the boss's skills. Partners hailing from the cooperation pays story feel that they owe allegiance to those who have aided them. Bosses relentlessly trade up.

KNOWLEDGE LEADER'S ACTS

Consistent with the anchor skills of the innovator in the portal to a new world story, knowledge leaders reinvent themselves and are drawn out of their preferred story by their creative curiosity and ceaseless pursuit of new and challenging horizons. When these are best realized in the network worldview, knowledge leaders prefer to stay there. In this skill transition the knowledge leader anchors in innovator's skills (⊠⊠) and develops reach by augmenting the anchor skill, when needed, with deal maker's skills (⊠$), collaborator's skills (⊠○) and along the diagonal, navigator's skills (⊠Δ). Knowledge leaders who develop their deal maker's skills are attractive as tacticians ($⊠) to buccaneers in the entrepreneurial worldview; those who intensify their collaborator's skills are potential diplomats (○⊠) or symbolic leaders representing inward looking communities and along the diagonal those with navigator's skills are sought after as strategists (Δ⊠) by bureaucratic leaders eager to add a modicum of innovative capability to a tradition-bound structure.

In the knowledge leader's ACTs (see Figure 7.5), the gradient "1A" ACT appended to the gradient "3A" finds the knowledge leader migrating from the anchor skill of the network worldview to the skills of the tactician in the entrepreneurial worldview. This occurs when networks become cash-starved.[30] The innovator enlarges his or her deal making skills in pursuit of resources. Networks thrive when the populace is optimistic and confident, not only regarding the future, but are also willing to throw ample time, money and energy into new solutions, products and services. Knowledge leaders are pressed to enlarge their deal maker skills when populations turn away from the future and insist upon the tried, tested and true. Innovation is cyclical. Populations oscillate between a breathless desire to push into uncertain territory then withdraw into a lengthy period of quietly absorbing the novelty. In the latter periods, knowledge leaders are pressed to increase their

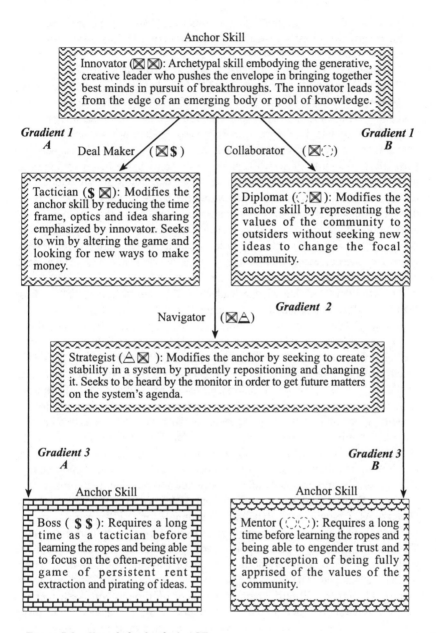

Figure 7.5 Knowledge leader's ACTs

entrepreneurial skills and both extract rents to sustain their projects and find ways to turn from costly research and development to less costly forms of operating creativity.

The gradient "1A", innovator (⊠⊠) → deal maker (⊠$) → tactician ($⊠) ACT when appended to the gradient "3A" knowledge leader ACT, tactician → boss ($$) speaks to the reinvention of the knowledge leader as the buccaneer. The leader's story is reinvented in the move from the wave pattern to the brick pattern in Figure 7.5. Buccaneer leaders are attracted to those who can raise money. Effective deal makers do just that. Buccaneers are particularly drawn to those who can do this when what is being sold is in its idea stage. In turn, deal makers in the network worldview are attracted to big money, especially during hard times within the portal to a new world story. In these circumstances, not only is remuneration better in crossing over to the entrepreneurial story, it is tied to a clear commission payment pattern; deal makers in the network worldview holding stock options stay where they are when the market evaluation of the agile network firms soars. They look elsewhere when these evaluations go into the trash heap.

The gradient "3A" knowledge leader's ACT from tactician ($⊠) → boss ($$) takes time. Tacticians look for ways bosses can use capital to enhance opportunity. They are bosses who think outside a specific entrepreneurial box by looking at how and when buccaneers ought to move to new options with a greater profit potential. They become exceedingly wealthy during periods in which new entrepreneurial business forms emerge. They often pilot these into boss's skills. The tactician, in modifying his or her skills to that of the boss, must learn to stay with what works and move away from the desire to try out something new. The boss only experiments when he or she is assured profits are forthcoming. At times, tacticians are lured by the excitement of the change itself. They wishfully see in it a fortune. Tacticians become bosses as they relinquish their fascination with change and focus solely upon change which is easily implemented and can, once put into practice, reap profits.

The reflective practice in the gradient "1A", gradient "3A" knowledge leader's ACT entails a rebalancing of the innovator's skill portfolio so that the bottom line business component rises to the fore. This generates tension. The innovator's emphasis is upon creativity. He or she seeks to push the project toward new heights and depths of experimentation – the cost, within reason, be damned. The innovator turned boss is preoccupied with the profit margin. He or she will push "beta" versions or prototypes with known errors into the market in order to both beat others to the punch and yield more profits. This "beta" version is justified by the innovator turned boss as an expedient means of getting the consumer involved and providing those in the project with useful feedback on how to improve future versions. A second and interrelated tension emerges. Innovators who have reinvented themselves as buccaneers will self-consciously play up innovations as radical even when they know them to be merely old wine in new bottles; the innovator recognizing the importance of his or her reputation in securing a leadership role as networks terminate and reconvene with an altered cast of characters is less likely to push in this direction. In a nutshell, the innovator intends to remain in the knowledge pool upon which the network is based; the innovator turned buccaneer will migrate to where there is more money to be made.

In the gradient "1B", innovator (☒☒) → collaborator (☒○) → diplomat (○☒) and gradient "3B" ACTs, diplomat → mentor (○○), one sees in outline how the four faces of capitalism portray the reinvention of the knowledge leader as a participative leader. This ACT entails transitioning from the wave pattern of the innovator to the scale pattern of the mentor's anchor skill in the communitarian worldview. This reinvention occurs under conditions quite distinct from those which mark the transformation from knowledge leader to buccaneer. Rather than pursuing immediate profits under adverse network conditions, the innovator in these ACTs seeks to create a cohesive community of capable creatives who will rise to the challenge of future problems and learn to handle new ventures. This creation of a communitarian culture in the midst of the loosely structured, temporary network solves the problem of how to care for, feed and motivate creatives. It also reduces the probability of creating a high-priced star system in the network's constant search for leading-edge talent. In this ACT, it is the culture and its intrinsic satisfaction that draws, retains and maintains the commitment of the best minds.

The reflective practice in the reinvention of the knowledge leader as a participative leader takes place on the boundary between the portal to a new world and the cooperation pays story. In the former, as denoted by the innovator with collaborator's skill, the knowledge leader who stresses teamwork, high involvement and idea sharing does so in order to increase the probability of this network beating other networks to a breakthrough. Even with the collaborator's skills, the knowledge leader will utilize short-term contracts and periodic culling of participants in order to keep the project focused. Those whose knowledge has been successfully absorbed by the network will be let go. In the cooperation pays side of the equation the emphasis is not upon collaboration in the hope of increasing the competitive advantage of the network in the short term; rather, it is upon increasing the cohesiveness of the culture in which the network generates a community capable of sustained innovation. The participative leader emphasizes process; the knowledge leader acknowledges process but reveres successful breakthroughs.

Knowledge leaders cross over into the cooperation pays story when networks begin to feel like communities and participants whose relationship to the network is transitory are made to feel like members. The diplomat, the worldly participative leader who has seen many different communities, is ideally placed as a figure to bring fragmented, *ad hoc* networks with their project base into the safe harbour of a creative, yet innovative community. The diplomat who understands various best practices, is versed in communicating and can act as an information conduit in bringing the network into acknowledging a shared set of values. The mentor embodies these shared values. The diplomat in a network once teeming with splinter projects and temporary contracts is the ideal candidate, over time, to act as the provisional centre. He or she is a magnet to creatives who must become technically proficient to attract intermediaries and investors. While the innovator → mentor reinvention is vital to those who seek to build a long-term creative culture, it can be argued that over time, within this ACT, radical innovation will give way to innovation. The innovator at the helm of a network possesses a desire to generate breakthroughs; the member in a community will interpret innovation as part of a longer learning process. Both vocabularies are partial to knowledge and flexibility. The former pushes competition; the latter extols cultural maintenance.

Along the diagonal in the knowledge leader's ACTs, knowledge leaders who attempt to take on the skills of bureaucratic leaders anchored in the monitor's skill will have trouble. Leadership reinvention here is problematic. The innovator transitions from the wave pattern of the built to last story, takes on the skills of the strategist, but fails to move to the dotted pattern of the anchor in the built to last story (see Figure 7.5). Innovators seek uncertainty in order to generate creativity; monitors abhor uncertainty in their systemic quest for order and stability. In the gradient "2" ACT, innovator (⊠⊠) → navigator (⊠Δ) → strategist (Δ⊠), the innovator with navigator skills can, in the right circumstances, make an excellent strategist in the built to last story. The innovator with navigator skills is a whiz at creating order in the midst of the blooming buzzing confusion of the typical project-based network. The navigator provides the basis for scheduling, coordinating and budgeting in a rather disorderly, anything goes, *ad hoc*racy. Large hierarchical systems seeking to purchase the potential to innovate by acquiring agile firms within the network worldview recognize the navigator as the leader. The navigator, unlike the innovator, collaborator or deal maker (the other skills in the knowledge leader's portfolio), has the basic figures needed to managed. These may not pass the standards of evidence needed in the hierarchical system, but they are vastly more reliable than the sales pitch of the deal maker, the visionary insight of the innovator and the "we will overcome by learning" message conveyed by the collaborator.

The reflective practice embedded in the innovator with navigator skills crossing from the network worldview to the built to last story involves the leader's willingness to move from provisional to contingent forms of analytic reasoning. As an innovator with navigator skills, the leader in the portal to a new world story employs quick and dirty measures or snapshots to capture the changing nature of orderliness in a highly dynamic network. Maps so created are tentative and exploratory. They are useful for a very brief time. As a strategist in the built to last story, the leader attends to options based on and grounded in data about the system and its operations. The data are clear within the rules of the system. The contingent policies and alternative strategies of the strategist are employed on an ongoing basis by those planning change in hierarchical systems. In this story, out of the box thinking helps portray a predictable or planned future using data from the past. Because of this difference between provisional and contingent reasoning, navigators who cross over to the built to last story must begin to take on the propensity for clear measurement and factual evidence required by those seeking to enhance the reliability of systems.

In all four ACTs – buccaneer, bureaucratic, participative and knowledge leaders – the contextual model of leadership permits one to examine how, and to some extent why, leaders move both into or out of stories other than those in their comfort zone. In some ACTs, leaders have the potential to fully reinvent themselves. Reflective practice accompanies leaders whose voyage propels them out of their worldview into unknown and beckoning territory. At first the tendency is to employ one's preferred story to map and make sense of the new territory. In time and with hard work leaders learn to hybridize stories, customizing them to the altering conditions about themselves and, in even more time, reconfigure their skill portfolio. The use of the four faces of capitalism is an important step in moving away from two strong problems which occur in most leadership books – first, the tendency to prescribe that a leader, for instance, requires vision without thoroughly underscoring how vision in the domain of the bureaucratic leader is totally at odds with that experienced by the knowledge leader, and second, to point out how important it is for leaders to develop new skills, but provide little direction as to which skills practising leaders can develop in tandem with others and for what purpose. Leadership is contextual. Learning is situational. Leaders who learn new skills put these two together.

CONTEXTUAL LEADERSHIP IN PRACTICE

This book ends where it started. We are reminded not only that there are no easy answers to leadership, no master story or narrative. Leaders come in many different sizes, packages and types. They speak different languages. Each of us prefers some version of the leader over others. In fact in the four faces of capitalism, or as my students continually call it – Wexler's wheel – we are known by the leaders we seek. As followers we are enticed by the winning ways of the bottom-line buccaneer. The buccaneer leader defines leadership in the act of winning. We are drawn to the bureaucratic leader in the quest to serve in a system that promises to reduce our anxiety by providing a clear routine and structure. We subordinate our desire to win in the belief that through our loyalty to the system and its provisions of security we will find security and long-term benefits. As members we are enchanted by the participative leader. He or she shares our values and credibly intimates that in becoming committee members of a community we will find meaning and purpose. We will be involved with others in a significant effort to learn, adapt to change, and realize our sustainable potential. We become participants and like to think of ourselves as free agents in the knowledge leader's network. The knowledge leader holds out the promise that we can become masters in a designed future. The excitement of joining in exploring the barely possible or just-imaginable intrigues those who see the leader as the explorer and prophet.

In the four faces of capitalism, I have tried to work with four archetypal stories of leaders within their worldview. These stories form the basic vocabulary for helping leaders and students of leadership map the variations within the theme of leadership. The model provides a field guide for how and why within each of these leadership stories leaders develop unique skills. The skills respond to the basic pulls – upward towards control, outward towards competition, inward towards culture or system maintenance and downward towards flexibility. The contextual model strongly fights our propensity to champion our preferred story as the genuine leader's story. It reminds us that those of us who would like to stay within our preferred leadership story can enlarge our within-story skills by accommodating the functional requisites or pulls other stories have "within" our worldview. Thus leaders within their comfort zone can develop skills which move out of their anchor skills and increase their reach. The model is systematic. Those who follow my reasoning will build techniques to systematically build within-story reach.

Leaders who develop reflective practice, self-consciously enter into ACTs or anchor cross-story transitions in which they not only increase their reach and hybridize stories, but also customize leadership skill portfolios in the act of reinventing themselves as leaders. The four faces of capitalism provide practising leaders with a field guide to reflective practice. While leaders in this model are ultimately not plastic they can become more cosmopolitan and realize their skills by developing a means of establishing ACTs which match their contexts. The model requires that the leader be able to read contexts and develop a course of action that resonates with both their unique worldview and their emerging skill set.

The model is also of use to those who seek to coach leaders and executives. Reaching for new skills within the model can be frightening, particularly skills along the diagonal wherein the acquired skill is in tension with the leader's existing skill sets. Leadership and executive coaches would do well to work with leaders seeking to enlarge their reach by showing them what it is that with their present skill system they can grasp. There is no affirmation better than succeeding in realizable victories before one takes on challenges far beyond one's grasp. Ultimately the coach's task is to help the leaders read their context and understand the moves open to them and the nature of the gradient required to acquire the skills.

In the end, the model celebrates the leader who can suture his or her version of success to their leadership story. The origins, plot, audience, nature of the protagonist, genre and lessons of the story are archetypically riveted. The leader with reach, however, customizes this to achieve success. Leaders do not find success, they make it and help others – followers, subordinates, members and participants – see it.

NOTES

1. Ronald A. Heifetz (1994), *Leadership Without Easy Answers*, Cambridge, MA: Belknap Press of Harvard University, p. 252.
2. Examples of solid work done probing reflective practice that the reader is urged to examine are Donald A. Schön (1983), *The Reflective Practitioner: How Professionals Think in Action*, New York: Basic Books; Marilyn W. Daudelin (1996), "Learning from experience through reflection," *Organizational Dynamics*, **38**(3), pp. 36–48; and David Golding and David Currie (2000), *Thinking About Management: A Reflective Practice Approach*, London: Routledge, which explores reflective practice in business leaders.
3. Paul Simon's treatment of leaders who pander, although filtered through an American lens, makes the point clearly that contemporary leaders frequently play to their followers, subordinates, members and/or participants. He explains why. See Paul Simon (2003), *Our Culture of Pandering*, Carbondale: Southern Illinois Press.
4. For an example of a challenging set of contemporary readings that discusses the relationship between cultural worldviews and success, see Robert J. Sternberg and Elena L. Grigorenko (eds) (2004), *Culture and Competence: Contexts of Life Success*, Washington, DC: American Psychological Association; Sydney Finkelstein's approach of finding out what we can learn about how we define success by looking at failed leaders is a very fruitful way to approach this position. See Sydney Finkelstein (2003), *Why Smart Executives Fail and What You Can Learn From Their Mistakes*, New York: Portfolio; or his brief treatment of this book in Sydney Finkelstein (2003), "Seven habits of spectacularly unsuccessful people," *Harvard Business Review*, **14**(4), pp. 39–50.
5. Alvin Gouldner first applied the distinction between cosmopolitans and locals in instrumental contexts a half century ago. See Alvin Gouldner (1954), *Patterns of Industrial Bureaucracy*, Glencoe, IL: Free Press. It has since been applied fruitfully to understand skill transitions and leadership. For example, see Walter R. Heinz and Victor W. Marshall (eds) (2003), *Social Dynamics of the Life Course: Transitions, Institutions and Interrelations*, Hawthorne, NY: Aldine de Gruyter; Robert J. House and Robert Widgar (1969), "Cosmopolitan and locals: Some differential correlations between leader behaviour, organizational practice and employee satisfaction and performance," *Academy of*

Management Proceedings, pp. 135–9; and Bronislaw Szersynski and John Urry (2002), "Cultures of cosmopolitanism," *The Sociological Review*, **50**(4), pp. 461–8.

6. Both Richard Scase and Richard Evans Farson argue, in very different ways, that developing a linear skill pattern as a leader leaves one entirely vulnerable in corporate settings. See Richard Scase (2002), *Living in the Corporate Zoo*, Oxford: Capstone and Richard E. Farson (1996), *Management of the Absurd: Paradoxes in Leadership*, New York: Simon & Schuster. Marvin Weisbord looks at skill development in the workplace as requiring the emotional intelligence needed to deal with rapid change while still maintaining close relationships and a good knowledge of one's capacities. See Marvin Ross Weisbord (2004), *Productive Workplaces Revisited: Dignity, Meaning and Community in the 21st Century*, San Francisco: Jossey-Bass.

7. The gradients in the four faces of capitalism can be likened to steepness when talking of learning curves. See Linda Argote (1999), *Organizational Learning: Creating, Retaining and Transferring Knowledge*, Dordrecht: Kluwer Academic Publishers, and Ezey M. Dar-El (2000), *Human Learning: From Learning Curves to Learning Organizations*, Dordrecht: Kluwer Academic Publishers.

8. For an introduction to the competing values schemata that I employ to deal with worldviews which lack a talking point, see the creative and, in my view, insightful treatment given by Robert E. Quinn and his various collaborators. See, for example: Robert E. Quinn, H.W. Rogers, H.W. Hildebrandt, P. Rogers and M.P. Thompson (1999), "A competing values framework for analyzing presentational communication in management contexts," *The Journal of Business Communications*, **28**(3), pp. 213–31; Randolph B. Cooper and Robert E. Quinn (1993), "Implications of the competing values framework for management information systems," *Human Resources Management*, **32**(1), pp. 175–201; and Robert E. Quinn and John Rohrbaugh (1983), "A spatial model of effectiveness criteria: Towards a competing values approach to organizational analysis," *Management Science*, **29**(4), pp. 363–77. More recent book-length efforts to put the competing values framework into use can be seen in Kim S. Camera and Robert E. Quinn (1998), *Diagnosing and Changing Organizational Culture: Based on the Competing Values Framework*, Reading, MA: Addison Wesley and Robert E. Quinn (2004), *Building the Bridge as You Walk On It: A Guide for Leading Change*, San Francisco, CA: Jossey-Bass.

9. Compare and contrast the vision skill of leaders in the four popular books on or about leadership. See James M. Kouzes and Barry Z. Posner (2002), *The Leadership Challenge*, San Francisco: Jossey-Bass; Fons Trompenaars and Charles Hampden-Turner (2001), *21 Leaders for the 21st Century: How Innovative Leaders Manage in the Digital Age*, Oxford: Capstone Publishing; Daniel Goleman, Richard Boyatzis and Annie McKee (2002), *Primal Leadership: Realizing the Power of Emotional Intelligence*, Cambridge, MA: Harvard Business School Press; and Robert H. Miles (1997), *Leading Corporate Transformations: A Blueprint for Business Renewal*, San Francisco: Jossey-Bass.

10. Entrepreneurs' identities change with the rising and falling fortunes of buccaneer leaders and the changing nature of their followers as they enter and exit firms in search of greater profits and opportunities. Robert Lord and Douglas Brown capture the basis of this idea in their recent book. See Robert Lord and Douglas Brown (2001), *Leadership Process and Follower Self-Identity*, Mahwah, NJ: Lawrence Erlbaum. Explore Michael A. Hogg (2001), "A social identity theory of leadership," *Personality and Social Psychology Review*, **5**(3), pp. 184–210; and Stuart Albert, Blake E. Ashforth and Jane E. Dulton (2000), "Organizational identity and identification: Charting new waters and building new bridges," *Academy of Management Review*, **25**(1), pp. 13–18, to piece together the social psychological aspects of leaders reinventing themselves.

11. The psycho-social aspects of 9/11 and the collective trauma therein are still being processed by contemporary thinkers. I have found Neil Smelser's (2004) piece "September 11, 2001 as cultural trauma," in Jeffrey C. Alexander (ed.) *Cultural Trauma and Collective Identity*, Berkeley, CA: University of California Press; and Norman K. Denzin and Yvonna S. Lincoln (2003), *9/11 in American Culture*, Walnut Creek, CA: Alta Mira Press, capture the complex, bellicose and security-seeking strivings that still accompany this event.

12. For a solid discussion of creativity in the competitive market context, see Stanley S.

Gryskiewicz (1999), *Positive Turbulence: Developing Climates For Creativity, Innovation and Renewal*, Greensboro, NC: Center for Creative Leadership; and with a nod to marketing, Mark Earls (2002), *Welcome To the Creative Age: Bananas, Business and the Death of Marketing*, Chichester: Wiley.

13. When I write that "bosses cannot reinvent themselves into mentors", I do not suggest it is impossible, but given the contradictions in values held by leaders in each of the varying anchor skills, it can only be accomplished when the leader is motivated to radically reorder his or her cultural assumptions. This entails a conversion process preceded by important life-changing antecedents. Urs Fuhrer (2003), *Cultivating Minds: Identity as Meaning-Making Practice*, New York: Taylor and Francis, captures the semiotic net we use to move from one worldview to another and the conditions which make this difficult. Manuel Castells (2004), *The Power of Identity*, Oxford: Blackwell, relates our efforts to change ourselves with our changing definition and understanding of power and its application.

14. In the combustible admixture of the entrepreneurial worldview and the buccaneer leader in gradient "2" ACTs making inroads into the cooperation pays story, money increasingly gives way to status and over time to the quest for meaningful relations. Robert D. Putnam (2000), *Bowling Alone: The Collapse and Revival of American Community*, New York: Simon & Schuster, argues that materialism alone alienates and deeply disenchants those who expect to find happiness in the heady mixture of rugged individualism and the singular pursuit of wealth.

15. Efforts to plumb the motives of ardent capitalists who act altruistically and philanthropically is a renewed topic of interest to leadership scholars. See Mark N. Wexler (2000), *Confronting Moral Worlds: Understanding Business Ethics*, Toronto: Prentice Hall; Michael Hopkiss (2000), *The Planetary Bargain: Corporate Social Responsibility Comes of Age*, Basingstoke, Hampshire: Macmillan Press; and, from a corporate communications perspective, Paul A. Argenti (2002), *The Power of Corporate Communication: Crafting the Voice of Your Business*, New York: McGraw-Hill.

16. Jeanne M. Plas (1996), *Person-Centered Leadership: An American Approach to Participatory Management*, Thousand Oaks, CA: Sage Publications, explores the antipathies between teamwork and rugged individualism that mark many contemporary businesses in America and elsewhere.

17. See John M. Clark, Bettina Cornwell and Stephen W. Pruitt (2002), "Corporate stadium sponsorships, signalling theory, agency conflicts and shareholder wealth," *Journal of Advertising Research*, **42**(6), pp. 16–32. These authors convincingly argue that corporate sponsorship of sports stadiums significantly enhances the stock price of sponsoring companies. The complex relationship in motives by buccaneer leaders is also discussed in arts sponsorship. See Mark W. Rectanus (2002), *Culture Incorporated: Museums, Artists and Corporate Sponsorships*, Minneapolis: University of Minnesota Press.

18. The difficulties encountered by ageing stars in executive and leadership roles are encapsulated in the first-rate treatment by Ann Howard and Douglas Bray. See Ann Howard and Douglas W. Bray (1988), *Managerial Lives in Transition: Advancing Age and Changing Times*, New York: Guilford Press. Harry Levinson and Manfred Kets deVries, two writers on leadership from a psychoanalytic orientation, take different perspectives in describing the ageing leader in a business context. Attend to Manfred Kets deVries (2003), "The retirement syndrome: The psychology of letting go," *European Management Journal*, **21**(6), pp. 707–16, and Harry Levinson (1969), "On being a middle-aged manager," *Harvard Business Review*, **47**(9), pp. 51–60.

19. Discussions of stakeholders broaden the view and scope of discussions of hierarchical systems by expanding the treatment of those who have a stake in the system from the shareholder to a long cast of characters including suppliers, contractors, clients, news media, activists, lobbyists and the like. For the seminal position on stakeholders, see Edward R. Freeman (1984), *Strategic Management: A Stakeholder Approach*, Boston, MA: Pitman. Don Tapscott and David Ticoll (2003), *The Naked Corporations: How the Age of Transparency Will Revolutionize Business*, New York: Free Press, discuss how and why increasing activism by formerly relatively passive stakeholders is leading to an accelerating demand for openness in corporate and bureaucratic governance.

20. Jon R. Katzenbach and Douglas K. Smith (1994), *The Wisdom of Teams: Creating the High Performance Organization*, New York: Harper Business, capture the basic argument for the preferred use of teams over individuals in task completion. For the argument on the creative potential of cross-functional teams, see Glenn M. Parker (2003), *Cross-Functional Teams: Working with Allies, Enemies and Other Strangers*, 2nd edn, San Francisco: Jossey-Bass.

21. For a useful discussion of why hierarchical systems purchase or go at innovation indirectly from an economist's position, see Walter Adams and James W. Brock (2004), *The Bigness Complex*, 2nd edn, Stanford, CA: Stanford Economics and Finance. From a behavioural orientation, attend to very useful compilations of readings in Andrew M. Pettigrew (ed.), *Innovative Forms of Organizing: International Perspectives*, London: Sage Publications.

22. Peruse Thomas W. Malone, Robert Laubacher and Michael S. Scott Morton (eds) (2003), *Inventing the Organizations of the 21st Century*, Cambridge, MA: MIT Press, especially the article by Thomas W. Malone and Robert Laubacher entitled "Two scenarios for 21st century: Shifting networks of small firms or all-encompassing 'virtual countries'," to capture some of the interesting work being done on the structure of new organizational forms in the network worldview.

23. For the growing field of strategic planning seen to formulate means of making bureaucratically structural systems more responsive and provide them with techniques to achieve competitive advantage, see Hugh Courtney (2001), *20/20 Foresight: Crafting Strategy in an Uncertain World*, Cambridge, MA: Harvard Business School Press, for an analysis of the motives, basic tools and processes, and Mike Freedman and Benjamin B. Tregoe (2003), *The Art and Discipline of Strategic Leadership*, New York: McGraw-Hill, for a more behavioural treatment of strategic planning.

24. Diversity in the community accelerates as participative leaders look for ways to cope with uncertainty and the use of relevant ideas outside the boundaries of the community. See the compilation of readings in Margaret S. Stockdale and Faye J. Crosby (2004), *The Psychology and Management of Workplace Diversity*, Oxford: Blackwell Publishing, and for an application to cognitive styles, see Michael J. Kirton (2003), *Adaptation–Innovation: In the Context of Diversity and Change*, London: Routledge.

25. Verna Alee (1997), *The Knowledge Evolution: Expanding Organizational Intelligence*, Boston, MA: Heinemann, captures the notion of intellectual capital in the ongoing relations between trusting members of a working community. Thomas A. Stewart (2001), *The Wealth of Knowledge: Intellectual Capital and the Twenty-First Century Organization*, New York: Currency Publishing, broadens this position to include collaborative forms of technology and structured routines in his highly readable treatment of intellectual capital.

26. We get a sense of the drive for fame and priority of discovery in White and Wright's conversation with contemporary innovators and leaders. See Shira P. White and G. Patton Wright (2002), *New Ideas About New Ideas: Insights on Creativity From the World's Leading Innovators*, Cambridge, MA: Perseus. David Giles explores the complex cycle of the perils of authenticity and the potential curbing of creativity that accompany the psychology of fame. See David Giles (1999), *Illusions of Immortality: A Psychology of Fame and Celebrity*, New York: St Martin's Press.

27. In the post-Enron, post-Parmalaat period, there is a discernible call for reforming corporate governance and accountability. See Jill Solomon and Aris Solomon (2004), *Corporate Governance and Accountability*, New York: John Wiley. For a solid set of readings using the Enron case to argue their position, see Christopher L. Culp and William A. Niskanen (eds) (2003), *Corporate Aftershock: The Public Lessons From the Collapse of Enron and Other Major Corporations*, New York: John Wiley.

28. The process of bureaucratization addresses the spread of the regulatory worldview and an increasing reliance upon formal structure, rules and objective measures to standardize events. See Sanford M. Jacoby (2004), *Employing Bureaucracy: Managers, Unions and the Transformation of Work in the Twentieth Century*, Mahwah, NJ: Lawrence Erlbaum, for a historical treatment of this concept, and Martin Kitchener (2000), "The bureaucratization of professional roles: The cases of clinical directors in UK hospitals," *Organizations*, **7**(1), pp. 129–44, for an example of this logic in a contemporary setting.

29. Failure or betrayal of trust is a difficult process to remedy. See Sally Bibb and Jeremy Kourdi (2004), *Trust Matters: For Organizational and Personal Success*, Basingstoke, Hampshire: Palgrave Macmillan; and the compilation of readings by Diego Gambieta (ed.) (1988), *Trust: Making and Breaking Cooperative Relations*, Oxford: Blackwell Publishing.
30. Colin Barrow (2000), *How to Survive the e-Business Downturn*, Chichester: John Wiley, captures the early days of the dot.com meltdown; Brigette Preissl, Harry Bouwman and Charles Steinfield (eds) (2003), *e-Life After the Dot.Com Bust*, New York: Springer, follow up the story three years later.

Bibliography

Ackoff, Russell L. (1999), *Re-creating the Corporation: A Design of Organizations for the 21st Century*, New York and Oxford: Oxford University Press.

Amar, A.D. (2001), *Managing Knowledge Workers: Unleashing Innovation and Productivity*, Westport, CT: Quorum Books.

Antonakis, John, Anna T. Cianciolo and Robert J. Sternberg (eds), *The Nature of Leadership*, Thousand Oaks, CA: Sage Publications.

Argote, Linda (1999), *Organizational Learning: Creating, Retaining and Transferring Knowledge*, Dordrecht: Kluwer Academic Publishers.

Argyris, Chris (1993), *On Organizational Learning*, Cambridge, MA: Blackwell Publishers.

Argyris, Chris (2004), *Reasons and Rationalizations: The Limits to Organizational Knowledge*. NewYork, USA and Oxford, UK: Oxford University Press.

Badaracco, Joseph (2002), *Leading Quietly: An Unorthodox Guide to Doing the Right Thing*, Cambridge, MA: Harvard Business School Press.

Badaracco, Joseph L. Jr and Richard R. Ellsworth (1989), *Leadership and the Quest for Integrity*, Cambridge, MA: Harvard Business School Press.

Bauman, Zygmunt (2000), *Liquid Modernity*, Oxford, UK and Malden, MA, USA: Blackwell.

Bauman, Zygmunt (2001), *Community: Seeking Safety in an Insecure World*, Oxford, UK and Malden, MA, USA: Blackwell.

Baumol, William J. (2002), *The Free-Market Innovation Machine: Analyzing the Growth Miracle of Capitalism*, Princeton, NJ: Princeton University Press.

Baxter, Stephen (2001), *Deep Future*, London: Victor Gollancz.

Bell, Daniel (1993), *Communitarianism and Its Critics*, Oxford: Clarendon Press.

Bennet, Alex and David Bennet (2004), *Organizational Survival in the New World: The Intelligent Complex Adaptive System*, Amsterdam and Boston, MA, USA: Butterworth-Heinemann.

Bennis, Warren (2003), *On Becoming a Leader*, Cambridge, MA: Perseus.

Bennis, Warren G. and Burt Nanus (1985), *Leaders: The Strategies for Taking Charge*, New York: Harper & Row.

Bennis, Warren G. and Robert J. Thomas (2002), *Geeks and Geezers: How Era, Values and Defining Moments Shape Leaders*, Cambridge, MA: Harvard Business School Press.

Bennis, Warren G., Gretchen M. Spreitzer and Thomas G. Cummings (2001), *The Future of Leadership: Today's Top Leadership Thinkers Speak to Tomorrow's Leaders*, San Francisco, CA: Jossey-Bass.

Birkenshaw, Julian M. (2000), *Entrepreneurship in the Global Firm*, London: Sage.

Bjerke, Bjorn (1999), *Business Leadership and Culture: National Management Styles in the Global Economy*, Cheltenham, UK and Northampton, MA, USA: Edward Elgar.

Black, J. Stewart, Allen Morrison and Hal Gregersen (1999), *Global Explorers: The Next Generation of Leaders*, New York and London: Routledge.
Blau, Peter M. and Marshall W. Meyer (1991), *Bureaucracy in Modern Society*, New York: Random House.
Boisot, Max (1995), *Information Space: A Framework for Learning in Organizations, Institutions and Cultures*, New York and London: Routledge.
Bolton, Bill K. and John Thompson (2004), *Entrepreneurs: Talent, Temperament and Technique*, Boston, MA: Elsevier Butterworth-Heinemann.
Boyle, Elizabeth and Stephen Mezias (2002), *Organizational Dynamics of Creative Destruction: Entrepreneurship and the Emergence of New Industries*, Basingstoke, UK and New York: Palgrave Macmillan.
Bozeman, Barry (2000), *Bureaucracy and Red Tape*, Upper Saddle River, NJ: Prentice Hall.
Brown, John Seely and Paul Duguid (2000), *The Social Life of Information*, Cambridge, MA: Harvard Business School Press.
Brown, Terence E. and Jan Ulijn (eds) (2004), *Innovation, Entrepreneurship and Culture: The Interaction Between Technology, Progress and Economics Growth*, Cheltenham, UK and Northampton, MA, USA: Edward Elgar.
Bryont, Jim (2003), *The Six Dilemmas of Collaboration: Inter-organization Relationship as Drama*, Chichester, UK and Hoboken, NJ, USA: Wiley.
Bryson, John Moore (1992), *Leadership for the Common Good: Tackling Public Problems in a Shared-Power World*, San Francisco, CA: Jossey-Bass.
Burns, James MacGregor (1978), *Leadership*, New York: Harper & Row.
Burns, James MacGregor (2003), *Transforming Leadership A New Pursuit of Happiness*, New York: Atlantic Monthly Press.
Burton-Jones, Alan (1999), *Knowledge Capitalism: Business, Work and Learning in the New Economy*, Oxford: Oxford University Press.
Butler, John E. (ed.) (2003), *New Perspectives on Women Entrepreneurs*, Greenwich, CT: Information Age Publishing.
Casson, Mark (2003), *The Entrepreneur: On Economic Theory*, Cheltenham, UK and Northampton, MA, USA: Edward Elgar.
Castells, Manuel (2000), *The Rise of the Network Society*, Oxford, UK and Malden, MA, USA: Blackwell Publishers.
Castells, Manuel (2004), *The Power of* Identity, Malden, MA, USA, and Oxford: Blackwell Publishers.
Caves, Richard E. (2000), *Creative Industries*, Cambridge, MA: Harvard University Press.
Champy, James and Nitin Nohria (2000), *The Arc of Ambition: Defining the Leadership Journey*, Cambridge, MA: Perseus Books.
Channer, Philip and Tina Hope (2001), *Emotional Impact: Passionate Leaders and Corporate Transformation*, Basingstoke, UK and New York: Palgrave.
Ciulla, Joanne B. (1998), *Ethics, the Heart of Leadership*, Westport, CT and London: Quorum.
Coates, David (2000), *Models of Capitalism: Growth and Stagnation in the Modern Era*, Cambridge, UK and Malden, MA, USA: Polity Press.
Cohan, Peter (2002), *E-Leaders*, Oxford: Capstone Publishers.
Cohen, Dan and Laurence Prusak (2001), *In Good Company: How Social Capital Makes Organizations Work*, Cambridge, MA: Harvard Business School Press.
Collins, James C. (2001), *Good to Great: Why Some Companies Make the Leap – Others Don't*, New York: Harper Business.

Collins, James C. and Jerry I. Porras (1997), *Build to Last: Successful Habits of Visionary Companies*, New York: Harper Business.

Conger, Jay A. and Beth Benjamin (1999), *Building Leaders: How Successful Companies Develop the Next Generation*, San Francisco, CA: Jossey-Bass.

Cooke, Phillip (2002), *Knowledge Economies: Clusters, Learning and Co-operative Advantage*, London and New York: Routledge.

Cooper, David J. (2003), *Leadership For Follower Commitment*, Oxford: Butterworth-Heinemann.

Cortada, James W. (2001), *21st Century Business: Managing and Working in the New Digital Economy*, Upper Saddle River, NJ: Financial Times/Prentice Hall.

Courtney, Hugh (2001), *20/20 Foresight: Crafting Strategy in an Uncertain World*, Cambridge, MA: Harvard Business School Press.

De Kluyver, Cornelis A. and John A. Pearce (2003), *Strategy: A View From the Top*, Upper Saddle River, NJ: Prentice Hall.

Dibben, Mark R. (2000), *Exploring Interpersonal Trust in the Entrepreneurial Venture*, Basingstoke: Macmillan.

Dilley, Roy (1992), *Contesting Markets: Analyses of Ideology, Discourse and Practice*, Edinburgh: Edinburgh University Press.

Dosi, Giovanni, Richard Nelson and Sidney G. Winter (eds) (2000), *The Nature and Dynamics of Organizational Capabilities*, Oxford, UK and New York: Oxford University Press.

Doz, Yves L. and Gary Hamel (1998), *Alliance Advantage: The Art of Creating Value Through Partnering*, Cambridge, MA: Harvard Business School Press.

Drucker, Peter F. (1998), *Post-Capitalist Society*, New York: Harper Business.

Drucker, Peter F. (1999), *Management Challenges For the 21st Century*, New York: Harper Business.

Du Gay, Paul (2000), *In Praise of Bureaucracy: Weber, Organization, Ethics*, London and Thousand Oaks, CA: Sage Publications.

Ellsworth, Richard R. (2002), *Leading With Purpose: The New Corporate Realities*, Stanford, CT: Stanford Business Books.

Emmott, Bill (2003), *20:21 Vision: The Lessons of the 20th Century for the 21st*, London and New York: Allen Lane.

Etzioni, Amitai (1995), *New Communitarian Thinking: Person, Virtues, Institutions and Communities*, Charlottesville, VA: University Press of Virginia.

Etzioni, Amitai (2004), *The Common Good*, Malden, MA: Pity Press.

Fahey, Liam (1999), *Competitors: Outwitting, Outmaneuvering and Outperforming*, New York and Chichester: Wiley.

Fairholm, Gilbert (1994), *Leadership and the Culture of Trust*, Westport, CT: Praeger.

Fairholm, Gilbert (1998), *Perspectives on Leadership From the Science of Management to Its Spiritual Heart*, Westport, CT and London: Quorum.

Fairholm, Gilbert W. (2001), *Mastering Inner Leadership*, Westport, CT: Quorum Books.

Fairhurst, Gail T. and Robert A. Sarr (1996), *The Art of Framing: Managing the Language of Leadership*, San Francisco, CA: Jossey-Bass.

Farson, Richard Evans (1996), *Management of the Absurd: Paradoxes of Leadership*, New York: Simon & Schuster.

Fiet, James O. and Jay B. Barney (2002), *The Systematic Search for Entrepreneurial Discoveries*, Westport, CT: Quorum Books.

Finkelstein, Sydney (2003), *Why Smart Executives Fail and What You Can Learn From Their Mistakes*, New York: Portfolio.

Fishman, Ethan (ed.) (2002), *Tempered Strength: Studies in the Nature and Scope of Prudential Leadership*, Lanham, MD: Lexington Books.

Fligstein, Neil (2001), *The Architecture of Markets: An Economic Sociology of Twenty-First Century Capitalist Societies*, Princeton, NJ: Princeton University Press.

Fombrun, Charles J. (1996), *Reputation: Realizing Value From the Corporate Image*, Cambridge, MA: Harvard Business School Press.

Frank, Robert H. and Philip Cook (1995), *The Winner-Take-All Society*, New York: Free Press.

Freedman, Mike and Benjamin B. Tregoe (2003), *The Art and Discipline of Strategic Leadership*, New York: McGraw-Hill.

Freeman, Edward R. (1984), *Strategic Management: A Stakeholder Approach*, Boston, MA: Pitman.

Freeman, Sue, Susan C. Borque and Christine Shelton (eds) (2001), *Women on Power: Leadership Redefined*, Boston, MA: Northeastern University Press.

Fritts, Patricia (1998), *The New Managerial Mentor: Becoming a Learning Leader to Build Communities of Purpose*, Palo Alto, CA: Davies-Black Publishing.

Frydman, Bert, Iva Wilson and JoAnne Wyer (2000), *The Power of Collaborative Leadership*, Boston, MA: Butterworth-Heinemann.

Fuhrer, Urs (2003), *Cultivating Minds: Identity as Meaning-Making Practice*, New York: Taylor and Francis.

Gambieta, Diego (ed.) (1988), *Trust: Making and Breaking Cooperative Relations*, Oxford: Blackwell Publishing.

Gardels, Nathan (ed.) (1997), *The Changing Global Order: World Leaders Reflect*, Malden, MA: Blackwell Publishers.

Gardner, Howard (1997), *Extraordinary Minds: Portraits of Exceptional Individuals and an Examination of Our Extraordinariness*, New York: Basic Books.

Gardner, Howard (1999), *Intelligence Reframed: Multiple Intelligences for the 21st Century*, New York: Basic Books.

Gee, James Paul, Glynda Hull and Colin Lankshear (1996), *The New Work Order: Behind the Language of the New Capitalism*, Boulder, CO: Westview Press.

Gerdes, Sarah (2003), *Navigating the Partnership Maze: Creating Alliances That Work*, New York: McGraw-Hill.

Gitlow, Abraham L. (1992), *Being the Boss: The Importance of Leadership and Power*, Homewood, IL: Business One Irwin.

Golding, David and David Currie (2000), *Thinking About Management: A Reflective Practice Approach*, London: Routledge.

Goldman, Alan (2002), *Practical Rules: When We Need Them and When We Don't*, Cambridge, UK and New York: Cambridge University Press.

Gottlieb, Marvin R. (2003), *Managing Group Processes*, Westport, CT: Praeger.

Grandstrand, Ove (1999), *The Economics and Management of Intellectual Property: Towards Intellectual Capitalism*, Cheltenham, UK and Northampton, MA, USA: Edward Elgar.

Greenleaf, Robert K. (1991), *Servant Leadership: A Journey Into the Nature of Legitimate Power and Greatness*, New York: Paulist Press.

Greenleaf, Robert K., Don M. Frick and Larry C. Spears (eds) (1996), *On Becoming a Servant-Leader*, San Francisco, CA: Jossey-Bass.

Gupta, Suman (2002), *Corporate Capitalism and Political Philosophy*, London and Sterling, VA: Pluto Press.

Hackman, J. Richard (2002), *Leading Teams: Setting the Stage For Great Performances*, Cambridge, MA: Harvard Business School Press.

Hambrick, Donald, David A. Nadler and Michael L. Tushman (eds) (1998), *Navigating Change: How CEOs, To Team and Boards Steer Transformation*, Cambridge, MA: Harvard Business School Press.

Hamilton, Richard (2001), *Mass Society, Pluralism and Bureaucracy: Explanation, Assessment and Commentary*, Westport, CT: Praeger.

Harkins, Philip (1999), *Powerful Conversations: How High Impact Leaders Communicate*, New York: McGraw-Hill.

Hassan, Robert (2003), *The Chronoscopic Society: Globalization, Time and Knowledge in the Network Economy*, New York: P. Lang.

Hay, Julie (1990), *Transformational Mentoring: Creating Developmental Alliances for Changing Organizational Cultures*, London and New York: McGraw-Hill.

Heifetz, Ronald A. (1994), *Leadership Without Easy Answers*, Cambridge, MA: Belknap Press of Harvard University.

Heifetz, Ronald A. and Marty Linksy (2002), *Leadership on the Line: Staying Alive Through the Dangers of Leading*, Cambridge, MA: Harvard Business School Press.

Heiskanen, Tuula and Jeff Hearn (eds) (2004), *Information Society and the Workplace: Spaces, Boundaries and Agency*, London and New York: Routledge.

Henderson, Keith and O.P. Dwiveda (eds) (1999), *Bureaucracy and the Alternatives in World Perspective*, Basingstoke: Macmillan.

Hirschorn, Larry (1998), *Reworking Authority: Leading and Following in the Post-Modern Organization*, Cambridge, MA: MIT Press.

Hjorth, Daniel (2003), *Rewriting Entrepreneurship: For a New Perspective on Organizational Creativity*, Malmo: Liber, and Oslo: Abstrakt.

Huber, George (2004), *The Necessary Nature of Future Firms: Attributes of Survivors in a Changing World*, Thousand Oaks, CA: Sage Publications.

Huber, John D. and Charles R. Shipan (2002), *Deliberate Discretion?: The Institutional Foundations of Bureaucracy*, New York and Cambridge, UK: Cambridge University Press.

Huseman, Richard and John P. Goodman (1999), *Leading With Knowledge: The Nature of Competition in the 21st Century*, Thousand Oaks, CA: Sage Publications.

Jacoby, Sanford M. (2004), *Employing Bureaucracy: Managers, Unions and the Transformation of Work in the Twentieth Century*, Mahwah, NJ: Lawrence Erlbaum.

Jaques, Elliott (1976), *A General Theory of Bureaucracy*, London: Heinemann.

Jaques, Elliott and Stephen D. Clement (1991), *Executive Leadership: A Practical Guide to Managing Complexity*, Cambridge, MA: Blackwell Business.

Johnson, W. Brad and Charles R. Ridley (2004), *The Elements of Mentoring*, New York: Palgrave Macmillan.

Jones, Sue (1996), *Developing a Learning Culture: Empowering People to Deliver Quality, Innovation and Long Term Success*, London and New York: McGraw-Hill.

Jones, Tim (2002), *Innovating at the Edge: How Organizations Evolve and Embed Innovation Capability*, Oxford: Butterworth-Heinemann.

Joni, Saj-Nicole A. (2004), *The Third Opinion: How Successful Leaders Use Outside Insight to Create Superior Results*, New York: Portfolio.

Judge, William Q. (1999), *The Leader's Shadow: Exploring and Developing Executive Character*, Thousand Oaks, CA: Sage Publications.

Kaplan, Robert S. and David P. Norton (2004), *Strategy Maps: Converting Intangible Assets Into Tangible Outcomes*, Cambridge, MA: Harvard Business School Press.

Keller, Suzanne (2003), *Community: Pursuing the Dream, Living the Reality*, Princeton, NJ: Princeton University Press.

Kets de Vries, Manfred (1993), *Leaders, Fools and Imposters: Essays on the Psychology of Leadership*, San Francisco, CA: Jossey-Bass.

Kikoski, Catherine and John F. Kikoski (2004), *The Inquiring Organization: Tacit Knowledge, Conversation and Knowledge Creation Skills For the 21st Century*, Westport, CT: Praeger.

Kirton, Michael J. (2003), *Adaption–Innovation: In the Context of Change and Diversity*, London and New York: Routledge.

Klein, Sherwin (2002), *Ethical Business Leadership: Balancing Theory and Practice*, New York: Peter Lang.

Klir, George J. and Doug Elias (2003), *Architecture of Systems Problem Solving*, New York: Kluwer Academic/Plenum Publishers.

Koehn, Nancy Fowler (2001), *Brand New: How Entrepreneurs Earned Consumers' Trust From Wedgwood to Dell*, Cambridge, MA: Harvard Business School Press.

Koestenbaum, Peter (1991), *Leadership: The Inner Side of Greatness*, San Francisco, CA: Jossey-Bass.

Kotter, John P. (1996), *Leading Change*, Cambridge, MA: Harvard Business School Press.

Kotter, John P. (1999), *John P. Kotter on What Leaders Really Do*, Cambridge, MA: Harvard Business School Press.

Kouzes, James M. and Barry Z. Posner (2002), *The Leadership Challenge*, 3rd edn, San Francisco, CA: Jossey-Bass.

Kramer, Roderick M. and Karen S. Cook (eds) (2004), *Trust and Distrust in Organizations: Dilemmas and Approaches*, New York: Russell Sage Foundation.

Krause, George and Kenneth J. Meir (2003), *Politics, Policy and Organizations: Frontiers in the Scientific Study of Bureaucracy*, Ann Arbor, MI: University of Michigan Press.

Krugman, Paul (2003), *The Great Unraveling: Losing Our Way in the New Century*, New York: W.W. Norton.

Laurie, Donald L. (2000), *The Real Work of Leaders: A Report From the Front Lines of Management*, Cambridge, MA: Perseus.

Lehman, Edward (2000), *Autonomy and Order: A Communitarian Anthology*, Lanham, MD: Rowman and Littlefield.

Lessem, Ronnie and Sudhanshu Palsule (1992), *Managing in Four Words: From Competition to Co-creation*, Cambridge, MA: Blackwell.

Lessig, Lawrence (2002), *The Future of Ideas: The Fate of the Commons in a Connected World*, New York: Vintage Books.

Lewis, Richard D. (2003), *The Cultural Imperative: Global Trends in the 21st Century*, Yarmouth, ME: Intercultural Press.

Lipman-Blumen, Jean (1996), *The Connective Edge: Leading in an Interdependent World*, San Francisco, CA: Jossey-Bass.

Lipman-Blumen, Jean (2004), *The Allure of Toxic Leaders: Why We Follow Destructive Bosses and Corrupt Politicians – and How We Can Survive Them*, New York and Oxford: Oxford University Press.

Lipman-Blumen, Jean and Harold J. Leavitt (1999), *Hot Groups: Seeding Them, Feeding Them and Using Them to Ignite Your Organization*, Oxford: Oxford University Press.

Lord, Robert and Douglas Brown (2001), *Leadership Process and Follower Self-Identity*, Mahwah, NJ: Lawrence Erlbaum.

Lovink, Geert (2002), *Uncanny Networks: Dialogues With the Virtual Intelligentsia*, Cambridge, MA: MIT Press.

Mandelbaum, Seymour (2000), *Open Moral Communities*, Cambridge, MA: MIT Press.

Mariotti, John (2002), *Making Partnerships Work*, Oxford: Capstone.

Maxwell, John C. (1999), *The 21 Indispensable Qualities of a Leader: Becoming a Person Others Will Want to Follow*, Nashville, TN: T. Nelson.

McGrath, Rita Guntler and Ian MacMillan (2000), *The Entrepreneurial Mindset: Strategies for Continuously Creating Opportunity in an Age of Uncertainty*, Cambridge, MA: Harvard Business School Press.

McKenna, Patrick J. and David H. Maister (2002), *First Among Equals: How to Manage a Group of Professionals*, New York: Free Press.

McLagan, Patricia and Christo Nel (1995), *The Age of Participation: New Governance for the Workplace and World*, San Francisco, CA: Berrett-Koehler.

Nanus, Burt and Stephen M. Dobbs (1999), *Leaders Who Make a Difference*, San Francisco, CA: Jossey-Bass.

Nicolini, Davide, Silvia Gherardi and Dvora Yanow (eds) (2003), *Knowing in Organizations: A Practice-Based Approach*, Armonk, NY: M.E. Sharpe.

Nooteboom, Bart and Frederique Six (2003), *The Trust Process in Organization: Empirical Studies of the Determinants and the Process of Trust Development*, Cheltenham, UK and Northampton, MA, USA: Edward Elgar.

Nutt, Paul C. (2002), *Why Decisions Fail: Avoiding the Blunders and Traps that Lead to Debacles*, San Francisco, CA: Berrett-Koehler.

Olmstead, Joseph A. (2002), *Leading Groups in Stressful Times*, Westport, CT: Quorum Books.

Omae, Kenichi (1999), *The Borderless World: Power and Strategy in the Interlinked Economy*, New York: Harper Business.

Patel, Keyur and Mary Pat McCarthy (2000), *Digital Transformation: The Essentials of e-Business Leadership*, New York: KPMG/McGraw-Hill.

Pearce, L. Craig and Jay A. Conger (eds) (2003), *Shared Leadership: Reframing the Hows and Whys of Leadership*, Thousand Oaks, CA: Sage Publications.

Popper, Michael (2001), *Hypnotic Leadership: Leaders, Followers and the Loss of Self*, Westport, CT: Praeger.

Putnam, Robert D. (2000), *Bowling Alone: The Collapse and Revival of American Community*, New York: Simon & Schuster.

Quinn, Robert E. (1998), *Beyond Rational Management: Mastering the Paradoxes of Competing Demands of High Performance*, San Francisco, CA: Jossey-Bass.

Quinn, Robert E. (2004), *Building the Bridge As You Walk On It: A Guide for Leading Change*, San Francisco, CA: Jossey-Bass.

Quinn, Robert E., Sue R. Faerman, Michael P. Thompson and Michael R. McGrath (2003), *Becoming a Master Manager: A Competency Framework*, New York: Wiley.

Ray, R. Glenn (1999), *The Facilitative Leader: Behaviors That Enable Success*, Upper Saddle River, NJ: Prentice Hall.

Reichmann, Thomas (1997), *Controlling: Concepts of Management Control, Controllership and Ratios*, Berlin and New York: Springer.

Reina, Michelle and Dennis Reina (1999), *Trust and Betrayal in the Workplace: Building Effective Relationships in Your Organization*, San Francisco, CA: Berrett-Koehler.

Robbins, Richard Howard (2002), *Global Problems and the Culture of Capitalism*, Boston, MA: Allyn & Bacon.

Roberts, John (2004), *The Modern Firm: Organizational Design for Performance and Growth*, Oxford: Oxford University Press.

Rosen, Bernard Carl (1998), *Winners and Losers of the Information Revolution: Psychosocial Change and Its Discontents*, Westport, CT: Praeger.

Salerno, Roger A. (2003), *Landscapes of Abandonment: Capitalism, Modernism and Estrangement*, Albany, NY: State University of New York Press.

Satha, Vijay (2003), *Corporate Entrepreneurship: Top Managers and New Business Creation*, Cambridge: Cambridge University Press.

Schön, Donald A. (1983), *The Reflective Practitioner: How Professionals Think in Action*, New York: Basic Books.

Schuler, Douglas (1996), *New Community Networks: Wired for Change*, Reading, MA: Addison-Wesley.

Schwartz, Peter (2003), *Inevitable Surprises: Thinking Ahead in a Time of Turbulence*, New York: Gotham Books.

Seeger, Matthew W., Timothy Sellnow and Robert Ulmer (2003), *Communication and Organizational Crisis*, Westport, CT: Praeger.

Segil, Larrain, Marshall Goldsmith and James Belasco (eds) (2003), *Partnering: The New Face of Leadership*, New York: American Management Association.

Seiling, Jane Galloway (2001), *The Meaning and Role of Organizational Advocacy: Responsibility and Accountability in the Workplace*, Westport, CT: Quorum Books.

Senge, Peter (1990), *The Fifth Discipline: The Art and Practice of the Learning Organization*, New York: Doubleday/Currency.

Shaviro, Steven (2003), *Connected, Or, What it Means to Live in the Network Society*, Minneapolis, MN: University of Minnesota Press.

Sifonis, John G. and Beverly Goldberg (1996), *Corporation on a Tightrope: Balancing Leadership, Governance and Technology in an Age of Complexity*, Oxford and New York: Oxford University Press.

Silzer, Rob (ed.) (2002), *The 21st Century Executive: Innovative Practices for Building Leadership at the Top*, San Francisco, CA: Jossey-Bass.

Simmons, Michael (1996), *New Leadership for Women and Men: Building an Inclusive Organization*, Aldershot: Gower.

Sison, Alejo G. (2003), *The Moral Capital of Leaders: Why Virtue Matters*, Cheltenham, UK and Northampton, MA, USA: Edward Elgar.

Sjöstrand, Sven-Erik, Jörgen Sandberg and Mats Tyrstrup (eds) (2001), *Invisible Management: The Social Construction of Leadership*, Boston, MA and London: Thomson Learning.

Sklair, Leslie (2002), *Globalization: Capitalism and Its Alternatives*, Oxford and New York: Oxford University Press.

Smits, Wendy and Thorsten Stromback (2000), *The Economics of the Apprenticeship Systems*, Cheltenham, UK and Northampton, MA, USA: Edward Elgar.

Soder, Roger (2001), *The Language of Leadership*, San Francisco, CA: Jossey-Bass.

Solomon, Jill and Aris Solomon (2004), *Corporate Governance and Accountability*, New York: John Wiley.

Spears, Larry and Michele Lawrence (eds) (2002), *Focus on Leadership: Servant Leadership for the Twenty-First Century*, New York: Wiley.

Spreitzer, Gretchen and Robert E. Quinn (2001), *A Company of Leaders Five Disciplines For Unleashing the Power in Your Workforce*, San Francisco, CA: Jossey-Bass.

Srivastua, Suresh and David L. Cooper (1990, *Appreciative Management and Leadership: The Power of Positive Thought and Action in Organizations*, San Francisco, CA: Jossey-Bass.

Starkey, Ken, Sue Tempest and Alan McKinlay (eds) (2004), *How Organizations Learn: Managing the Search for Knowledge*, London: Thomson.

Starratt, Robert J. (1993), *The Drama of Leadership*, London and Washington, DC: Falmer Press.

Steger, Ulrich (2003), *Corporate Diplomacy: The Strategy for a Volatile, Fragmented Business Environment*, Chichester and New York: Wiley.

Sterling, Bruce (2002), *Tomorrow Now: Envisioning the Next Fifty Years*, New York: Random House.

Sternberg, Robert J. and Elena L. Grigorenko (eds) (2004), *Culture and Competence: Contexts of Life Successes*, Washington, DC: American Psychological Association.

Stewart, Thomas A. (2001), *The Wealth of Knowledge: Intellectual Capital and the Twenty-First Century Organization*, New York: Currency Publishing.

Stivers, Richard (2004), *Shades of Loneliness: Pathologies of a Technological Society*, Lanham, MD: Rowman and Littlefield Publishers.

Strebel, Paul (2003), *Trajectory Management: Exploiting the Right Drivers for Business Leadership*, London: Wiley.

Tannen, Deborah (1998), *The Argument Culture: Moving From Debate to Dialogue*, New York: Random House.

Taylor, William Cooke (1996), *Going Global: Four Entrepreneurs Map the New World Marketplace*, New York: Viking.

Teece, David J. (2000), *Managing Intellectual Capital: Organizational Strategies and Policy Dimensions*, Oxford: Oxford University Press.

Terry, Larry D. (2003), *Leadership of Public Bureaucracies: The Administrator as Conservator*, Armonk, NY: M.E. Sharpe.

Terry, Robert W. (1993), *Authentic Leadership: Courage in Action*, San Francisco, CA: Jossey-Bass.

Tichy, Noel M. and Eli Cohen (1997), *The Leadership Engine: How Winning Companies Build Leaders at Every Level*, New York: Harper Business.

Torbert, William R. (2003), *Action Inquiry: The Secret of Timely and Transforming Leadership*, San Francisco, CA: Berrett-Koehler.

Trompenaars, Fons and Charles Hampden-Turner (2001), *21 Leaders for the 21st Century: How Innovative Leaders Manage in the Digital Age*, Oxford: Capstone Publishing.

Tsoukas, Haridimos and Jill Shepherd (eds) (2004), *Managing the Future: Foresight in the Knowledge Economy*, Malden, MA: Blackwell Publishers.

Ulrich, David, Jack Zenger and Norman Smallwood (1999), *Results-Based Leadership*, Cambridge, MA: Harvard Business School Press.

Von Krogh, Georg, Kazuo Ichijo and Ikujiro Nonaka (2000), *Enabling Knowledge Creation: How to Unlock the Mystery of Tacit Knowledge and Release the Power of Innovation*, New York and Oxford: Oxford University Press.

Wade, David and Ronald U. Recardo (2001), *Corporate Performance Management: How to Build a Better Organization Through Measurement-Driven Strategic Alignment*, Boston, MA and Amsterdam: Butterworth-Heinemann.

Wall, Stephen J. (2004), *On the Fly: Executing Strategy in a Changing World*, Hoboken, NJ: John Wiley.

Weick, Karl E. (2001), *Making Sense of the Organization*, Oxford and Malden, MA: Blackwell Publishers.

Weick, Karl E. and Kathleen M. Sutcliffe (2001), *Managing the Unexpected: Assuring High Performance in an Age of Complexity*, San Francisco, CA: Jossey-Bass.

Weintraub, Jeff and Krishan Kumar (eds) (1997), *Public and Private in Thought and Practice: Perspectives on a Grand Dichotomy*, London and Chicago: University of Chicago Press.

Weisbord, Marvin Ross (2004), *Productive Workplaces Revisited: Dignity, Meaning and Community in the 21st Century*, San Francisco, CA: Jossey-Bass.

Wenger, Etienne, Richard McDermott and William Snyder (2002), *Cultivating Community Practice: A Guide to Knowledge*, Cambridge, MA: Harvard Business School Press.

Wexler, Mark N. (2000), *Confronting Moral Worlds: Understanding Business Ethics*, Toronto: Prentice Hall.

White, Shira and G. Patton Wright (2002), *New Ideas About New Ideas: Insights on Creativity From the World's Leading Innovators*, Cambridge, MA: Perseus.

Young, Stephen (2002), *Moral Capitalism: Reconciling Private Interest With the Public Good*, San Francisco, CA: Berrett-Koehler.

Zachary, G. Pascal (2000), *The Global Me: New Cosmopolitans and the Competitive Edge: Picking Globalism's Winners and Losers*, New York: Public Affairs.

Index